THE
SEARCH

THE
SEARCH

The true story of a D-DAY survivor,
an unlikey friendship, and a lost
shipwreck off Normandy

JOHN HENRY PHILLIPS

ROBINSON

ROBINSON

First published in Great Britain in 2022 by Robinson

1 3 5 7 9 10 8 6 4 2

A CIP catalogue record for this book
is available from the British Library.

ISBN: 978-1-47214-618-2

Typeset in Adobe Garamond Pro by SX Composing DTP, Rayleigh, Essex
Printed and bound in Great Britain by Clays Ltd, Elcograf S.p.A.

Papers used by Robinson are from well-managed forests
and other responsible sources.

Robinson
An imprint of
Little, Brown Book Group
Carmelite House
50 Victoria Embankment
London EC4Y 0DZ

An Hachette UK Company
www.hachette.co.uk

www.littlebrown.co.uk

For my mum, dad and brother

CONTENTS

LCH 185's Journey

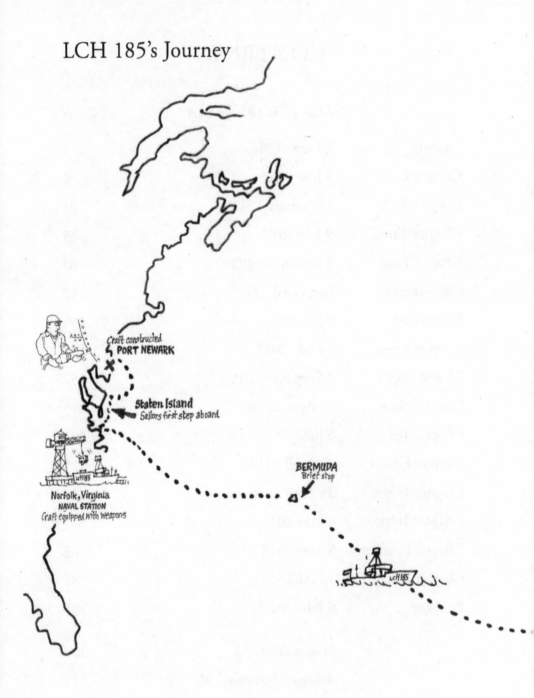

Craft constructed
PORT NEWARK

Staten Island
Sailors first step aboard

LCH185

Norfolk, Virginia
NAVAL STATION
Craft equipped with weapons

BERMUDA
Brief stop

LCH185

Prologue

25 June 1944

Hanging on desperately to the metal railing, Patrick Thomas reaches into the dark water below and begins to untie his brand-new leather boots. His hand is shaking from the panic. Water is already up to his knees. The teenager knows that if he doesn't get the boots off, the weight will pull his shirtless body to the bottom of the English Channel. He reaches up to touch his aching forehead, feeling the warmth of fresh blood. Bringing his trembling hand down to his face, Patrick sees a watercolour of crimson and grey trickle through his fingertips. Tins of paint stored in the bow have burst open in the explosion, covering the men as they desperately try to escape. He gazes across the deck. It is a shambles. Thick steel has been sliced like butter. A dying man nearby is being comforted in the arms of his petrified friend in their final moments. Patrick's boots will not budge. His hand is too wet and shaking too violently. The landing craft is rising up out of the water and beginning to turn over.

The boy turns to take one final look at the vessel. What was once a lifeless grey machine has become a home for those now clawing to get away. Coming from all walks of life to train and serve together, they have crossed the world and survived three campaigns, but the war at sea did not end with the landing of troops on to French beaches. Enemy attacks have been constant ever since, and now their time is finally up.

Patrick looks towards France. His childhood in Shrewsbury seems a world away. With a deep breath, he closes his eyes and launches himself hopelessly into the harsh, emerald sea. Plunging beneath the waves, piercing the water like a bullet from the weight of his boots, death is waiting at the bottom. The surreal tranquillity of a moment cradled by the water feels like a dream as the sea holds him silently in its grasp, coaxing the sailor down.

Punching up through the waves, Patrick fights his way to the surface, straight back into the hideous scene that exists above the peaceful world below. The stern has begun to sink, pushing the bow up towards the sky. An enormous vessel now looms over the 5-foot, 3-inch lad, threatening to crush his small body into the water as he lies on his back to stay afloat. Debris is smashing into the sea at an alarming rate and with a vicious ferocity. Patrick is just a child. He's green as grass. They all are. One shipmate is an eighteen-year-old with high qualifications in music who once played at Portsmouth Cathedral before joining the crew. He can't even peel a potato. Another young man still gets seasick while dry docked. What are they doing here?

Frantically swimming away from the metal hailstorm, Patrick spots a lifebelt floating gently across the surface. He knows it belongs to Jack Barringer from the scribbles and personal markings gained during the hours of boredom at sea. Patrick knows Jack well, having trained for the war with his brother Les. The two telegraphists have become fast friends on the landing craft. He grabs the lifebelt and pulls it close, cherishing a brief moment of relief as the weight lifts away. The struggle is halted for a matter of seconds, until a horrific scream rings out over the drone of the sea. Patrick looks up slowly, scared of what will greet him. He is aghast to see Jack crying out for help, badly injured and struggling to swim. Patrick's head is wounded, but he thinks he can stay afloat on his own. The sea off Normandy is filled with ships as far as the eye can see. If he can just keep treading water then he'll surely be rescued eventually. If Jack lives, his injuries might get him sent home, back to his wife and young child. He might see his brothers again.

Patrick quickly attempts to gauge the distance. With as much might as a small, injured sailor can muster, his arm goes back, then sharply forward for the throw. As he moves his hand back to launch the lifebelt to Jack, Patrick is startled by something nearby. A sailor is thrashing forward with both arms, screaming in terror. His legs have been shattered in the explosion. As the man gets closer, he begins to grab ferociously at the lifebelt. Patrick knows that the weight of the two sailors will pull them down. At just nineteen, the innocent boy from Shropshire is faced with an unimaginable choice. Which man should he save? His best friend Jack, who has taken the teenager under his wing, and who Patrick knows has a wife and child waiting in England; or the man nearest to the lifebelt and closest to saving? He closes his eyes and makes a decision that he will never be able to forget. There is no right answer. Either outcome will haunt the boy for decades to come.

On the sinking craft, a radio operator with one blue and one brown eye runs to a hatch on the upper deck. He climbs down a small chain ladder that hangs on by a single link to try to save those trapped below. When he arrives, he sees that the room is completely destroyed. The sight that greets him is sickening; boys still in their teens crying out, mangled within the twisted metal of the craft as if they are one and the same. As he stands frozen still, the companionway door bursts open and water begins to rush in. The terrified man rushes back up the ladder, leaving the dying crew to their fate. Their bodies are never found.

A sailor pulls Patrick out of the water on to an LCG(L) – a Landing Craft Gun (Large). He stumbles across the deck, where he notices Stan Jennings checking his watch. Saltwater has flooded the face, freezing the hands forever at 13:04. It has taken four minutes for the craft to all but disappear. Patrick shakes himself off, looks to the water and watches as the landing craft he has called home for so long sinks to the bottom of the English Channel. Adam Christie is sitting on the upturned hull with his arms crossed as it goes down. He has accepted that death is inescapable. Patrick never sees Adam again.

The small number of survivors are moved across to an LST(L) – a Landing Ship Tank (Large). Patrick is rushed down into the bow. Moving through the cramped guts of the craft, he sees bright lights hanging over an operating table. Watered-down blood puddles across the floor as a man lies on a white slab surrounded by medics. Patrick has part of his hair shaved and a bandage wrapped around his forehead. He goes to the upper deck to be interviewed about the sinking, answering as best he can with the shock of it all. From the shore a gun battery opens up. The shells drop all around the craft, coming closer with each hit.

The pressure in Patrick's head builds. Less than an hour ago, he was almost torn to pieces in an explosion, then somehow avoided near certain drowning. Now, on board what is supposed to be the safe haven of a rescue ship, he is going to die. Patrick thinks of Jack and Les Barringer. He thinks of the friends who had been by his side for so long. Adam Christie and Alan Maxwell; John Brothers and Dennis Piper; Robert Bell and James Armstrong.

The shells keep coming, explosions bursting just inches from the craft. He thinks of the rest of the thirty-five friends he has just lost in four short minutes, of the screaming and the blood and the grey paint. He thinks of the man with the broken legs, of the lifebelt and the choice he was forced to make. The pressure builds and builds until the teenager throws himself on to the cold, wet deck and hopes to God that somehow, someway, he can dig himself a foxhole through the wood with his bare hands. His entire body begins to shake. Patrick feels completely helpless. He is just a small cog in an enormous war machine, destined to become another statistic.

As a telegraphist, Patrick has been working two hours on, two hours off. On his breaks, he catches up on desperately needed rest. This morning the sun was shining, so he headed up top, unrolled a camp bed, took off his shirt and closed his eyes. Every other day since leaving England, he has taken his nap below deck with the rest of the men. The boy should have drowned. Patrick Thomas should have become a name on a memorial by the sea. On quiet nights alone, he will sit and ask himself, 'Why me? Why did I live, when so many died? Was it something outside myself?' All three of Mrs Thomas's sons are fighting in the war. Unbeknown to any of the siblings, their mother kneels by the bed each night and prays for their safe return.

Patrick continues to shake, but the shells never hit. They either have your name on or they don't. He cleans himself up and dries off, then attends the funeral of one of his shipmates. It must be the poor young man he saw lying on the operating table. Perhaps it's the radio operator who had tried to rescue the trapped men. There is a short service by the captain of the LST(L), and the man's body, sewn up in canvas and draped in a British flag, is slipped off the stretcher into the sea to be reunited with the rest of the crew. Patrick watches on as the nameless sailor floats beneath the waves into a forgotten corner of history that so many victims of the Second World War will occupy.

Chapter One

5 June 2016

Elderly men in black blazers shuffle past on walking sticks. The sound of rattling goes with them, medals earned in distant battles dangling proudly from chest pockets. Frail old boys who were warriors once, and in occasional moments can still be glimpsed as the young men they used to be. So strong in the past, but now wishing to shed the thick coat of time, they are wild at heart with heads full of life, held back only by their failing bodies. One by one they go, through the foyer of the Royal Maritime Club towards the pavement outside. The journey ahead will be tiring, but this is what the members of the snail-paced procession have waited for all year. It will be a trip to feel alive. A chance to be appreciated and remembered.

Before them lies a glorious return to the beaches and fields of a foreign land that to a rapidly dwindling few takes on an almost religious significance. Normandy means something to each person that enjoys its calming sands but, to a small number of elderly comrades, its importance can't be shared. Hedgerows where a friend was lost, a church tower where a sniper was dodged, a street corner where a bottle of wine was enjoyed in the madness, the grave of a friend lost long ago. Each ageing soldier is drawn back to a time, a place, a story from a short period that defines a long life.

With the last of the veterans helped down the front steps, I sit on top of my battered suitcase and try to imagine the lives of each person. Attempting to unravel the story told in the medals, I do it no justice. The campaigns do not tell the tale of the man. Reaching the group outside, we disperse across a convoy of vehicles and prepare to head for the harbour. I cram my luggage into the boot of a 4 x 4, pull open the door and jump in. To my right sits a small man with neatly combed white hair and untamed eyebrows.

'Nice to meet you. I'm John.'

His eyes stay glued to the seat in front. There's no response to my introduction.

'Hello. I'm John!' I say again, but still nothing.

'You'll have to speak loudly!' comes a voice from the front passenger seat. It's the man's carer and family friend, a woman named Margaret.

'Try to look him in the eye when you talk. He needs to see your lips move. He's very, very deaf.'

Thanking Margaret for the tip and worrying if I've come across as rude, I gently tap the man on his knee. He turns to look my way and, realising that I've been trying to introduce myself, springs to life.

'Sorry, sorry! My hearing is bad. Going up and down on those submarines, I think it must have damaged my eardrums.'

He's well spoken with a slight hint of a rural accent.

'That's fine, don't worry,' I say, taking a split second to register the point about submarines. This is certainly not a normal introduction.

'My name is John. I suppose we'll be travelling to France together.'

'John! I'm Patrick. Patrick Thomas,' he replies with a smile, emphasising his surname. He reaches up to fiddle with his hearing aid, cursing its uselessness in the process.

My eyes wander down to the crest on the chest pocket of his blazer. I see an image of some sort of ship. Beneath is embroidered the words 'Landing Craft Association'. Above is a gold brooch in the shape of a dolphin, a sure sign of a former submariner. Patrick's medals are dull, unpolished and held together with Blu-Tack. Among the ramshackle awards is a single red ribbon in pristine condition, from which hangs a white and green cross inscribed in French. It is the medal of the Légion d'honneur, the highest order of merit awarded by the French government.

I'm here volunteering with a charity that has secured enough funding to take sixteen Normandy veterans back to where they once fought. The men come from right across the UK, with one elderly soldier travelling from as far as Australia on his own. It's the first time the veteran has returned to France since the war and, after the trip, the frail man will travel with his wheelchair to Wales to see his relatives. He knows, as do they, that once he returns to Australia, they will not see each other again.

Veterans started returning to France almost as soon as the last bullet was fired. Some of the earliest photographs show men still wearing parts of their army uniform. The soil calls these men back. It always has. It will keep calling them back until the last soldier closes his eyes for the final time.

Although a number of volunteers and carers are on the trip, I'm the only one here on my own. I stumbled across the charity online just before starting my first job after university and offered to help. I almost pulled out at the last minute, worried that taking a week's leave from work so soon after starting would look bad. But I didn't. Something in my head was telling me that I couldn't miss this trip. With a thud the car bounces across a metal ramp and on to the ferry. Our convoy parks in the belly of the ship, where small groups of veterans and volunteers wander slowly towards the elevators. Not wanting to burden Patrick with my presence, I veer off on my own. The crossing will take five hours. I haven't been on a ferry since childhood and I'm unsure if seasickness is something I suffer from. I watch the sea pass by the square windows that line the ferry. The waves are choppy. Saltwater hits the glass like rain in a storm. It feels strangely cosy.

It soon seems safe to assume that illness isn't an issue I have to endure, and so I head to get some food. Carrying my tray through the dining hall, I search for a place to sit. Patrick's face pops up from across the room. We meet eyes, but I quickly turn away, not wanting to accidentally invite myself over. He immediately begins waving for me to join. I place my tray down on the cramped plastic table and take a seat. He's busy eating gammon and chips with a wincingly large mountain of salt dumped on top. I tuck into my plate of fresh prawns and try to think of something to say.

'You were in France then, Patrick?' I shout. 'Seventy years ago?'

'Oh yes! Sword Beach, in the first wave. On board the landing craft LCH 185,' he says, gently putting his cutlery down on to the plate to speak. I'm glad that I'm familiar enough with the terminology to know that LCH stands for Landing Craft Headquarters, so I don't have to ask him to explain.

'I've never met someone who was in the first wave of D-Day before. Where did you go after that? Into Normandy?' I ask.

'No, I was always on the craft. We were sunk two weeks after D-Day on the twenty-fifth of June 1944. I was one of the only people to escape.'

Patrick goes quiet. His eyes drift to the sea beyond my shoulder. Even so soon after meeting, it's clear that he is trying to hold back tears. I struggle to understand how our lunch has so easily taken a turn towards a story this bleak. The conversation comes to a halt. Neither Patrick nor I know what to say next. As we eat, I look up at the elderly man sitting before me and wonder what exactly happened to him. When the time feels right, as something in the air seems to say that we're nearing the shore, I stand up.

'Well, Patrick, I'll see you later! I'm going up top to watch our approach to France. I want to see what you saw on D-Day,' I say.

'Right oh! I'm off to shed a tear for Nelson,' he replies.

I laugh along and pretend to know what he means. Up on the deck, the wind is brutal. Puddles rip into the air and morph into a salty mist that blinds the few determined passengers out here. As the ferry nears Ouistreham, German fortifications on the beach begin to appear from the shadows. The concrete looms through the morning mist, still standing guard, crumbling apparitions of a war fought long ago.

In the gravel car park of an old hotel complex, I watch as each volunteer is given a set of room keys before swiftly leaving to unpack their bags. The crowd disperses until only I remain. It dawns on me that my name has been left off the rooming list.

Just my luck, I think to myself.

The organiser recommends that I knock on the door of one veteran who he thinks might have a spare room. I agree, but all I can think about is how awkward this will be. Dragging my luggage across the car park, dust and gravel are sent flying as I bounce the suitcase into the air each time the wheels get stuck. Each of the veterans has been given a suite on the ground floor. The stairs would have been too much for them. Reaching my destination, I find the door of the small chalet wide open. Rather than finding it inviting, the door being ajar seems far worse. I can't even knock first. Creeping through the entrance, I try to make as much noise as possible. I cough, bump into things and rattle my suitcase on the tiled floor but, despite my efforts, no one is stirred. A toilet flushes in the bathroom across the hallway and the door creaks open slowly.

Oh God, I think. *A stranger is about to find me lurking in their hotel room.*

While I panic over what to do next, out hobbles a short, elderly man midway through buttoning up his perfectly pressed beige trousers. I laugh as he lifts his head to meet my eyes and I realise that the man staring back at me is Patrick Thomas.

'John, is it? I was just shedding a tear for Nelson!'

So now I know what that means.

Patrick doesn't look annoyed, thankfully, but he certainly looks confused as to why I'm here.

'I have nowhere to stay and I heard you have a spare room,' I shout.

His grandson laughs from a sofa in the living room. Jason is in his forties, which reminds me of how big the gap in age was between my own grandfather and me. He has driven himself over from England, taking his work van across on the Eurotunnel.

'We have a straggler, Grandad,' he says. 'A poor little orphan looking for a bed.'

Patrick chuckles as he tucks his shirt in.

'You can stay with us then!' Patrick says, grinning from one wrinkled cheek to the other as he walks into the kitchen to join Jason and Margaret.

'Thank you!' I shout, but he can't see my lips.

The wooden steps creak as I lift my luggage up a narrow staircase. Standing by the bed, I look from the window out on to a lake and the endless countryside of Normandy.

Later that day, we all squeeze back into the car to head for the first stop of the trip. Everyone is exhausted, myself included.

No one really wants to be on the road again this soon, but the destination has been specifically requested by Patrick. With a tight schedule for the next week, this is the only time we can go.

Ranville War Cemetery is found in the first village to be liberated on D-Day. The British 13th Parachute Battalion took it back from the Germans in the early hours of the invasion. The cemetery walls are the colour of sand, glistening in the sun and turning dark in the rain. Grass pathways and flowers are kept so immaculately that the grounds could easily be called art and the gardeners artists. On the other side of the wall stands the original Ranville church, where forty-seven casualties of the Second World War are buried alongside civilians from the village. The war cemetery has a calmness to it. There is a beauty to each perfectly kept grave of one of the thousands of British troops that rest here. For countless living veterans returning through the decades and the families of those that were killed, Ranville holds huge significance. It is where loved ones lie. Beneath these matching headstones are fathers, sons, friends and comrades. There are Germans here too. Enemies long ago now rest together in eternity.

Arriving at the cemetery, cars and minibuses empty on to the street as our group circles together. There are sixteen veterans here, as well as forty volunteers and family members. We silently walk through the gate and beneath the archway that leads to the graves. Veterans meticulously thumb through the book of names kept behind a small metal door by the entrance, before setting off in various directions. Patrick seems different to the others. There is no need to check for what he's looking for; instead, he determinedly walks across the grass towards the furthest wall. I trail behind, keeping a respectful distance. Turning right, Patrick looks at the names on each grave before stopping in front of one in particular. He doesn't need to read the inscription.

'Jack Barringer,' Patrick says, letting out a deep sigh. Sensing my presence, he turns in my direction.

'I knew Jack well. We were on the same craft.'

Gently stepping beside the graves until I reach Jack, I lower my head to read the inscription.

J. BARRINGER
LEADING TELEGRAPHIST. R.N.
P/SSX.30514
H.M.L.C.H. 185
25th JUNE 1944. AGE 29

'We were at D-Day together and trained in Scotland before that. We were both telegraphists. I knew his brother Les, so Jack took me under his wing.'

I nod, but ask no questions. Patrick is visibly upset and I don't want to pry. If he wants to tell me more, he will. As I look up from the grave and stare at row upon row of young lives cut down before their prime, I'm reminded just how much we take simply being alive for granted.

'When I was in the water, I saw Jack nearby. He was hurt badly and couldn't swim. I tried to give him a lifebelt, but another man was going to grab on to it and sink us both.'

Patrick's words grow quieter with each syllable as his thoughts trail off.

'I had to let him have it. There was no choice. He would have pulled us both down. When I looked back, Jack was gone.'

Tears slowly drift down his cheeks. This grave is taking him back to that moment, back to fighting for his life in the rough English Channel.

I'm twenty-four years old, standing with a veteran in his nineties as he cries by the headstone of a friend killed seven decades ago. The man still hurts. There are no words I can utter that will help.

'That's . . . terrible,' I say. It's all I can think of.

'He was ten years older than me. I was nineteen. He had a wife and a child. I don't think anyone else ever comes to his grave. I suppose his family are out there somewhere,' Patrick says.

I nod again in agreement, trying to hold back my own tears.

'There were hardly any survivors. I must be the only one left now, I'm sure of it.'

I lift my arm and place it on Patrick's broad shoulder. This situation is new to me. It's overwhelming. We solemnly walk back towards the entrance with our hands clasped behind our backs, before taking one final look back from the gate.

It is said that you die twice. Once when you take your last breath, and again when your name is spoken for the final time. Driving along the coast, I wonder for how much longer Jack Barringer's name will be spoken.

At dinner, Patrick tells me all of the war stories he can remember, the good and the bad. He seems relieved to have someone to tell. I'm grateful for the chance to learn from someone who has seen so much through the years. I think my age allows him to open up, as if his knowledge is being passed on to a younger generation and ensuring that the past will not be forgotten.

Over the following days we attend a number of commemorations together. I push him in his wheelchair in veteran parades and stand by his side as he poses for photographs with people from all over the world. We eat breakfast, lunch and dinner together. In the afternoons, we have cups of tea in the sunshine and look out across the fields of France. I seem to never stop asking questions. It's like I'm making up for lost time. I learn about Patrick's job with the Post Office after the war. We speak about my career and hopes for the future. The gap in our years that was so clear when we first met in the back of the 4 x 4 floats away. We bond with the excitement of new friendships and laugh with the joy of old pals. It's hard to pin down why we get along so well. I can't explain it.

On the final evening of the trip, the two of us attend a reception with the mayor of Arromanches, the town that overlooks the British landing area of Gold Beach. Having drank all the complimentary champagne we can manage, partying like the war has only just ended, I watch in awe as, now freshly watered, Patrick all but jogs through the cobbled French streets on our way back to the hotel.

The ferry trip home is filled with contemplation. I'd not expected to be left off the rooming list, and I definitely hadn't planned to become such close friends with a man who was in the first wave of D-Day. Patrick and I spend most of the journey sitting next to each other in silence, staring out through the giant windows that line the bow of the ship. He's probably thinking of the friends he lost in Normandy, but I'm thinking of him, of how long this friendship can actually last. Parting ways in Portsmouth, it seems likely that Patrick and I will never see each other again. I've met plenty of other Second World War veterans in the past. One in particular, Marvin Hardy, comes to mind. I met him in 2014 by chance in a café at Pegasus Bridge in Normandy. He was American, wearing his combat jacket, something that separates the US veterans from the shirt-and-tie-wearing Brits. Marvin had served in the 2nd Infantry Division, landing on Omaha Beach on D-Day plus 1. He was wounded in France, but made it back in time to fight in the Battle of the Bulge. It was the first time Marvin had been back, and he was surprised to receive such a warm welcome from the French. I wasn't surprised at all. Veterans are often treated by the locals as if they're still heading towards the Eiffel Tower on the back of a jeep to liberate Paris.

Marvin and I chatted for a while in the sun by the water. As I listened to his memories of Europe and England, he pulled out three pebbles from his pocket, picked up that morning at Omaha Beach. Holding them out in his fragile hand, Marvin pointed to each one. Two grey ones for his daughters, one red for the blood his friends had shed on French soil. I emailed Marvin soon after I got back to England, but he had died. It was as if returning to a former battlefield was a dying wish and a last box to tick. Go back, say your goodbyes, bury old ghosts, then disappear. Driving back to my house in Suffolk, that's all I can think about.

The first time I ever learned of the war, I was standing on the green in the village that I grew up in. Tearing open one end of the paper packaging, I pull out the necessary parts to build a styrofoam Spitfire. In my tiny five-year-old hands, I hold a tail, the fuselage and a red plastic propeller to attach to the nose. My grandparents, Dick and Betty, bought me the gift for a few pence from the petrol station on the way to the green. It was on a display stand right by the counter. On one side of the packaging is the dramatic scene of a dogfight over Britain, sending my imagination running. I carefully push the pieces together, trying not to bend anything. My brief role on the assembly line complete, I climb to the top of a hill and gently grip the base of the Spitfire like a dart. With one eye shut, I concentrate enough to go slightly dizzy, aiming at the imaginary landing strip just a few metres ahead. Holding my elbow perfectly still, I reach my hand behind my head and bounce it back and forth while planning a perfect flight. Everything seems ready for take-off, but as the launch begins, all of my careful preparation collapses when my arm comes forward with such a childlike velocity that my entire body spins around.

Stunned, I watch as the plane steers at a right angle towards the clouds. Time slows to an unbearable pace as I wonder how it has all gone so horribly wrong. My new pride and joy twists and turns before finally undertaking a backwards loop-the-loop towards the ground. With a silent explosion, the smiling pilot crash-lands nose first into the runway. I look at the crash site. Sprinting down the hill, I drop to my knees to examine the debris field and search for any survivors. Staring down at the tragic sight before me, it's clear that the plane has suffered terribly from its collision with the earth. Cupping the wreckage in my palms, I try to assess the damage. The tail has snapped, not completely off, but bent enough to never take to the skies again. My upset must be obvious because, as I look up, my grandmother is staring down at me.

'Don't worry,' she says. 'Grandpa fixed planes in the war.'

'The war' is uttered so often and with such casualness that I never think to question what it means. 'That's from the war,' my parents often say as we drive past dilapidated buildings. The war, despite ending almost fifty years before I was born, is all around us in Suffolk. It's in the pillboxes watching over the fields that we play in. It's in the abandoned airfields and bombed-out manor houses that my friends and I explore in the summers. It's in the leftover animosity towards the still-active United States airbases. It hangs from flags on church walls and on memorials in every village that we pass through. It is, most vividly, in the memories of our grandparents. I never stop to wonder which war, because it's never *a* war, it's *the* war, but the day of the mini-Spitfire crash landing is the first time I learn that it has something to do with my own family and my own history.

My grandmother turns to face her husband, who is standing in an olive wax jacket and a flat cap.

'You can fix this, can't you?'

'Yes, I can fix that. Don't worry!' he says.

The three of us walk the short distance to my house, where my grandparents rummage through the cupboards. With his thick hands, Grandpa gently bends the tail back and tapes it into place. I reach out my hand, taking the Spitfire back with a quiet 'thank you'.

'Jolly good!' he replies.

Out in the back garden, I send the plane up a few more times before quickly growing bored and moving on to the next activity. What my grandparents say to me that day is immediately forgotten about in the excitement of a summer without school, but it periodically pops into my mind over the years. By the time I'm old enough to understand who my grandparents are, they already seem ancient. I can't remember them ever not having white hair or being unsteady on their feet. The war that they speak about seems far from my childhood in the 1990s, but it isn't. They have both lived through it. Grandpa really did fix planes in the war and now, five decades on, he's fixing a toy Spitfire for his grandson.

Years later, when I'm twenty years old, my grandfather dies at the age of ninety-six. To die so old is no tragedy, but it hits me hard. It isn't my first brush with grief, but it's the first time I really consider what death actually means. I'm fine for a while but, in bed one night, existential thoughts arrive and they linger for months. I can't stop myself from stressing all night about what it means to die. For my grandfather, it meant rapidly losing his faculties over the space of a few days, before unceremoniously dying in a hospital bed on a weekday afternoon.

The first time I visit him on the ward is the first night of his hospital stay. He chats as normally as a frail ninety-six-year-old can. The other patients are asleep. On the second night, the atmosphere is completely different. My grandfather doesn't know where he is. The other patients are awake and confused. One man tries to walk through a door in a wall that doesn't exist. Another asks me if I'm his son. A patient gets out of bed and walks toward us. Grandpa has a look of fear in his eyes that I have never seen before. A nurse mentions, after the patient is returned to his bed, that the man had tried to attack my grandfather the night before. He can't help it. None of them can.

Despite his rapid deterioration, Grandpa gets up each day, puts on a shirt and tie, and sits in the chair by his hospital bed. He is old-fashioned in every way. He was born during the First World War, and his own grandfather served in the Metropolitan Police during the 1800s, once making the cover of the *Illustrated Police News* after helping to solve a murder in Fulham. His father was wounded in the trenches of the Great War. Grandpa is from a different era and has always seemed it.

Each night I head to the hospital for a chat. Sometimes he asks if we can leave to go and grab a pint. Sometimes he asks when he'll be going home. Sometimes he asks me who I am. One evening a nurse explains to my dad and me that my grandfather had been refusing treatment.

'Whenever we come over to give him his medicine, he tells us that he doesn't want it. He says that he fought in the war and doesn't have to do anything he doesn't want to do.'

It seems odd. I know that he served in the Second World War as an RAF airframe fitter, but he has rarely spoken about it. I have a recollection of him mentioning seeing a few of his friends die, but I never knew how. I know very little about that time period, but try the next evening to ask what I can.

'Where were you during the war?'

'North Africa. Then we landed in Sicily and chased them right up into Italy,' he says, slowly motioning with his shaking hands across an imaginary map of the Mediterranean. 'I got malaria.

They flew me in a Dakota to Tunisia. I still wake up sweating in the night.'

I nod along, unsure how to reply. I don't know enough about the Second World War to ask any more.

He dies the next day; a rapid descent into senility and then gone. For months I can't shake the thought of that miserable ward and the sad, anticlimactic ending to a long life. At the funeral, a relative I'd never met before spoke of witnessing my grandfather's return from the war. He burst into the village pub and drunkenly sang 'Danny Boy' on top of the piano. It's such a different image to the old-fashioned grandfather I grew up with.

The guilt of knowing that I've become yet another person who has failed to ask his grandfather about the war is immediate. My dad never asked much about it either, nor did he ask his own grandfather about the First World War. I decide to learn what I can, reading book after book about campaigns right across the world. I take trips to French battlefields. The first time I step foot on the Somme, I find bits of rusty barbed wire, grenades and soldiers' boots sticking out of the ploughed ground. It's eye-opening to see such a tangible link to history right there by my feet. Like so many children, I was fascinated by archaeology. Finding those artefacts brings that love straight back.

Preserving the stories of past wars for future generations becomes my passion. I gain a new sense of purpose in meeting increasingly ageing veterans to record their stories, often for the first time and, more often than not, the last. A year later, I begin a degree in archaeology. Trips to Normandy and the Somme fill my downtime. I kayak solo along the River Kwai in Thailand, retracing the steps of my great-uncle who was captured by the Japanese and forced to build the infamous Death Railway. After graduation, I start work as a professional archaeologist. It is a childhood dream achieved. Guilt and sadness underline everything I do in my career, but that only makes me more determined.

After meeting Patrick in Normandy, I return to England and go back to work. It's deflating after such an incredible experience. The next six months are spent working on a cliff that overlooks the North Sea. It's a nightmare of a job; a large-scale, laborious slog of an excavation, bogged down with over-the-top health-and-safety precautions, horrific weather and less than thrilling archaeology. Arriving before sunrise, our first task each day is to chip the ice away from whatever needs excavating, and then we start digging in the dark. As the months go by, I grow tired of the situation. This version of archaeology is not what I ever imagined myself doing.

My eyes always find the sea. It is an escape from the monotonous days of dirt and exhaustion. With every lift of my mattock, I glance out at the water and slam the blade down into the rock-solid ground at my feet. The sea has never really gripped me before. I had always associated it with tame but enjoyable days at the seaside rather than a great horizon to explore, but the more I look out across my colleagues over the cliff towards the water, the more the view begins to mean something else entirely. Container ships, sail boats and fishing vessels all slowly drift by as I imagine myself dropping tools, swimming out to climb aboard and sailing away. The sea, from my clifftop lookout, becomes a way of escape.

Since hearing Patrick's story, I've been unable to shake it. The tale is so melancholic, a story of death on a scale far greater than I've heard from the mouths of other veterans. Drowning is an unimaginably horrific end to a life. It's impossible to fathom such horror. In all the time I have spent learning about the Second World War, those at sea have never really crossed my mind. Perhaps the battles on land are easier to follow. Certainly, the archaeology is much easier to uncover. Ships in the war have for me been exactly that. They are ships, great hunks of metal floating on the ocean. The individual men occupying those ships are something that I've never really thought about. It's naive of me to have overlooked it, because when a ship went down, it wasn't just a vessel. People went down with it. Real people with hopes and dreams, parents, partners and children. Those left behind were scarred deeply and rarely had a place to mourn. To look into the crying, vulnerable eyes of an old sailor still suffering each day with a tragedy long assigned to the history books is enough to not only change my view, but make me want to do something about it.

While the excavation lingers on, my fascination with the sea moves from the ships above to what might be found below. As my mind wanders, I picture myself learning to dive and exploring the seabed. Down there, I'm discovering new worlds in my head far away from the workplace. Patrick and LCH 185 are in my thoughts often as I stare out at the water. Somewhere between this muddy corner of England and the end of that shimmering horizon must be Patrick's shipwreck. I occasionally asked Patrick what he thought might have happened to the craft after the sinking. He thinks that it was simply lost and that no one has ever attempted to find it. After all, 185 went down during a war. Vessels were dropping like flies. It would be so different if a ship sank today and most of the crew were never seen again. The loss would make the news across the globe, but in 1944 it was merely another statistic.

Not long after Germany and Japan surrendered, the world moved on. The story of 185 was known only in the minds of those few that either survived or witnessed the sinking. They returned to normal life, to civilian jobs and a world in which every person had their own war story. Few wanted to talk about it and even fewer wanted to listen. In my childhood fifty years later, one of the country's most popular sitcoms – *Only Fools and Horses* – had a running joke about an old naval veteran boring his relatives with tales from the war. The change came with the passing of time. When once there were millions of veterans the world over, it was only as they dwindled to a small handful that their stories became unique and rare. It has since become a desperate and necessary race to record the last memories of those that survived. Stories like Patrick's, once unremarkable, are now incredibly important to those who care enough to try to preserve the memory of that time in history.

I read books on shipwrecks during my evenings after work and watch Jacques Cousteau documentaries on my phone during lunch breaks. My fascination with the world beneath the waves grows daily. It gets to be such an interest that I buy a dive watch, an old-school and outdated means to time dives underwater. I wear it to work, but whenever I check the time, I'm confronted with a constant question. Am I a fraud? How can I wear a watch built to go to the bottom of the world's oceans, but not be able to dive? It doesn't sit well with me. As foam from the North Sea curls my hair, I wonder whether or not the wreck of LCH 185 can actually be discovered.

In December 2016, I travel down to Portsmouth to join Patrick for a Christmas dinner. The same charity that organised the trip on which we met has brought the veterans together for a festive celebration. It's wonderful to see Patrick. He has grown an enormous beard since we last parted ways, making him look every bit the old sailor he is. We pick up exactly where we left off in France. There is plenty of laughter and alcohol. Songs are sung, war stories are exchanged, crackers are pulled over the delicately balanced glasses of wine and port clustered together on cluttered white tablecloths. Most of all, there is great relief in my heart to still have all of the ageing veterans here with us. I never experienced as much joy with my grandfather, mostly because I was a child when he was still active. We did share a few laughs in his final years, but he was reserved by then; an inaccessible soul from an unrecognisable time. My friendship with Patrick is youthful and energetic. He is old but modern, and not just because an iPad never seems to leave his side. We stay late into the night, huddled by the hotel bar, half-cut and sharing stories as torn party hats slowly fall down our foreheads.

The following June I find myself back in Normandy. This time I've gone on my own. The plan is to enjoy the wonderful atmosphere of the annual event and catch up with the friends I made last year. Patrick is still alive, thankfully, and the two of us have chatted frequently. His telegraphy experience has seamlessly been reapplied to the excellent use of his iPad. We've been exchanging countless emails, sharing photographs of our lives, of his days out and what I've been excavating at work. I've learned of his time in the Far East after Normandy, frying eggs on submarine hulls, and having his entire body covered in ringworm. But no matter how much we speak about his time after France, his thoughts always return to 25 June 1944. Patrick had kept the story to himself until his nineties, assuming that no one cared, but when the seventieth anniversary of D-Day came around in 2014, his perception began to change. It was time to open up.

On the morning of the anniversary of D-Day, I attend a remembrance service at Bayeux Cathedral. Patrick is seated at the front. As the service concludes, he is wheeled down the aisle towards the door.

'John!' he calls out, almost dropping his walking stick from his lap in the frantic race to shake my hand.

'Patrick!' I shout. 'I'll catch up with you later.'

'Good on you, blue!' he says. It's another one of his wartime phrases, this time picked up somewhere in Australia towards the end of the conflict.

After leaving the cathedral, I drive to Lion-sur-Mer, a town located in the Sword Beach sector where Patrick had been on D-Day. This is also the town that Patrick associates with the sinking of 185 because the craft never seemed to stray too far from its initial destination. Most veterans have a town that they think of when remembering the war. For Patrick, it is Lion-sur-Mer. Walking along the seafront, my eyes find the roofs of the stunning houses lining the promenade. They are beautiful in their grandiosity and charming in their fragility. There is something a bit different about this town. It is more real. Lion-sur-Mer was a seaside resort before the war and quickly returned to its tourist origins afterwards. The locals wanted to rebuild and quickly get back to their pre-war economy. As a result, the town hasn't become such a huge part of the business that is D-Day tourism. First-time visitors will often visit Omaha Beach or Sainte-Mère-Église, the US areas seen in television shows and Hollywood movies. For that reason, there are fewer memorials here; aside from the occasional information panel, a visitor might struggle to even know that the first British troops to step foot in Normandy did so in this town.

Before reaching the beach, I spot a small triangle of grass overlooking the water. It looks like the perfect spot for a memorial to be placed. I'm amazed no one has put one up here. As my boots pass over the sand, families play with their dogs and a group of women enjoy an exercise class. In the very water where soldiers had once been mowed down is now a group of windsurfers. Seeing the beach used for leisure seems fitting. This is freedom, the *joie de vivre*. Down at the water's edge children are playing with a frisbee. I take off my shoes and curl my toes into the sinking sand. Removing a red paper poppy from the lapel of my jacket, I kneel down to place it on to the water, watching as the delicate flower drifts out to sea. My eyes look to home. LCH 185 can't be far away from where I'm standing.

In the afternoon, the weather is appalling. I find Patrick among the busy streets of Arromanches. The rain is relentless and the annual veterans' parade has been postponed. We're sitting in the conservatory bar of Hôtel de Normandie, struggling to keep warm and dry. Patrick is disappointed, having waited all day for the parade to take place. This is a highlight of the trip and all of the veterans feel similarly, but, after an hour of boredom, word begins to spread that much like on D-Day, with a brief gap in the weather, the parade will take place after all.

I quickly rush into position, taking my spot behind Patrick's wheelchair. He finds being pushed degrading, but the long walks are becoming increasingly difficult with old age. The brass band kicks into song as we slowly march through the town square. The awful weather has kept the usual audience away. Instead, there is only a scattered handful of people watching. It's a sorry sight. The veterans deserve more than this. We defiantly walk the short route before taking our seats for the ceremony. The weather immediately worsens as rain starts to pour down harder than ever. Huddled beneath stretched-out ponchos or battling umbrellas in the wind, we listen as a local dignitary speaks of the town's determination to keep the memory of the war alive. Everyone here, from local children to the veterans themselves, knows that time is running out on these moments. With the speeches finished, a singer dressed in 1940s clothing takes the microphone and begins to sing Vera Lynn's 'We'll Meet Again'. The assembly stands up, joins hands and sings together. It's a cheerful moment, but one filled with an undercurrent of upset. In 365 days' time, when the parade rolls around once more, some of these proud veterans will no longer be here.

Patrick and I hang around for a short while as the crowd leaves, placing some flowers at the Landing Craft Association memorial while we wait. Patrick explains that the association recently shut down due to a lack of veterans still alive. That must be a common story. He gets back into his wheelchair, and I begin to push him towards the street. Upon turning the corner, we're both left speechless to discover that the previously deserted roads are now filled with hundreds of people. Despite the storm, the locals have come out to ensure that every last veteran is applauded back through the town. Patrick places his hands on the side of his wheelchair and slowly but firmly pushes his fragile body up and on to his feet.

'I want to walk,' he says.

Seeing how much this means to him, I take a few steps back and watch with tears in my eyes as this lone, elderly man hobbles down the road, drenched in the cheers of the enormous crowd. Women blow kisses and men shake his hand. Children are waving flags and holding signs that read 'Merci!' People hang out of upstairs windows to shout phrases of gratitude. It is a moment in time that I know can never be replicated.

We head to Arromanches town hall that evening to watch a few of our friends receive their Légion d'honneur medals. I'm still filled with pride from the parade and happy to have been reunited with Patrick. We watch the presentation, then head outside to mingle. The storm has passed, leaving in its wake a perfect French evening. The ostentatious town hall is made of stone, reflecting the sun on to the street. I look at Patrick, who appears small and frail in his wheelchair.

'You deserve a memorial, Patrick,' I blurt out.

'What do you mean?' he asks.

'LCH 185. It's a tragedy. What happened to you and your friends is so awful. There should be a memorial to remember your shipmates. What if I build one?'

'I'd like that,' he says with a nod of his head.

We both fall silent. How hard can building a memorial be? I think of the sea, back to those long days spent staring out at the water. My eyes move down to my wrist, where I see my dive watch poking out from beneath my shirt.

'What if the wreck of LCH 185 could be found?' I ask.

Patrick doesn't hesitate with his answer.

'That would be amazing, John. To know where my friends are resting after all these years.'

Carried away with the emotion of the day and slightly fuelled by champagne, I utter words that shock not only Patrick, but myself.

'Then I'll do it. I'll find the wreck for you.'

'I would be delighted,' he says gently. He doesn't think I really mean it, but I do.

I have no idea how to search for a shipwreck. I can't dive and I've never run my own expedition before. On the other hand, I am a professional archaeologist. Uncovering artefacts is my bread and butter. Perhaps most importantly, I care enough to try. It is no doubt a cliché, but true nonetheless, to say that we get one chance in life to live the way we want to live. So few opportunities appear that allow us to make any sort of difference. I haven't known Patrick for long, but the impact that our friendship has already had on my life is immense. I feel like I owe it to him to at least try to bring some closure to his story. Patrick, my grandfather and the rest of their generation have been forgotten in the fast-moving modern world. One by one they die, taking with them a life of untold tales, but Patrick is still here for a little while longer. With my own grandfather gone and his war stories taken to the grave, I have a shot at redemption.

Chapter Two

14 January 1943

The noise is always there. A constant soundtrack for the workers that clock in and out each day to earn a living. The crackle of welders, the dull thuds and chiming rings of hammers hitting steel and the piercing snake-hiss of steam. High up above seagulls cry out as they glide down to rest on the creaking skeletons of giant ships lining the water like piano keys. There is never silence. For employees at the Federal Shipbuilding and Drydock Company, the smell of oil and smoke doesn't ever truly leave their clothes. The men are never far from the shipyard long enough to get clean. Numbered badges pinned to mucky overalls are stained from the constant filth of the job. It is a hectic place to work; a dark and dirty world of sweat and soot located on the water's edge at Kearny Point, New Jersey.

The company managed to ride out the Great Depression, but as the war worsened, the business fell into disarray. Sixteen thousand employees went on strike in the sweltering heat of August 1941, causing almost half a billion dollars' worth of contracts to crumble. Those in charge were spooked, and so too was the US government. President Franklin D. Roosevelt attempted to control the situation by ordering the navy to take ownership of the shipyard. Rather than give in to the workers' demands, the owners chose to allow the takeover to go ahead.

It lasts just 134 days until, on 6 January 1942, the original owners are handed back control of their own business. They decide to expand, opening a second site on the former grounds of the Submarine Boat Corporation at Port Newark, an old First World War shipyard also in New Jersey, where business booms. When employees aren't on strike or when the company isn't the topic of dispute between the US Navy, the owners and the unions, the shipyard makes great strides. By the end of the year, production increases rapidly. More vessels are built, and at a faster rate, than anywhere else in the world. On 28 March 1943, the shipyard successfully launches two destroyers and two destroyer escorts, adding to the new record of eleven launches in twenty-nine days. In July, the company announces that USS *Dashiell*, a destroyer weighing over 2,000 tonnes and measuring more than 100 metres in length, has been built in just 170 days. Within two months, four destroyers are launched on the same day in what Charles Edison, Governor of New Jersey and former US Secretary of the Navy, calls the 'equivalent to a naval victory'. These impressive achievements are both the talk of the town and the topic of proud headlines in local newspapers. The company has become a powerhouse.

This inspiring increase is needed not just for the war, but for morale. While the worst of the Battle of the Atlantic is over, the conflict is far from finished. More ships mean more power, and as fighting rages across the world's seas, the company has become an enviably streamlined conveyer belt of desperately needed war machines. Soon Allied forces will head for Europe; the shipyard is producing the vessels needed to take the fight to the enemy.

The term 'landing craft' often conjures up images of the British Landing Craft Assault (LCA) or the US Landing Craft Vehicle Personnel (LCVP), both of which are short, barge-like vessels equipped with bow ramps designed to place troops directly on to beaches. There are, however, many types of landing craft manufactured in all kinds of shapes, sizes and roles. While LCA carry out their task excellently, at just under 13 metres long and capable of carrying only thirty-six troops, the craft leaves a clear need for a new vessel able to disembark more troops. In response, the Landing Craft Infantry (Large) – the LCI(L) – is born.

The LCI(L) is 48.31 metres long, weighs 419 tonnes when fully loaded, and is armed with four 20-mm anti-aircraft guns. The craft can be run by a crew of twenty-one men and three officers. From walkways located on each side of the bow, it is possible to disembark close to 200 men. It is a vast improvement, one that, it is hoped, will significantly boost the efficiency of amphibious landings. In December 1942, construction of LCI(L) 185 takes place at Port Newark, taking less than a month to complete. A British-designed but US-built craft, 185 is transferred on 13 January to the Royal Navy under the Lend-Lease Act. In time, it will be rechristened as a Landing Craft Headquarters and known as LCH 185.

As a group of British sailors prepares to cross the Atlantic, among them is twenty-year-old Adam Christie with his friend Frank Gammal. Adam has a young, round face and dark, wavy hair. He grew up in a small fishing village on the east coast of Scotland, where the sea was within view for most of his childhood. It was only natural that he should join the Royal Navy when the war erupted. The small but excited group of lads arrives in Greenock, western Scotland, where they are greeted by the scars of a war they are shortly to join. Greenock serves as a base for the Home Fleet, and is where the Atlantic convoys assemble before heading out to sea. Eight months previously, on 6 and 7 May 1940, roughly 300 Luftwaffe aircraft had bombed the town in an event that became known as the Greenock Blitz. Although targeted for the town's naval use, the majority of bombs landed on residential areas, killing 271 and injuring over 10,000 people. As Adam Christie heads aboard the ship, he can't ignore how deadly war can be, even in remote parts of his home country.

On board, most of the sailors have never left Britain, but now find themselves heading for New York City. The luxury ocean liner beneath their boots was launched as *Empress of Japan* in 1929 for the Canadian Pacific Railway Company. Costing £1.5 million to construct, the ship left Liverpool for Quebec on its maiden voyage on 14 June 1930, before successfully completing fifty-eight trips in eight years. The *Empress* was once both the largest ship in the Pacific Ocean and the fastest. With the capacity to reach an average speed of 21.02 knots, in 1931 it made the trip from Yokohama, Japan, to Vancouver, Canada, in a record-breaking 7 days, 8 hours and 27 minutes. On one notable occasion, the ship carried the US All-Star baseball team to perform for the Japanese. Among them was none other than Babe Ruth.

By November 1939, *Empress of Japan*'s civilian days are over, as news arrives that the ship is to be requestioned by the military. From Shanghai, the *Empress* journeys to Esquimalt, British Columbia, to be converted into a troop carrier. With its stunning white exterior now painted grey and loaded with Australian soldiers, the ship is ready for war as it heads for Suez, then rescues families from Singapore as the Japanese approach. By October 1942, hostilities with Japan are grievous. With Pearl Harbor having occurred just ten months previously, *Empress of Japan* is deemed to no longer have a name fit for purpose. Breaking both tradition and rule to never rename a ship, the decision is personally approved by Winston Churchill.

Renamed *Empress of Scotland*, the ship goes on to carry 30,000 troops across the water during 1943 and 1944.

No amount of military conversion can strip away the luxury of the *Empress*'s former life as an ocean liner. The men are thrilled to be aboard something so fancy as they settle in for the long journey ahead. Following their own successful crossing to North America, one filled with boredom and clock watching, they dock at 35th Street, Brooklyn, New York, at the South Brooklyn Marine Terminal. Beneath the unreal sights of the city, the men are surprised to receive a small stipend from the US government arranged by the Royal Navy. For a group of young British servicemen in New York City with a cash handout from Uncle Sam, the possibilities are vast. Chances for troublemaking are everywhere.

Adam and the gang head first to Asbury Park, New Jersey, where they are put up at the Monterey Hotel, one of many that line the promenade. Like the *Empress*, the hotel once represented luxury. This area of coast is known for its large, extravagant hotels decked out with ballrooms, golf courses, swimming pools and an elite clientele with a love for leisure. The building is vast in size with impressive white brick walls, beautiful gardens and an ornate tower overlooking its two wings. The hotel is situated right on the water, serving as a perfect setting to relax in the sun. Upon its opening, advertisements boasted of 'daily concerts' and 'hot and cold sea water in all rooms'. The Monterey is a hotel designed to escape into, to leave the hustle of the city for a break by the sea. How devastated the patrons and how pleased the sailors were when the building was taken over and made an official US Navy training headquarters.

The group relax at their new digs for a short rest before heading back to the city. They have so far travelled on a converted luxury cruise ship and been billeted in a hotel with a swimming pool, a far cry from life at home in a country that has already been at war for years. Despite the tantalising life of luxury dangled before them, the sailors know that they are here on an important mission: to collect new, flat-bottomed landing craft and take them back across the ocean for use in the war in Europe. The men head to Staten Island, where the landing craft have been brought up from the shipyard. There, hiding among the jumble of ships, is a number of LCI(L). The group split out across the craft to form small, makeshift crews. Adam Christie takes his first step on to the deck of LCI(L) 185, boarding a craft that will go on to define the lives of so many that live and die within its metal hull.

Safely aboard their new homes, the crews take the vessels out for practice runs on the water to go through emergency procedures. They then head to the naval yard at Norfolk, Virginia. On arrival, to add to the money already received in New York City, Adam Christie and the boys are given packets of cigarettes. They are put up at the Naval Station Norfolk while the craft are being fitted out with everything from flare plates to plastic armour. At Seawalls Point Magnetic Range, the vessels are calibrated and degaussed, then moved to the Naval Ammunition Depot at nearby St Julien's Creek. Here, the 20-mm Oerlikon anti-aircraft guns are bolstered with additional small arms.

Like thousands of their US counterparts, the group immediately head to the nearby Ocean View Amusement Park. The park was almost closed down before the war, but military brass at the nearby base have successfully persuaded the owners to keep it open. It's a convenient way to keep the men together in one place under the watchful eye of the navy, and while it might not keep them out of trouble, it at least keeps the trouble behind closed doors. Vast crowds of excited sailors in white uniforms quickly resemble a rowdy snowstorm as they head towards the park each day. The British men among them stand out not just for their unusual accents, but for the blue uniforms that only they wear.

The vendors have soon caught on to the wants and needs of this young clientele. Away from their hometowns, destined for war and faced with the prospect of not coming back, fairground rides are no longer cutting it. They want something with a bit more of an edge. Amusement attractions, once an innocent activity, are quickly redesigned to include gambling activities. The situation spirals and before long burlesque shows are being put on for the troops. The 12-foot-high screen put up along the seafront keeps the appetising view of so many uniformed military men out of sight of the German U-boats waiting hungrily in the water, but it doesn't stop the images of debauchery from being spotted by the locals. The United Civic Organizations of Ocean View write a letter to the park to say that they are 'alarmed and aroused . . . over the new low in morality, vulgarity, obscenity and depravity that has not only been permitted but encouraged'.

For a group of sailors fresh off the boat from the UK, Ocean View is exactly what they were hoping for. The British sailors endeavour to spend their money, smoke their cigarettes, befriend the locals, and enjoy the amusement park for everything it has to offer. Adam Christie has a professional photograph taken of himself in full military uniform sitting on a stern-looking prop of a frowning half-moon. The photograph remains in his possession for the rest of his life, a reminder of when he once briefly lived the American dream.

Although the men are on duty, it is still a welcome rest from the strain of life on the Home Front, but as enjoyable as it is to be this carefree in the United States, the fun can't last. The landing craft are needed on the grand stage of a world at war. Before leaving, the sailors are given new patches for the shoulders of their uniforms with a symbol made up of an albatross, an anchor and a submachine gun. It represents Combined Operations, the coming together of the military's three branches, of which the men are now a part.

Freshly assigned, they set off like immigrants in reverse, leaving the coast of New York, destined for Europe. The men have spent thirty days in the States. Sixteen LCI(L) move together in convoy on the long journey. This isn't the first time a large group of landing craft has made the crossing. Rather, it is the sixth delivery from the US. The convoy is unescorted and unprotected. Those on board are well aware that U-boats may lurk beneath them. With vast expanses of water meeting the eye from every corner of the craft, each step of the journey is tense and anxious.

The trip is too far to be undertaken in one go, and a stop in Bermuda is made. The convoy spends a short time at the subtropical island's dockyard, where the men take in the sights and sounds of a place like no other the crews have ever seen before. From Bermuda, they move towards the Mediterranean. The convoy stops off briefly at Gibraltar before heading towards the recently captured Algiers. It is here that the craft are sorted into groups, known as Operation Flotillas, ready to be assigned to future landing forces. Close to the port town of Béjaïa, the vessels are put to the test during landing training, where they fare well enough to undertake real assignments. Some of the craft are involved in missions to drop female guerrilla fighters on to the island of Crete and deliver food to the starving population of Malta. From Algiers, the convoys navigate the coast of North Africa to Tripoli, then on to Malta to begin preparations for the landings at Sicily. Operation Husky is to be the first time that LCI(L) are used in a real landing, leaving an element of the unknown and a fear that the vessels will crumble in a battle situation.

From the glorious harbour of Valletta, the craft cross the water towards the coast of Sicily at the western end of the 105-mile stretch of landing beach. It's assumed by some that due to previous failures to beach successfully in such shallow water, the LCI(L) will have to unload troops onto smaller vessels offshore to take them up to the sand. The crossing takes place at night. It is windy, which causes many of the landing craft to arrive behind schedule. Some of the new craft face issues almost immediately. At least one finds itself stuck on a false sandbar; another has its controls destroyed by Italian fire from the beach; two collide during the first wave, causing one to lose both of its troop ramps. In a particularly devastating event, an LCI(L) attempts to disembark as close to the shore as possible, but its troops are dropped into deep water. At least three men drown.

Despite this, the landing craft prove a success. Most disembark troops safely, some even directly on to the beaches. Many successfully use their guns to fire on to enemy positions. LCI(L) 185 does its job well, adding to the landings at Sicily, which ultimately end in Allied victory. The enemy is chased right across the country in a matter of weeks, causing them to retreat across the Strait of Messina into mainland Italy. Christie and the crew ready themselves to go again.

The calm Mediterranean waters gently sway vessels in the harbour. In the distance rest large battleships. Two LCA filled with men float on each side of the hulls. All around are Arabic buildings. At Tripoli, the crews are experiencing wonderful cultures first hand. They can't wait to tell their loved ones about it when they next write home. Palm trees dance in the warm wind of early autumn as sand-coloured military vehicles unload men and equipment on to the hot concrete. The windscreens are covered in dust. Drivers can only see through small spaces created by the wipers. A long line of soldiers, three-men wide in places, creeps from the city streets right up to the deck of an LCI(L), which is back in Tripoli in readiness for an invasion. The men wear berets but have metal helmets strapped to their backs. Wearing light uniforms, most carry heavy haversacks, some with battered white ceramic drinking cups rattling on one side. Rifles draped over their shoulders, men split the load of large metal boxes between them. One soldier carefully places a Royal typewriter on to the craft. The troops are mainly British, but a few US soldiers line up alongside. As they pass by the bow, '185' is painted in large black numbers. From the deck, the crew look down at those set to join them and call out a mixture of directions and friendly greetings to the troops about to walk the short wooden ramp on to the deck.

During the Allied invasion of Italy, known as Operation Avalanche, the craft will be a part of the Northern Landing Force. Its destination is Salerno. On 9 September 1943, surrounded by ninety-five other LCI(L) packed with soldiers from the British 46th Division, 185 heads across the water. The task at hand is once again to successfully disembark its cargo of troops on to the beach. Crews are experienced now, as are the infantrymen preparing to disembark. They have been fired upon before, but fear is still abundant on the journey. The dark atmosphere has subsided ever so slightly due to an armistice between Italy and the Allies the previous day, resulting in Italian troops pulling out of the upcoming battle. As the craft move in formation through the waves, there is jubilation on board, even talk of wandering into

Italy without any hassle from the enemy. The Germans, however, are quickly plugging positions left by the Italians. They will not be going down without a fight.

Choosing to forgo any pre-landing naval or aerial bombardment in order to preserve the element of surprise, the Allies do not control the skies above. As the flotilla heads towards the Italian coast, it is quickly spotted by German aircraft overhead. Reaching the shallows, British ears are filled with the haunting sound of loudspeakers taunting their arrival. The enemy is ready. Machine-gun posts are zeroed in on the landing beaches. Artillery surrounds the coast. LCI(L) 185 is once again heading into the thick of it.

When troops reach the beach, initial defence is lighter than expected. The enemy still puts up a fight, but troops are successfully disembarked nonetheless. Subsequent waves of craft and men ready themselves to enter the fray, but progress is slow, and the 16th Panzer Division soon counterattacks. They are quickly repelled by naval bombardment. Ships offshore prove invaluable, dropping over 11,000 tons of explosives on to the enemy. Five Landing Craft Tank (Large) – LCT(L) – and the hospital ship *Newfoundland* are lost, but still the beaches are secured. Although Allied casualties start to mount up as the battle progresses inland, 185 has once again proven its worth in an initial landing.

From the coast of Italy, the craft are called back to Britain. There is a sense among the men that a landing in France is on the horizon. By now, the crew of 185 have been continuously on board since leaving the coast of North America. Large numbers of troops have briefly occupied the vessel and left its bow to head towards the enemy. The craft has become quite literally the crew's home.

On the journey back, the convoy moves through the Bay of Biscay. Suddenly from above, enemy aircraft scream through the air and attack. LCI(L) 309 is hit, quickly sinking in the unfathomable depth of the bay, never to be seen again. LCI(L) 185's crew jumps into action to try to save as many survivors as possible. They save eighteen men, but four are killed, with another later dying of his wounds. Their efforts are hindered when their own craft becomes a victim of the attack. It is struck by the enemy, losing its ability to steer. The vessel is dangerously close to sinking but is quickly stabilised and carefully towed until repairs can be made. Back in working order, 185 arrives into the harbour at Poole in Dorset, where all involved are shaken up from the experience.

It has been a challenging eighteen months. Adam Christie and the group that left Scotland as fresh-faced sailors have sampled the delights of New York City, enjoyed the beautiful climates of Bermuda and Gibraltar, and practised landings at Algiers. They have fought for real in both Sicily and Italy and rescued drowning men, but for 185 life at sea is far from over. By late 1943, the Allies are well versed at putting large numbers of troops on to enemy beaches using landing craft. Now with LCI(L) truly battle tested, and the need to land in France becoming more pressing by the day, the craft are called upon once again.

Safely back in England, the craft are assigned to Force S. LCI(L) 185 will now cease to exist. Instead, along with LCI(L) 269, it will be converted into a Landing Craft Headquarters, with the two becoming sister ships. These craft will for all intents and purposes be in charge of the initial landing at Sword Beach when the time finally comes to land in Normandy. Although they will keep their pennant numbers, the craft will need to undergo a physical conversion in order to take on this role.

LCI(L) are designed to carry and disembark as many troops as possible. Large open spaces fill the bow of the craft, leaving ample room for soldiers. The main conversion to a Landing Craft

Headquarters is to fit out the two Troop Deck areas into a number of Wireless Offices, Operations Room and Officers' Quarters. This scales down the capacity of the craft from nearly 200 to 50, but these rooms are crucial to the purpose of an LCH. During the landing, the vessels will send, receive and relay information. The need to exchange messages across the assault force is of utmost important to the success of the invasion. These newly created rooms will be filled to the brim with wireless telegraphy and radio equipment.

The exterior of the craft is also changed, with a large tripod foremast fitted to the middle of the deck. To this are mounted the extra aerials needed to run all of the communication equipment. This addition makes a Landing Craft Headquarters stand out clearly in the chaos of craft seen in Force S. It is unique, making it easier for those following it to spot, but the foremast will also be an obvious target for the enemy. Final alterations to come later on will not be to the craft itself, but to the type of men who will work within it. Hundreds of troops tightly fitted into an LCI(L) will be swapped out for a much smaller number of thoroughly trained, highly skilled telegraphists and radio operators with the ability to work the new equipment. With these alterations made, LCH 185 is born.

The scale of the Allied invasion at Normandy can't be overstated. Operation Neptune is the largest amphibious operation in any war in history. The broad objective will be to successfully establish the Allies on mainland Europe in order to ensure an offensive push into the Continent. In total, 6,939 vessels will be present, 4,126 of which will be some form of landing craft. There will be a further 1,213 warships, 864 merchant vessels and 736 ancillary craft. During the landings, 156,000 troops will disembark on to the beaches, while a further 195,700 naval personnel will be spread across vessels in the English Channel. The assault will be split into two task forces.

Western Task Force will attack the two US-designated beaches to the west. Eastern Task Force will attack the two British beaches and one Canadian beach further east. Within these task forces will be the Assault Forces J, G and S, with L serving as a follow-up force.

LCH 185 will be in Group One of Force S, which consists of the ships HMS *Dacres*, HMS *Glenearn*, HMS *Battleaxe*, HMS *Cutlass* and HMS *Empire Broadsword*. There will be a further two Landing Craft Navigation and one motor launch to guide the way to France; eight Landing Craft Tanks to launch Duplex Drive tanks; three Landing Craft Support (Large) – LCS(L) – to provide cover for those on the beach; three Landing Craft Gun (Large) – LCG(L) – to fire upon enemy defences; and ten Landing Craft Personnel (Large) – LCP(L) – to shuttle troops and provide smoke cover, with LCH 185 overseeing it all. After Group One has successfully disembarked, 185 will then head back in repeatedly with the other seventeen landing groups that are to follow. The commander on board will assess everything from enemy resistance to water conditions in order to make crucial decisions in the heat of the moment.

The plan for D-Day is exactly that. It is a plan written up in clandestine meetings by those in positions of power. The difference between a plan in war and the actuality of a battle is enormous. Situations can change in a split second, if not derailing the entire operation, then at least throwing it in an entirely different direction. The landings have been meticulously planned right through to the most minute of details. Every single man will know his role and will have rehearsed it relentlessly. Each individual vessel and person has a job to do, and, when the time comes, so many practice landings will have taken place on British shores that, for those heading across on 185, it should feel like another day at work.

For the hardened crew, who have already survived Sicily and Italy, they know what to expect. For most of the telegraphists and wireless operators that will soon step aboard, D-Day will be first the time that they have ever seen the enemy. There will be machine guns on clifftops, enemy planes overhead, mines strapped to deadly defences and heavy artillery all coming together in a terrifying orchestra that aims to send them to the seabed. If 185 makes the wrong calls, relays the wrong information or the craft is sunk, the landing at Sword Beach will be in jeopardy.

The Allied invasion of Normandy has been an inevitability for years, building for almost as long as the war has lasted. By June 1940, the German army had stormed across Europe, chased 338,000 British troops back into the English Channel, and successfully taken control of France. As the last man boarded the final ship at Dunkirk, leaving behind vast amounts of equipment, vehicles, machinery and men, both sides knew that it wouldn't be the last time commonwealth feet would touch European sand. In March 1942, Hitler ordered the construction of the Atlantic Wall, an awe-inspiring series of concrete fortifications snaking along the coast from the bottom of France to the tip of Norway. The defences were built because it was a case of when, not if, the Allies would be returning to mainland Europe. Winston Churchill knew this when he formed the Combined Operations Command in 1940, in order to take the fight to back to the Continent in the future.

Pressure was building from Franklin D. Roosevelt and Joseph Stalin as early as 1942 for Churchill to land in northern France. Two plans were drawn up, codenamed Operation Roundup and Operation Sledgehammer. The former called for a large-scale invasion of Europe in the spring of 1943, while the latter differed by calling for an invasion as early as autumn 1942. Sledgehammer didn't plan for an immediate push across Europe. Instead, the Allies would secure and hold a beachhead at Cherbourg to which supplies and men could be transported periodically across the English Channel. When enough power had amassed, an offensive breakout could take place in the spring of 1943.

Both plans were the topic of discussion and dispute. The British viewed an invasion of France that early in the war as premature. The Allies lacked the huge amount of resources that the plans called for. Everything from landing craft to equipment and infantry came up short in comparison to those needed. Roundup would require 5,800 aircraft, 48 divisions' worth of soldiers with enough landing craft to carry them across the water, and the destroyers and cruisers to support them. Similarly, with Sledgehammer, the Allies lacked the force needed to not only take Cherbourg, but to then hold it. Such a condensed area of Allied troops in Europe cut off from Britain would be prone to attack by air, sea and land. It could end in disaster.

Both plans were deemed feasible at various stages, and even seriously considered, but Churchill resisted. Having fought on French soil during the Great War, he was keenly aware of the possibility of a bloodbath on foreign land. A repeat of the first day of the Somme on 1 July 1916, which ended with 60,000 British casualties, would be a disaster that he could do without. Instead, Churchill pushed to take the fight to the Mediterranean, referring to it as the 'soft underbelly' of German-occupied Europe. Fighting in the Mediterranean, it was reasoned, would allow the Allies time to gather enough supplies to eventually invade France with an overwhelming force, while giving the Americans, who were still new to the war, much-needed time and experience in battle.

In November 1942, the Allies successfully invaded North Africa. Sicily followed in July 1943, and Italy two months later in

September. With the Mediterranean now in Allied hands, Stalin and Roosevelt ramped up the pressure on Churchill, insisting that the Allies invade France sooner rather than later. A few months earlier, Frederick Morgan, a British general, was made Chief of Staff to the Supreme Allied Command and was tasked with creating the plan for an invasion of northern France. What he came up with went against what the Germans were expecting. Between South Foreland in Kent and Cap Gris-Nez in the Pas-de-Calais are just 18 nautical miles of water. On a clear day, one can occasionally be seen from the other. Calais is the most obvious place for an invading army to land. Germany knows that. As a result, the area is heavily fortified, but Morgan instead chooses Normandy. Operation Overlord, as it is now known, is set for May 1944. It is a simple premise. With a stronghold on the mainland in place, German forces can be pushed back across Europe. In doing so, each country on the way to Germany can be liberated from Nazi rule. Once fought back to Berlin, with the Russians closing in from the east, the Nazis can be toppled and peace in Europe restored.

Britain is referred to as the world's biggest aircraft carrier in the war years. In the build up to the invasion, it is an island filled to the brim with servicemen and women. Dwight Eisenhower himself jokes that the only thing keeping the UK afloat is the barrage balloons. By the time D-Day arrives, there will be over three and a half million military men and women in Britain, of which one and a half million will be involved in the invasion itself. The numbers, it is hoped, will be overwhelming, beating the Germans into submission.

Chapter Three

9 July 2017

Time is not on my side. Patrick is ninety-two years old. He is in good health, but I've learned first-hand that elderly veterans can be dancing in a bar one night and gone the next. If I had forever, sooner or later LCH 185 would be found, but without Patrick around to witness it, the discovery will mean far less. Second World War shipwrecks are often just piles of rusting metal, ship-shaped if you're lucky, resting on the seafloor. They will eventually corrode away, disappearing to nothing. Of course, discovering any wreck is important, but with the last survivor of the sinking here to see it, that pile of rusting metal holds a much deeper meaning. LCH 185, if found, represents a link to the present day that can never be repeated once the final witness has died. Archaeologically, anything I uncover will be measured by length and width, but Patrick's memories mean that the story is still alive. Deep beneath the surface, the remains of 185 hold within it anecdotes of laughter and sadness, mundane days spent doing chores, and the voices of men that were never heard again. Patrick remembers it all.

I wouldn't want to raise the wreck if it still exists, or even disturb the site. Simply locating the vessel, seeing it on the seabed and showing Patrick whatever is down there, will be enough to finish the story. I want to locate the wreck with Patrick by my side. I want him to witness the location of the place he called home for so long being discovered. That way, he can know once and for all where his friends were lost; know where his fellow sailors were once held together within 185's crumpled bow until their bodies disappeared with time, returning to nature with the flow of the sea. To find the wreck could bring closure to the trauma of the sinking, and end a chapter of my friend's life that is still left as a blank space on the page. If Jack Barringer's family are out there, if the families of any of those who died that day still remember their loved ones, perhaps finding the wreck could bring them all peace. I hope it will.

But I didn't just promise to find the wreck, I promised to build a memorial to the crew. Building a monument to those who died on 185 would give the story the recognition it deserves and ensure that the memory of the tragedy never fades. If I could pull off such a feat, Patrick would be able to unveil it in tribute to the friends he lost that day, fulfilling his duty as the last member of the craft's crew. I'm going to have to deliver both of these promises in order to call the search for 185 a success. But these are two different worlds. One of diving and adventure, and one of bureaucracy and red tape. It will be tough to navigate both sides of the project at once, but I can't let my friend down.

The search begins immediately after I drive off the ferry on to British soil. After a few days at work, I take the four-hour journey to Eastbourne. Patrick has lived in the quaint seaside town for decades, drawn to its coastal setting by his definitive younger years spent at sea. Pulling into a quiet cul-de-sac, I knock on the door. There's a long delay as I wait for the ageing sailor to slowly hobble his way through the house.

'Patrick! Good to see you again,' I shout.

We shake hands, then move through to the living room. He offers me a glass of wine from an already open bottle. It is 10 a.m. and I'm driving. I ask for a cup of tea instead. It's just the two of us at his house today. Away from the excitement of the Normandy celebrations, I find a different atmosphere altogether. It has never occurred to me that when D-Day veterans aren't drinking with dignitaries or accepting cheek kisses from French women, they mostly sit alone in silence in their empty houses.

As I look around at the fading photographs of a long life scattered around the living room, I think back to times spent at my own grandparents' house. Of all the times I visited, one stays with me the most. I had been sitting in the living room for an hour when my grandfather came through. He sat down with a look of surprise, having not realised I was there.

'Sorry, John,' he said. 'I take my time getting ready these days. It makes the days go by faster.'

I can still hear the tiredness in his voice.

After a quick catch up, turning down more offers of wine, Patrick and I sit down to discuss his time during the war. He decides to start at the very beginning with his life as a young boy. Time is short and I have a busy day ahead, but when a D-Day veteran wants to tell you his story, it's hard to cut them short.

'People asked me why I joined the Royal Navy,' he begins. 'Well, otherwise I would have gone into the PBI, the Poor Bloody Infantry. They were always up at the sharp end!'

Patrick Thomas is born on 20 October 1925 in Shrewsbury, Shropshire. A largely uneventful upbringing in a quiet corner of England, he is raised in one of the earliest examples of a council house, built to clear out the slums, a common story right across the country. Even as a child, Patrick notices that his surroundings are far from those of a prosperous family. The house is in a state of much-needed repair, but the family always find themselves with enough of what they need. The boy is happy, despite the hardship.

The family home is 3 miles from the local primary school. On his first day, Patrick's older brother Fred is given the task of escorting him to class. As the two young lads skip through the country lanes, they have no idea where life will take them in just a few short years. Patrick will land at Sword Beach and Fred at Gold. Neither will know that the other was in France until long after the landings are over.

Reaching school, after settling in to his new surroundings, Patrick and the rest of the children are given chalk to write the numbers one to nine. He struggles with the eight, before realising that he can take a shortcut by drawing two noughts on top of each other. A perfectionist at heart, he is pleased when the teacher finally shows him the correct way. Patrick wants to do it properly. At lunchtime, a child invites him round for dinner after school. The possibility of a new friendship is exciting, especially on the first day, but upon arrival at the boy's house the child promptly runs away, leaving Patrick bawling in the street. He is a small-statured and cheery-faced chap. The child that he is will never truly leave his face as he gets older. People will always find him to be adorable. Standing in the street, tears streaming, the boy is spotted by two girls who kindly walk him back to school, right into the comforting arms of his mother. He relishes the attention.

After a dramatic start to the education system, Patrick spends his days in class restlessly watching the clock, waiting for the bell to ring. With the end of the day comes freedom to wander the countryside with his best friend, Len. The boys sneak off to the cattle market, taking in the sounds and smells of rural life, clambering up to peer over gates at the cows and pigs. They sometimes venture further out, down to the weir to play in the water, but a destination isn't needed to make them feel like they are on a big adventure. To simply wander through the picturesque town, free of parental smothering, is enough to be content. It's liberating to be out and alone with Len, at least until Patrick's sister Sheila is sent out to find them, dragging the small adventurers straight back home.

Before long, Patrick moves up to senior school. Not just a sign of growth; this is the historic moment when he is finally allowed to wear trousers instead of shorts. A smartly dressed young man at last, just like his father. He attends Monkmoor Senior Boys School. By the standards of the day, the building is far ahead of its time. Designed by a Swiss architect, the school is based on the collegiate quadrangle concept, with a covered walkway that snakes around the outside. Mr Hipwell is the loathed headmaster, feared by both pupils and staff alike. If you are sentenced to be caned, Hipwell is the designated punisher whose ghoulish figure frequents the covered walkway. Children hear him long before they see him, the haunting sound of a wooden leg echoing down the hall. Thump. Thump. Thump. His students won't forget the noise of the headmaster hunting his prey. The classrooms are glass panelled. He stops to stare into each room as the thumping falls silent. Hipwell has arrived. A boy is spotted not paying attention. The headmaster strides into the classroom unannounced and orders the pupil to his office to be caned. The punishments are not always in private. Humiliation is just as key to the discipline as the hitting itself. Patrick and his classmates are occasionally called to the assembly hall to witness a boy being escorted on to the stage and given six whacks of the cane in front of the entire school. The sound of the child pleading and the painful sense of second-hand embarrassment will stay with those who see it for a lifetime.

Patrick is a smart child, having gained top grades on his entrance exams to the school, something that will fare well in his future life as a telegraphist. The war, after all, is not far away. A contingent of Germany's Hitler Youth visit the school to compete with the local boys at the annual sports day. The Germans are smartly dressed in military-style uniforms and excel at every sport they take part in. Patrick watches in awe as the Hitler Youth members tear win after win from the grasp of the Shrewsbury boys. Discus and javelin, in particular, leave the home team thrashed.

Although passionate about learning, Patrick has to leave school at fourteen to find a job and earn a living. Such is the way of life for many in the 1930s, but despite heading out into the world he is determined to not limit his prospects, choosing to pay a shilling a term to return to school in the evenings. Years later, Patrick will discover that some of his teachers fought, and were killed, fighting in the same war that claimed so many of his own friends' lives.

As news of Hitler's rise to power reaches the English countryside, Patrick's mother is concerned. The '14–18 war', as many of that generation know it, is still fresh in her memory. 'Cannon fodder' is a term used in the Thomas household frequently. War comes quickly and, on 3 September 1939, Patrick sits with his family around the radio. They listen with anticipation as Neville Chamberlain announces that Britain is at war with Germany. There is immediate dread. Every person in the country knows what those words mean. Many have been here before. Whether it is young men knowing they will be heading to war, mothers learning that their sons will be in the firing line, fathers remembering the horrors of the last time, or those destined to stay at home knowing that everything is about to get much harder – for every single person, life will not be the same for a very long time.

* * *

Ever the gentleman, Patrick has prepared a three-course meal for my visit. He cooks me a steak, with dessert a homemade trifle soaked in enough alcohol to make me think I should have just drunk the wine anyway. We reminisce about our times in Normandy while both trying to ignore the elephant in the room: that I am here to start an expedition to search for the wreck of LCH 185. Both Patrick and I know that we have to discuss it at some point, so I cut to the chase. As he clears the dinner table, I spread out a handful of maps I've brought with me. Some are wartime, others are modern, but all of them show the stretch of land and water known as Sword Beach. Patrick calmly walks over to me and wisely gazes across the table at his former battlefield like an artist preparing his canvas.

'Where did you land, Patrick?' I ask.

I already know the answer, but I want to familiarise him with the maps.

'Lion-sur-Mer. Which is about . . .' He trails off as his finger moves across the table.

'Here!' he says.

'Where do you think the craft sunk?' I ask.

'Ah, well, it must have been somewhere around here,' he replies, pointing to a patch of water about 5 nautical miles off the coast of France.

It's a promising start, but too vague to really do anything with. After such a long time, it's understandable that Patrick doesn't remember exactly where he was. During our email exchanges, he had casually mentioned that a sailor he later worked with at the Post Office had seen 185 sink. The man watched as the craft went up in a sheet of flames, clouded by a column of water bursting into the air, before vanishing. Patrick's colleague, he claimed, was stationed on one of the Gooseberry harbours, lines of half-submerged ships used as breakwaters off of the landing beaches.

If true, this means that the craft had to have gone down east of the Gooseberry at Sword. Another clue came when Patrick mentioned that the LCG(L) he was pulled on to was then shelled from Le Havre, meaning that it must have been within firing range of the guns in that location. This gave a very wide and incredibly rough search area, but it was at least something I had to go on before visiting Patrick at his home. His finger, luckily, has just landed right in that spot.

'We were following LCH 269, our sister ship. I feel we couldn't have been far from the Gooseberry, that's my feeling,' he says.

The vast search area has just been propped up by Patrick's own recollection, but still the position might be wrong. LCH 185 may have been destroyed beyond recognition during the war, or lifted and moved after hostilities ceased. If this is the right area, I face such a huge expanse of water that to pinpoint a single wreck will be like looking for a needle in a haystack full of needles. I once read of a man who spent decades diving in search of sunken US tanks off the coast of Omaha Beach, only for archaeologists to then find them using sonar. The data showed that he had been within touching distance of the vehicles on a number of occasions, unable to see his holy grail through the gloom of the English Channel. It will be hard, perhaps even impossible, but I can't stop now. My promise has been made, and the wheels of the search are moving forwards.

We move to the sofa to continue our conversation. I listen carefully for any crucial pieces of information that could prove useful later on. Patrick recalls the difficulty with which he adjusted to life after the war. How exactly those who fought managed to return home from such traumatic events is something often overlooked. We see brave men fighting wars in films and read of their heroics in memoirs, but think little of their lives afterwards.

'When I was eventually demobbed, it took me a long time to settle down, because I'd done so much in such a short time in the Royal Navy. I must confess that I drank too much. I never drank pints, I drank buckets,' he says with an uneasy laugh.

Patrick has never told me this before. No doubt in the age in which we now live, he would likely have been diagnosed with post-traumatic stress disorder and offered help, but back then he was left to drink away the memories. Growing up, I had two great-uncles who were prisoners of war in South-east Asia. I once arranged to speak to one of them about the prison camps, but with the day approaching I instead received a phone call from my grandmother.

'He can't do it, I'm afraid,' she said. 'Ever since he promised to speak, he's had dreams of his captors every night.'

Like countless others, my great-uncles were told simply to not talk about the camps when they got back to England because not only would no one be interested, few would even believe that something so awful could have actually occurred.

'The thing to remember is this,' Patrick continues. 'When I was demobbed, there were thousands of others who had also been demobbed. They all had a tale to tell. I never used to speak about it, I never dreamt of speaking about it. The medals came in a little square box. I opened them once and had a look at them but, after that, I didn't look at them again for about thirty years. I never thought any more about it.'

I nod my head, remembering how my grandfather wore his medals on just one single occasion. When he died, I found his dog tags in a bedside drawer. I didn't know he still had them. The war was rarely mentioned in personal terms, but it was never far out of reach.

'You see, we change as we get older. I rarely gave it a thought all those years. You don't. It's at the back of your mind. You don't think about it any more, but I couldn't really forget it. I never spoke about it to anybody, I didn't tell anybody. It's only in recent years that I've thought about it. It's very difficult to recall feelings about your shipmates from all those years ago. I never used to get emotional, but I suppose now I've grown older, I tend to get more emotional when I think back. Knowing what happened to those men. My age, most of them. I was nineteen at the time. Some were younger, of course.'

Patrick is visibly upset as he speaks.

'If I could find the craft, would it matter to you?' I ask. 'If I could pinpoint where the craft is, you could know where your friends are resting and get some closure, perhaps.'

'I'd love to know! I'd love to be able to find where it is. I get a feeling there wouldn't be a lot of it left. I could be wrong, I don't know. If ever you could find LCH 185, I would be delighted! I would absolutely love that.'

Patrick reaches beside the sofa and brings up a small envelope yellowed by time. This is the first time he has tried to read the letter since it first arrived in 1944. It was written to Patrick from Les Barringer, asking about the fate of his brother Jack. Fighting through the tears, he struggles to get to the end.

The conversation winds down with a light-hearted chat. Patrick shows me a photograph of what he was told is 185 storming towards Sword Beach. He was sent it after the war by someone who took the photo from the deck of another landing craft. I look down at the grainy image. The motion of the water is vivid. If this is 185, the craft is clearly heading at some speed through the chaos of the first wave of the landings.

We drink tea before heading out to my car. Despite his age and frailty, Patrick will be joining me for the first part of the expedition. Helping him into the passenger seat, I load his wheelchair into the boot and drive to Portsmouth.

'It's like we're on a road trip together!' I shout towards his ear.
'Yes!' he nods.
We both laugh.

The journey is short, from one coastal town to another, and we soon
arrive at the Historic Dockyard. The town has a long, impressive
history. The entire identity of the area is built around the navy.
It seems as if every pub sign and street name makes reference to
sailors or the sea. Memorials to those lost in wars fought on the
water are everywhere. The Historic Dockyard is a living museum
and still an active naval base. It isn't uncommon to see a modern
sailor walking by in full uniform as you explore the old buildings.
Heading towards the entrance, we pass a pub called the Ship and
Castle. Patrick spots it right away, calling up from his wheelchair
with excitement as the memories come flooding back.

'That's the pub we used to drink in, I'm sure of it!'

There are historic ships of all shapes and sizes wherever my eyes
turn. It's a task to not get swept up in the atmosphere of expeditions
at sea, but Patrick and I aren't here to be tourists. We're here because
it was in this dockyard that 185 and its crew impatiently waited to
head to Normandy on the eve of D-Day. The heads of other visitors
spin as we move along the path, pushing the wheelchair towards
our destination. Patrick is an ordinary-looking elderly man dressed
in civilian clothes. There is no blazer and certainly no medals. He
is never one to unnecessarily wear his 'shrapnel', as he refers to it,
but a man of Patrick's age, with a beard so definitively that of an
old sailor, stands out as a veteran immediately. Strangers stare and
smile as we move. Patrick gives his adoring public a wave back.

HMS *Victory* shadows over us. It is an iconic landmark in
Britain, having served as Lord Nelson's flagship at the Battle of
Trafalgar. We look insignificant as we pass the giant wooden hull.

Victory's grand exterior is still breathtaking even centuries after the ship was last used in battle.

'I suppose I'll go and join my old shipmates!' Patrick shouts, waving towards the salmon-pink bow of Nelson's old ship.

'You're not that old!' I reply with a laugh.

We slowly wheel along, until eventually coming to a stop at a deep void in the ground. This is a dry dock, a place for ships to be taken out of the water. In fact, it is the exact dry dock into which 185 was pulled for preparations the day before the landings took place. I push the wheelchair as close as it can get to the edge before moving to stand beside Patrick. When I've visited this spot as a tourist in previous years, it has never been that impressive – just a large hole in the ground where the Historic Dockyard now stores a First World War ship for guests to stare down at. I did not expect to feel much when visiting it today but, to my surprise, as I look down at the concrete walls with my friend by my side, the weight of the moment is enormous. It was here that Patrick Thomas, Jack Barringer and the rest of the crew of 185 were once preparing for war. I turn to take in the surroundings. *Victory* is right by us. Nelson's ship was here in 1944, covered in the scars of a recent Luftwaffe attack.

'I can't be precise where we were, because there were ships everywhere, as far as the eye can see,' Patrick says, motioning to the harbour beyond the dry dock. 'We must have set sail in the very early hours of the fifth of June. The sea was a bit bumpy. I'd got my sea legs by then you see, John!'

'And which way is Normandy?' I ask.

'I've lost my Boy Scout thing on that one!'

We burst out laughing before going quiet. I can feel the emotion seeping out of Patrick a few feet below me in his wheelchair. His thoughts journey back to the war, back to being a teenager in uniform. This was the last piece of Britain that his feet stepped on before heading to battle. For the majority of his crew, it was the last corner of home they ever saw. This mundane old concrete, trodden on by hundreds of people every day, was the last goodbye. For the old sailor, it represents the finality of a grand farewell to England.

'I never thought that after seventy-three years . . . I'd be here again,' Patrick says.

He has been gently crying.

'LCH 185 is out there, somewhere!' I say.

'Out there . . . somewhere,' Patrick says in a whisper.

We join Patrick's grandson Jason for lunch, before the two of them head home. As we part ways, I know that by the time I return from France, there is a possibility that I'll be bringing news of the wreck with me. I travel the short distance to a private marina behind a coded gate. Crossing over a metal bridge, I walk along a slippery wooden jetty in the hammering rain. The vessel I'm trying to find immediately stands out against the backdrop of pristine white yachts with its matte grey exterior covered in stencilled numbers. HMS *Medusa* appears from the misty landscape like a smoke-breathing dragon. The craft was designed as a Harbour Defence Motor Launch (HDML), a type of vessel originally intended for use as an offshore anti-submarine screen, but quickly swept up for use in amphibious landings. Like 185, Medusa is a veteran of D-Day. Its role had been to arrive a full twelve hours before US forces reached Omaha Beach to serve as a marker at the entrance to a crucial channel cleared of mines. Made entirely of wood, Medusa is now the last survivor of the original 464 HMDL manufactured.

Having never stepped foot on a Second World War vessel before, I feel honoured to head aboard. Carefully treading the uneasy wooden plank, I teeter above the gloomy water, trying not to lose my grip. Among the glass bottles and plastic bags that so commonly float through British marinas, I watch as a couple of neon-pink jellyfish peacefully dance beneath me. Making my way across the deck, beside ropes and cogs and bits of machinery, I open the hatch and head below. Waiting for me are two people I've arranged to meet in the hope that they might hold information on what problems may face me in this early stage of the expedition.

'Room for one more?' I ask, casually attempting to hide the fact that I've just smashed my head on the low ceiling.

Mike Perrin and Alan Smith are leaning up against the wheel of the ship as they chat among themselves. Alan is the chairman of a trust that looks after *Medusa*, and Mike is an old friend of mine from university. He is the only maritime archaeologist I personally know, so was naturally the first person I thought to call about the search. After introductions and a quick catch up, Mike blurts out the question on both of their minds.

'What's happening?' he asks.

Mike is clearly excited at the prospect of an adventure.

'Well . . .' I say, before pausing. I'm hesitant to explain, knowing exactly how I'm about to sound. 'This might be a bit crazy, but I want to find my friend's sunken landing craft. I'm hoping to find it and build a memorial to his shipmates while he's still with us. It's a bit of a race against time.'

'Do you know where the boat is?' Mike asks.

'Not exactly. I've got some ideas where it might be, and I've spoken to Patrick extensively about where he thinks it could be.'

Mike looks both concerned and enthralled. To be an archaeologist you have to have an innate sense of adventure inside you. No matter what anyone in the profession claims, we all secretly wish that the job could be at least a bit more like the movies.

Alan moves to a wooden drawer and pulls out a large map of the Normandy coastline. The map is used whenever his crew of volunteers are tasked with taking *Medusa* across the Channel, a challenging trip even now. It gives potentially life-saving information not just on water conditions, but on any hazards to avoid as well. As I try to make sense of what I'm seeing, I notice that scattered across the paper are tiny black drawings of a sinking ship. To my surprise, the map highlights wrecks in the area, but I can't see the symbols anywhere near Lion-sur-Mer. Worryingly, the chart doesn't show a Gooseberry harbour at Sword Beach either. I raise my concerns, but Alan confidently points out that the map only highlights hazards. If a wreck isn't tall enough or in a dangerous enough position to snag passing boats, then it isn't a hazard, and there is no need to mark it as one.

Steadying myself on the gently rocking boat, I remember something Patrick repeatedly mentioned the first time that we met. He holds a strong belief that at some point after the conflict the wartime wrecks off Normandy were systematically destroyed. Patrick was told this by a diver who had supposedly seen the evidence for themselves. The news hurt him deeply. Perhaps that is the reason why no wrecks are shown near to where 185 is supposed to have sunk. I researched Patrick's theory before beginning the expedition and, sadly, it seems to be true. Licensed by the French government, teams of divers had salvaged some, or possibly all, of the wrecks. Information on the salvaging is hard to come by. It isn't something that people boast about. What is clear is that, at some point in the 1970s, it was decided that as the English Channel is relatively shallow in places, it was too dangerous to continue to allow contemporary boats to pass so closely above jagged wrecks. The Channel is a busy crossing and almost always filled with pleasure cruisers, fishing boats, passenger ferries and enormous cargo ships.

To have any of these sink would be a national disaster. Hitting one of the wrecks from the war could very well cause such an incident.

France suffered terribly during the Second World War, with at least 20,000 civilians being killed in the Battle of Normandy alone. Immediately after its conclusion, the war was not yet history, it was the reality of a horrifying time that Europe had lived through for years. People were keen to move on. They needed to. There are photographs of landing craft, tanks and even large ships corroding away on the landing beaches years after the war ended. These days any of those vehicles would be seen as historically important, but back then they merely represented a recent trauma. When the decision was taken to salvage the wrecks, veterans of the war were not nearing a hundred years old. They were middle-aged men still yet to retire from their post-war civilian careers. Patrick and his fellow veterans are the last remnants of battles fought seven decades ago. They know, as do the public, that soon they will be gone. Back in the 1970s, veterans were just normal people living perfectly normal lives. The wrecks were understandably seen in the same light. Europe needed to rebuild. That is why Patrick thinks that, if 185 could be found, there wouldn't be much left of it.

'Mike, if you were to look at this and had to find a small landing craft in the middle of the English Channel . . .' I ask, not needing to finish the question.

'Do you dive?'

'No,' I say.

'Well, step one!'

We both laugh, knowing how bold it is to think that I can not only locate the wreck of 185, but do it without any diving experience at all. Mike explains that, while studying maritime archaeology, a lecturer had told him that it is 'easier to make an archaeologist a diver than it is to make a diver an archaeologist'.

'So, there is incredible hope!' he says.

We discuss the hurdles that I may come across. My first step is
to learn to dive. That will be easy enough to arrange. People learn
to dive every day, but learning in a swimming pool and diving
in the English Channel for an archaeological expedition are two
very different things. Conditions off the coast of Normandy are
infamous as a dreaded combination of strong currents, bad visibility
and dark waters. There's a reason that people who learn to dive for
pleasure often do so in places like Thailand or the Bahamas. The
surroundings are stunning and the clear blue water is filled with
exotic fish. Those that dive in the English Channel are more likely to
be doing so for an archaeological purpose, like myself. Once able to
dive and if a potential wreck is located, I will still need to undertake
a full survey in order to uncover the small details and measurements
that can confirm the identity of anything found on the seabed.

As I rest my shoulder on the steamed-up windows of *Medusa*,
I question whether I've taken on too much. Archaeology is
my vocation, but I've given little thought to the most obvious
difference. Maritime archaeologists use almost identical techniques
to those used on land, but they work underwater and are restricted
by the time it takes for a tank filled with oxygen to deplete. It is
so similar, but so very different. The odds are stacked against me;
the likelihood of someone with zero diving experience successfully
running a multi-country, full-scale search expedition is slim.
Still, that doesn't really matter. I've promised Patrick that I'll try.
Waving goodbye to Mike and Alan, I hurry from *Medusa* back on
to the now pitch-black jetty and walk a short distance in the rain
to another ship at the end of the marina.

Ducking to avoid another ceiling collision, I order a pint and head
through the wooden doors into a room that visibly slopes at one

end. The ship moves as the storm outside gains momentum. It's hard not to imagine how much worse this would be out on the open water. The ship I'm now aboard was built in 1947 for use as a light vessel, a floating lighthouse, in the Channel. At some point in its life, the hull was painted lime green and the ship renamed *Mary Mouse 2*. These days it is a floating restaurant, with framed black and white promotional headshots of former radio presenters spread across the walls. I spot the face of John Peel, the DJ who lived for much of his life close to my hometown in Suffolk.

Waiting for me at one end of the room, sitting at a table dented and stained from many drunken nights on the water, is Stephen Fisher. At the start of the expedition, I knew that I'd need help to uncover the exact history of 185 on D-Day. I have a decent amount of historical knowledge, as well as personal recollections from Patrick, but my archival searches for the craft have been repeatedly turning up blanks. Stephen, who is both an accomplished naval historian and a maritime archaeologist, read about my project and kindly got in touch to offer a helping hand. With bleached-blond hair spiked high into the sky and wearing a beaded necklace, he is not what I expect to see, which is exactly what I like about him.

A large map is spread across the table with a chunky laptop pinning it down. Papers are scattered all around and I struggle to find a place to put my drink in the middle of the organised mess. Introducing myself, I take a seat. Straight away Stephen launches into the treasure trove of information he's managed to uncover.

'It's kind of difficult to find out about individual ships, because they gave them new numbers called Landing Index Table Numbers.'

I have no idea what he means or where this is going, but nod along and hope to make sense of it as we go.

'So, on D-Day, LCH 185 wasn't LCH 185?' I ask, confused.

'No,' Stephen says. 'It still had its identity painted on the hull, but it also had a second number. They called them Fleet Numbers. That's the number you need. By comparing information in different documents, we can start to work out that puzzle and come up with the other identity of 185.'

I had no idea that on D-Day landing craft were given a new number just for that one single day. Stephen has discovered that it's possible to crack the key to these numbers by carefully combing through the original documents and maps. Initially, we take a report filed by the senior officer on board 185, Commander Edmund Currey, and find it to confirm that the vessel served as the headquarters craft in Group One of the landing. This shows definitively that 185 was in the very first wave at Sword Beach. Although we don't dwell on the confirmation for long, it's an amazing feeling to be able to show in the official documentation that Patrick was right up at the front of the invasion. The report goes on to state that, alongside Currey, Brigadier George Erroll Prior-Palmer also crossed the Channel on 185. Prior-Palmer was the commanding officer of 27th Armoured Brigade, which was destined to land in Group One. Everything is lining up. Next, perhaps most crucially, is a document showing the devolving chain of command needed in case any senior officers were killed or injured. It shows that Brigadier Prior-Palmer, who we now know was on board 185, was assigned to a craft with the Landing Index Table Number 501. In a eureka moment, these combined documents reveal that LCH 185 was actually known as LCH 501 on D-Day. With this uncovered, what exactly 185 did on 6 June can be gradually teased out of the eerie silence of history through maps and documents spread across the table.

Wind rumbles the hull of the ship. The storm is battering the vessel now, dimming the room as it rocks us in the marina.

In the hour I have before needing to catch a ferry to France, Stephen and I begin to unravel the story of LCH 185 for the first time since 1944.

Chapter Four

3 September 1939

When war breaks out, Patrick is too young to serve. He tries to sign up for the Royal Navy at sixteen, but is told to wait another two years. In the meantime, he takes a job at the Post Office as a sorting clerk and telegraphist, a role that will come in handy later on. Waiting to come of age, Patrick joins the Home Guard, serving alongside his own father and a number of much older men who had fought in the 14–18 war. Together they patrol Shropshire, guarding their beloved countryside from a future German invasion that may or may not arrive. Patrick and his fellow citizen soldiers are taught by a Republican veteran of the Spanish Civil War how to strangle a man with piano wire, how to attack someone's eyes with needles, and the correct way to attach a homemade sticky bomb to an enemy tank. Fear of the enemy crossing the English Channel is real, and this odd mix of young bucks and old soldiers take the role very seriously.

After a time spent using whatever gun-shaped alternative can be found, the group are sent Ross rifles from Canada. They are hard to get on with, thought of as overly heavy, too big and impossibly greasy. Excitement spreads through the group when a number of British Lee Enfield rifles arrive, most of which are left over from the last war. For the veterans in the group it feels like being reunited with an old friend. In decades to come, history will paint the Home Guard in a naive, perhaps even hopeless light but, for the men involved, their skill, belief and commitment to their country are real.

The group travel to firing ranges often, where in Patrick's words he goes 'charging about with the old boys'. During one training exercise, the men run towards a pretend enemy position from deep within the camouflaged cover of a forest. They head for a house, having attached firecrackers to their rifles to simulate live fire. Patrick is confident that, had the attack been genuine, they would have defeated the enemy with ease: the Germans, rather than succumb to the overwhelming superiority of the British fighters, would have died laughing. As soon as the drill ends, the veterans head for the pub. Patrick follows on, happy to be joining in the camaraderie and thrilled to be a part of something. For a young man wanting to go to war, the Home Guard is a great opportunity to feel like he's making a difference.

By the time Patrick's eighteenth birthday comes around, he's more adamant than ever that doing his bit for king and country is the right thing to do. Britain is an island filled with veterans. It is built on stories of war and of men that carved their names into history. For Patrick and many his age, it seems a shameful proposition to let such an important moment pass them by. How can they speak of the war in years to come if they never actually live it? Both Patrick's brothers have already joined up, putting even more pressure on the young lad. But while most are keen to have a tale to tell, the bleak reality is that, once the war is over, for many it will never be mentioned again.

* * *

Having at last successfully signed up to serve with the Royal Navy on 26 March 1943, Patrick is sent away to begin his training. The gruelling journey from a fresh recruit to the front line will halt at many destinations, the first of which is the seaside town of Skegness in Lincolnshire. Picked up by bus at the train station, Patrick makes the short journey along the coast to his new home. Through the window, beyond the road flickers the shimmering water of the North Sea. Spring is almost here, coming closer with each turning tide. On the other side of the bus the view is much less optimistic. Behind an 8-foot-tall barbed wire fence is HMS *Royal Arthur*. It sounds like a ship, and newsreels joke that before long the Nazis will no doubt claim to have sunk it. The press are right in their prediction; Germany does exactly that on two separate occasions, but *Royal Arthur* isn't a ship at all. It is a stone frigate: a training base. The site began life as a Butlin's holiday camp when it first opened in 1936, but was subsequently requisitioned from the hands of its owners by the Admiralty at the outbreak of hostilities. For thousands of young men, this base is where their war will begin.

Once through the entrance, large metal gates are closed behind the recruits with the rattle of chains and an echoing ding of iron. From the inside the gates are unclimbable, looming high to guard a deeply inescapable situation. Civilian life is gone now, left on the other side. All that remains is the sound of holidaymakers gently riding up over the wall on the sea breeze. Lads from all corners of the United Kingdom have come together as one in a polyphonic expression of differing British accents. It doesn't pay to be well spoken here. Those that sound even slightly posh are labelled 'lah-de-dah ratings' in a heartbeat. Patrick is pleased to get by, safely blending in with his Shropshire twang.

The bright colours and eye-catching decor that once greeted enamoured families has long since been replaced with the same military grey that serves as a backdrop for the war for so many that wear a uniform. The words on the sign that greets new recruits, leftover from *Royal Arthur*'s holiday camp days, read:

Our true intent is all for your delight

In the stark light of a wartime present, the message taunts those about to move into the cramped wooden chalets that line roads turned sodden from the constant treading of hundreds of leather boots. Duck boards have been placed in the pathways to try to halt a rapid descent into a quagmire, but it has little effect. Recruits have no choice but to settle into a constant presence of thick, sticky mud on everything they own, including the new uniforms they have just been to collect. Hammocks hang like beige bunting from beamed entrance ways, chosen straight away as a perfect spot to practise putting up sleeping quarters. Down the treacherous mudslide path are shared toilets stocked with sharp newspaper and a smell to avoid at all costs.

Patrick's class of enthusiastic young faces are known as HO ratings, short for Hostilities Only. These are not career sailors, and they receive a suitably lacklustre welcome from the petty officer in charge. Dusty Miller enjoys tormenting recruits. It's light-hearted, but he means it, calling the hopefuls 'bloody crows' and 'civvy swine'. They have been 'raised under the regime of the petticoat', he reckons. Still, in Patrick's eyes Miller is a decent old boy. He takes his time with them, making sure the recruits understand what they are being taught. Despite his teasing, Miller's orders are always enthusiastically met with cries of 'Aye aye, chief!' from the wide-eyed hopefuls.

The huts are not meant for this time of year. They were built for the summertime stays of families wishing to cherish a break in the sunshine. Gaps around the doors are wide enough to ensure that the occupants shiver through the night. It's far from unusual for two recruits to huddle together beneath their combined blankets in an attempt to escape the cold. If they make it through the night to reach 06:30, after next to no sleep, the day begins with a violent banging so hard it seems to rattle the brain. Miller takes great pleasure in manoeuvring through the mud, foot by careful foot, hammering each chalet with a large stick to ensure everyone is awake. A rare moment of morning peace can be briefly found in steaming cups of cocoa before a day of hardship begins.

As training starts, there is a constant threat of German bombing raids hanging over the stone frigate. Bombers have already killed twelve civilians in a raid on the town, and claimed the lives of four sailors in a direct hit on *Royal Arthur*. Dinners are regularly interrupted by blackouts and enemy planes passing overhead. The deafening sound of air-raid sirens is not a rare occurrence, but training never stops for long. Each day consists of boat drills, rifle drills, signalling training, marches, seemingly endless running and everything else needed to turn a young man into a fully fledged seaman. Mundane chores need to be done as well. Each man takes their turn sweeping the chalets. Football matches are played to build unity and teach healthy competition, providing at least some minor enjoyment to cling onto.

There is a swimming pool teasing passersby with its perfectly inviting turquoise water that reflects the high afternoon sun. Staying at a former Butlin's camp complete with chalets, a pool and the sounds of seagulls in the air, recruits could almost be on holiday, if only the rest could be blocked out. The pool is used, but not for leisure. Instead, it is loaded with wooden boats and used for rowing practice or swimming lessons. All of this will come in handy should the men ever find themselves manning a lifeboat or trying to escape a sinking ship.

Patrick soon meets a man named Les Barringer. The two become fast friends, sticking together in the tough months to follow. They learn fast as they grow close. Recruits eat, work and sleep side by side. It's easy to form bonds behind the barbed-wire fence. Patrick doesn't find training that challenging, but his patience is pushed to its limit on the afternoon that he heads to collect his oilskin coat from the storage room. Putting it on, happy to be reunited with his favourite piece of clothing, he reaches into a pocket and is confused to find his hand sinking into a warm puddle. It doesn't take long for Patrick to clock what has happened. Someone has urinated in the pocket to prove that the coat really is watertight. The teenager is gutted.

Each recruit is given a shift on watch. When Patrick's turn arrives, he takes great pleasure in finally being the one to bang on the doors himself.

'Wakey, wakey, wakey!' he shouts.

A wash of obscenities greets his ears in return.

After successfully completing a series of interviews, Patrick is quickly earmarked for wireless telegraphy training. Before leaving, the class poses together for an official photograph in full uniform. Patrick stands at the back with his arms crossed as he grins widely for the camera. Les Barringer is a few rows away.

On 7 May 1943, the two are sent by train up to Dundee, Scotland. Carriages are filled to the brim with military personnel. Men in every colour of uniform cram the aisles, squeezed together like cattle, holding on tightly overhead. In Dundee, the students are billeted in the Mathers Hotel, a grand building sitting on the corner of a road junction. From here on out, students are expected to act as if they are on a vessel. Everything in the hotel must be referred to by its equivalent section of a ship. Bunk beds are installed, corridors become gangways, hotel rooms become cabins, and the dining room becomes the mess hall.

Compared to HMS *Royal Arthur*, the food at the hotel is an improvement, but the kitchen staff have struggled with a huge infestation of cockroaches for months. By the time Patrick arrives, it is all but over, but had the new arrivals known the true extent of the issue they may not have felt so comfortable. One woman who had trained at the hotel was horrified to find clearly recognisable parts of a cockroach in not only her breakfast but the mashed potato served at dinner as well. Eating the bread was a risk. Tearing open a freshly baked roll could reveal an entire body of one of the creatures.

At the Mathers Hotel, Patrick and Les are now enrolled in Marconi College, named after the pioneer of radio, Guglielmo Marconi. Here they learn how to operate wireless telegraphy equipment. Patrick takes to it with ease, having gained experience already while working as a telegraphist at the Post Office. At night, the students try to escape to local dances, but the hotel doors are always locked dead on 23:00. A mad dash across the city usually follows any night of escape. The scene is a stark contrast to what the hotel has been used to, having been caught up in the temperance movement. The building doesn't serve alcohol and won't until the 1950s.

After six months the class take their final exams. Patrick passes with flying colours, and is now a qualified and highly skilled wireless telegraphist. The Royal Navy has invested a lot of time and training into the teenager as an answer to a demand for telegraphists right across the military. The graduates are rightfully confident in their ability and aware of the importance that their role holds, but still know that the first true test will come when under enemy attack. Doing their job in battle will change everything, and that inevitability looms closer with each passing day.

The paths of Patrick Thomas and LCH 185 are beginning to converge. So far the man and the machine have been on two separate journeys, but they are now both heading towards the invasion of Normandy. LCH 185's crew are hardened veterans of two campaigns. Those already on board know each other well, but will soon have to accept fresh faces: graduates of training programmes, not grizzled soldiers. All that is left for 185 to do is welcome those with the ability to operate the new communication equipment to step aboard.

At Dundee, Patrick and Les Barringer are separated. Les is drafted to the destroyer HMS *Savage*, joining the Arctic convoys to Murmansk, Russia. Patrick is sent even higher into Scotland. In November 1943, he once again finds himself on a train filled with troops. His destination this time is Invergordon, Ross-shire. The journey takes twelve hours, including a brief stop off in Edinburgh where passengers are treated to breakfast. It is the first time that Patrick has salt on his porridge, in what turns out to be a surprisingly definitive culinary experience. Invergordon is large for a settlement on the water's edge not too far from the Scottish Highlands. During the Great War, the town had been a Royal Navy base but, with the outbreak of the Second World War, the location was considered to be within flying distance of the enemy. As a result, the base has been deemed unsafe. Instead, the area is used for amphibious aircraft, such as the Catalina and Sunderland flying boats. These planes patrol the Scottish islands, often going as far as the Norwegian coast. Despite this change of use, Invergordon is still important to the navy. Four miles outside of the town, at a place called Inchindown, is one of five large-scale fuel depots built in Scotland to refuel naval ships. The depot has been built to be bombproof, consisting of six enormous tanks, five of which are capable of holding 32 million gallons of fuel. From these tanks fuel can be sent directly from the depot to Invergordon through underground pipes in order to refuel docking naval ships.

Upon arrival, Patrick is saddened to find that the town is completely dry. There are no pubs open for business and all of the hotels are temperance buildings. Patrick and a few others are quickly marched off to an RAF naval base on the outskirts of the village of Alness. If Invergordon was bleak, on the rocky edge of the North Sea surrounded by nothing but hills and sheep, this place seems like a wasteland. The men are informed that they are to be housed in cold and cramped Nissen huts. Opening the creaking wooden door, an alarming sight greets those that peer inside. There are no beds. They are expected to sleep on the concrete floor and to try to warm up by the barely working stove in the middle of the hut.

This is cold enough to freeze a brass monkey!, Patrick thinks.

He has slept in holiday chalets in Skegness and hotel rooms in Dundee. They weren't perfect, but even for fit young men preparing for war, sleeping on a damp concrete floor is a step too far. Instead, they gather together and go searching for something, anything, better than this. Somehow a number of iron beds, broken into pieces, are located. In the dead of night the beds are snuck back to the huts, where in the light of the stove they are carefully reassembled in the hope that life can be as pleasant as possible. The next morning, Patrick and his roommates, like seeing an oasis in the desert, awake to discover that the camp has a small canteen selling ice-cold beer to thirsty servicemen.

Five men journey from Alness to Chatham, England, to pick up LCH 185 and LCH 269. On the train, the group are tasked with deciding who will go to which vessel. LCH 185 is the more senior of the two vessels, by nature of the captain – the skipper –

on 185 being more senior than the skipper on 269. With this, a petty officer, the highest ranking serviceman present, heads to 185 and takes with him a leading signalman whom he knows from a previous ship. Jack Barringer and another telegraphist head to 269.

Patrick and Jack have met at the camp. The name Barringer stood out to Patrick, and the two were soon bonding over memories of training with his brother Les back in England. Jack is a telegraphist as well, but he is far from new. A decade older than Patrick, he joined up in 1939 and has served throughout the war. Patrick is in awe of the man. He has a family. He is brave. Jack has already served on HMS *Capetown* with the Eastern Fleet and escaped from Singapore as it fell, jumping on to a motor boat to soar away one step ahead of the Japanese. He found nothing to eat or drink on board but a crate of port, which he quickly consumed. Jack has lived it for real already. He is a veteran; an adventurer who has seen the world.

The two Landing Craft Headquarters hug the coast back up to Scotland. Upon safe arrival into Invergordon, Patrick and the others have travelled to greet them, ready to be assigned to one of the two craft. Patrick is put on to 185. Jack sees this, and asks one of Patrick's shipmates if they can swap. The man agrees. Together Patrick and Jack step aboard LCH 185 for the first time, unknowingly sealing their fates in an instant. Jack isn't meant to be on 185. He swapped to be with his friend Patrick. That quick switch is made so casually that, if both crafts survive the war, the decision will never be thought of again.

With telegraphists and radio operators assigned, the crafts head to join the steadily gathering Force S, making the short journey around the coast towards a fishing village called Inver, where rehearsals for the invasion are set to begin. Inver has barely 1,000 residents. A fishing village through and through, it is quite normal for those that are born in Inver to die in Inver. That isn't seen as a bad thing. As an entire landing force navigates its way through rough seas towards a bay that residents have built their lives around for centuries, never could the villagers have known that the war is about to have such an immediate effect.

Until now, the conflict has not really altered the lives of those that call Inver home, but that is about to change overnight. On 11 November 1943, residents are called to the local hall. As they gather together, most taking their seats know each other well. There is a mixture of excitement and concern. It isn't normal for a sleepy village on the east coast of Scotland to call an emergency meeting. What could possibly be this important? Through the doors of the hall the villagers are greeted by military personnel. Sir Andrew Thorne, General Officer Commanding (GOC) Scottish Command, and Lord Rosebery, the Regional Commissioner of Civil Defence, bluntly inform the locals that they have until 12 December to evacuate the area. There is shock and upset in the room.

Movement in and out of the village is immediately restricted to just two time slots a day. Fifteen square miles of exclusion zone are cordoned off around the village. Two schools fall within the no-go area and are immediately forced to close. Inver Primary School stops teaching its fifty-six pupils, ending the education of a huge chunk of the local population's younger generations. There is no reason given for this turmoil, no explanation for lives being turned upside down in an instant. It is crucial to the war effort, they are told, and nothing more is said. A few miles behind Inver, the residents of a hamlet named Kintessack are also ordered to evacuate. They are given one week less than Inver to clear out. The war has arrived with a disturbing thud.

It will be years before anyone here finds out exactly why they are being made to leave. They have no idea that their homes are earmarked for military training. There are grumbles and there is agony. People are hurt to be carted out of their homes, but there is no choice. Britain has been at war for years already and, eventually, leaving is reluctantly accepted as a part of life in these times. The small number of villagers knuckle down, packing up entire lives into suitcases ready to leave everything behind. Some of the more elderly of the village wonder if they'll ever return. Everyone else wonders what exactly they might one day return to.

Inver's residents have always earned a living fishing or farming. Everything they know and love, and everything they have worked for, is in the village. As well as the trauma that comes with being forced to leave their homes, the locals are faced with another issue. What are they to do with the livestock kept on the land? What about the crops growing in the arable ground? Solutions come, but at a loss. Livestock is sold off in the nearby town of Dingwall, with animals put up at heavily discounted prices to get rid of them as quickly as possible. It's an everything-must-go sale taking place outside of the usual trading season. Sellers aren't allowed to advertise for the event in case the unusually timed and suspiciously large auction draws attention. Over 9,000 items of livestock are sold. The chickens aren't put up for sale; no one knows where their next meal will come from once the village is locked off. To prevent crops rotting in the soil, hundreds of Italian prisoners of war are brought into the area by the military to salvage as much as possible in the little time available. Such is the secrecy of the plans for the area that only approved farmers brought in from around the country are allowed to take part. Inver school records low attendance, with many of the children sent to help on the farms.

With the melancholy process of preparing to leave complete, the residents of Inver set off to begin a new life of uncertainty. Most find a place to stay with friends or family as close to home as possible and set about waiting eagerly to return. The village means so much to its people. Inver is where babies were born and the elderly passed away, where marriages took place and laughter filled the houses. Now it is merely a stage set. An empty village, a body without its soul, and that is exactly what the Royal Navy needs to rehearse for D-Day with live rounds.

The village is located in the Dornoch Firth, part of the broader Moray Firth, a triangular-shaped inlet that leads out to the North Sea. The coastline has been earmarked for its similarities to what the Allies will face in Normandy. Bookended at one end by the Tarbat Peninsula, the area of coast shares clear similarities to the landing beaches, and importantly for amphibious landings consists of a long, sandy beach stretching for miles. Behind the beach are undergrowth, fields and eventually a series of small villages. The area lacks the large bluffs often found in Normandy, but otherwise serves as a perfect fill-in. As Force S moves into the bay, eleven-year-old Rosemary Mackay and her twin sister are awoken at two in the morning by their father. Against their mother's wishes, he scoops them up in blankets and carries the girls outside to watch the ships arrive. This is history in the making, and he doesn't want his children to miss it.

By December, winter has truly set in. Thousands of 3rd Assault Division troops have arrived. In the bay floats a colossal display of destroyers, cruisers and landing craft. Up here on the Scottish coast, life is extremely tough this time of year. Each rising sun brings another cold, damp day to toughen up or break the troops. When rehearsals begin there are only six hours of sunlight per day. The sea is consistently choppy. Ships shell the beach with live munitions and soldiers attack with real bullets. This is the real deal, the closest thing men will get to a firefight before the genuine invasion takes place.

Patrick never touches land. The craft has been designed for men to live on for as long as is necessary, and there is no need to leave. The fresh graduates are as intimidated by the salty veterans as they are by the live shells passing overhead, but the old sailors take them under their wings before long. Floating off the coast of Scotland, they do everything on the craft, living and working with the constant sway of water. In the process, the crew form a bond unimaginable in civilian life.

In the Moray Firth, practice landings take place each day. It is hypnotising in its regularity and quickly becomes a routine. Rehearsing is relentless. Roles become second nature. Crossings of the English Channel are simulated again and again in the bay, dropping troops and tanks on to the beach to head towards pretend enemy positions inland.

Back at Marconi College, Patrick had been briefly put on to a fleet sweeper to get used to working at sea. It was the first time he had ever been on the open water. He was forced to undertake his duties with a sick bucket between his knees. Patrick's only experience on a boat before the war had been crossing the Mersey in Liverpool during his youth. Now floating in the Firth, Patrick is out on the waves for only the second time in his life. It is hard going to say the least. The current is violent, the wind sharp and frozen, and storms are ever present. After the war is won, Winston Churchill will claim that the winter storms in Scotland prepared those involved for the 'rough-and-tumble of D-Day'.

The crossings start at Fort George, an eighteenth-century fortress built to guard the area in the aftermath of the Jacobite rising in 1715. From there, the vessels head across in formation.

Seasickness is abundant, but there is no choice but to push on. Deep within the brutally rocking bow of 185, Patrick can barely relate to his jovial days in the Home Guard.

In February 1944, Patrick watches on as two floating tanks are overcome by the waves and sink to the bottom of the bay. The crew of LCH 185 rescue some of the men that manage to escape, and together the tank and landing craft crews share the Admiralty's generous rum ration. When the dust settles on the catastrophe and survivors are counted, a soldier is found to have drowned. Three more tanks will go on to sink, causing concern to those in charge of the invasion. If the tanks fail in Normandy, infantry troops will be landing unprotected on the beach. Not long after, the crew collect the body of a man who has been accidentally shot in the head. It is Patrick's first brush with a dead serviceman, but casualties are not uncommon during the rehearsals; accounts of accidental friendly fire on landing craft and vessels sinking in the bay are part of everyday life.

Conditions never let up. It is always cold. The men are constantly damp. During one landing a soldier named Peter Brown launches into the shallows. With sodden clothes he heads with his unit towards their target, a small wood a few miles inland where they set about digging a slit trench to hunker down for the night. As darkness falls, the men are chilled to the bone and soaked through. They fear not making it to sunrise, but breathe a sigh of relief when the exercise is called off in the early hours of the next morning. In celebration Peter and his comrades light an enormous bonfire, pass around their rations of rum, and try to bring themselves back to life.

The crew of LCH 185 practice putting portable generators and wireless sets on to the beach before transporting them further inland. Jack Barringer is one of those chosen to take part. Having set up the equipment, he rehearses sending messages to a man named Peter Dwyer on board LCH 269. They become good friends through the experience, bonding over the question that hangs above both of their heads. When D-Day comes, will they be the ones to do this task for real in the heavily defended, sniper-ridden towns of Nazi-occupied Normandy?

Towards the end of March, the biggest rehearsal yet takes place. It involves 234 Stuart tanks and an entire division of infantry. On the water are hundreds of landing craft, destroyers and cruisers. This is the big one. LCH 185 is right there in among the explosions. By now, every man knows their role and often the roles of their comrades. Patrick is on autopilot with his head down. All he can do is try to block out the noise. He knows that if he can't hack this, he'll die in France. The sounds are deafening and the scenes chaotic. One woman living just 200 metres outside of the exclusion zone is left stunned when a live shell smashes through her roof while she is enjoying a cup of tea.

With rehearsals complete by early April 1944, Force S begins slowly to move out. The area remains in military hands to allow live shelling practice to continue but, by May, the bay falls silent once more. Force S now heads south towards England. When the villagers steadily begin to return, they are unsure what to expect. Apprehension and worry weigh heavily on the residents, who wonder whether there will be anything left to call home. It has been all but impossible to not damage houses during the rehearsals. Despite the military's stance that buildings were not used for target practice, returning locals find the village in an immensely sorry state. Houses and barns are either destroyed or badly damaged. Broken tanks sit in the road. Pavements and roads are torn up. Beaches are covered in barbed wire. The government will eventually agree to pay for rebuilds and repairs, but a roof over one's head is not enough in such a rural area. Villagers had hastily dug up crops and sold their livestock for a pittance. Immaculately kept, purebred cattle and pigs are now gone, and poultry has long since been consumed. Fields have been utterly devastated by a furious flurry of naval shelling, tank tracks and soldiers' boots. It will take years to get answers and even longer for the soil to recover. Live rounds will continue to be ploughed up for decades.

Force S leaves Inver with the majority of men unaware of the destruction they have caused to strangers' lives. There was an inkling that the houses on the shore belonged to someone; a faint voice whispering that something doesn't seem quite right, but this is war and there is a job to be done. It never crosses Patrick's mind that everyone from children to the elderly had been dispersed right across the countryside, hoping for a day when they could return home.

The trip along the coast of Britain is a slow and extremely tense journey that leaves crews plenty of time to wonder how far in the distance D-Day might be. Travelling down towards Portsmouth, the Germans are but a stone's throw across the water in France. To lessen the chances of being spotted, the assault force does not travel together. LCHs 185 and 269 move in a convoy of around a dozen landing craft, once again unescorted and justifiably fearful of enemy attack. It is a very real threat. Just a few weeks before, nine E-boats had managed to get across to England, sneaking towards Exercise Tiger, a large-scale US dress rehearsal for the invasion. German torpedoes sunk LST(L) 507 and LST(L) 531 and damaged two other LST(L)s. In total, 749 men were killed.

To break the journey up, the convoy pulls into Harwich in Essex. For the first time in months, the crew are allowed to leave their vessels. Naturally, they head for the nearest pub. On the way, Patrick witnesses two young women fighting on the docks. There is blood and hair flying everywhere and a circle of rowdy men cheering on the melee. The young lad is shocked at a sight so far removed from his upbringing in the Shropshire countryside. Despite all that he will see before the war is over, that image will stay seared into his memory for the rest of his life.

Chapter Five

Late April 1944

The slow journey from Scotland has been filled with tension, and the crews are happy to be at their destination and finally out of dangerous waters. As the convoy pulls into Portsmouth, scattered across the water is an awe-inspiring assembly of ships and landing craft. A constant symphony of engines and seagulls fills the air as the smell of diesel fumes and saltwater infiltrates the noses of the new arrivals. Surprisingly, Patrick doesn't give much thought to the intimidating scene gathering in every direction. The country has been at war for so long by now. The teenager has seen every type of ship imaginable and witnessed every variation of military vehicle the army could ever possibly conjure up. As a sixteen-year-old boy in the Home Guard, he was already learning to kill. This is just how life is now. Weapons of war have become mundane in their normality. Patrick, like Jack Barringer and the millions of men spread out across the world, is just looking forward to the whole thing being over and done with.

With LCH 185 back in England, D-Day can't be far away. The crew prepare for an unknown wait, resting quietly in the water as the build-up to the invasion intensifies. Every person involved in the landing has trained extensively. They are ready and raring to go. Many are keen to get it over with. Those on board 185 know that this is the final wait, one last breather before France. The thought of what is to come sits heavily on the minds of the men. Some have been in battle before and know first-hand how dangerous it will be. Patrick has never been fired upon by the enemy and isn't sure what to expect, but he knows that when he next leaves England, there's a strong chance that he won't return.

Aside from rare but well-received breaks, used more often than not to head for the nearest pub in order to sample the local ales by Brickwood brewery, the sailors are almost always confined to the craft. A huge proportion of the country is filled with camps surrounded by barbed wire and guarded by armed soldiers. It's as obvious to any civilian as it is to the troops that the invasion is imminent. It seems like military uniforms and olive-drab vehicles are down every side street and occupy every field. In the harbour the men spend most of the time in a state of boredom. Aside from daily duties, there is little to do but wait.

To relieve some of the tension, a telegraphist named Stan Jennings hatches a plan to get the lifeboat off the stern and lower it down for a row in the harbour.

Seeing an opportunity for a rare spot of fun, Patrick agrees, and the two sailors set about lowering a wooden lifeboat from the stern of 185 into the still water below. The lifeboat is a rickety old thing, and they soon realise what a poor decision they have made. Next to every other vessel, the wooden boat is minuscule. Waves churned up by huge ships toss the lifeboat around like a rag doll. Boats in harbour are not static, they sway and groan. Being crushed to death between two immense hulls seems imminent as Patrick and Stan are pulled slowly towards the ships like a fish sucked into the enormous jaws of a whale. As destroyers bear down on the two terrified sailors, they know they're in trouble. Hidden from view among the vast walls of steel, they are about to be flattened. Kicking into fight mode, Patrick and Stan row as frantically as a couple of telegraphists can row. Battling the current, desperately pushing against the powerful pull of the fearsome ships, they manage to somehow propel the lifeboat out of the way just in the nick of time. The two men quickly clamber back up on to the landing craft, knowing that they have somehow managed to cheat death before D-Day has even begun.

Towards the end of May, with the invasion closing in and a lockdown of the area inching nearer, the crew are given forty-eight hours' leave. They are told to not under any circumstances leave Portsmouth. The chance of information leaking out is too high to risk. Patrick naturally ignores the order almost as quickly as he hears it and, ever the homebody, boards a train to London. The platforms at both Portsmouth and Waterloo are filled with military police on the lookout for any servicemen or women who might have snuck away from their designated areas. In London, the MPs seem to turn a blind eye to Patrick as he strolls towards his connecting train. Steam fills the air and rises to the ceiling as the telegraphist moves discreetly through the crowd, expecting to feel the grip of authority on his shoulder at any second. Instead, he makes it on to the train and heads for Shrewsbury.

Spending the night with his parents, Patrick chooses not to mention the impending invasion. He doesn't want to worry them. Mrs Thomas's other two sons are out there somewhere, fighting the Germans. One of Patrick's brothers will be landing at Gold Beach, just a few miles along from Sword. The landing is top secret. Patrick knows that, and so do his parents. Patrick isn't allowed to tell them anything, but why would he want to? If the enemy somehow finds out, they'll be expecting it. At the front of the first wave, 185 will feel the brunt of the leak in the devastating form of fatal machine-gun nests and gun batteries.

Early the next morning Patrick and his parents say goodbye. The teenager knows it might be the last time he ever sees them. They know it too. The landings in France have to come at some point soon. The British public can't avoid seeing the build-up of hundreds of thousands of troops along the coast.

Patrick avoids being stopped once again on the way back to Portsmouth, making it back just in time to step aboard 185 before the deadline hits. The size of the growing armada might not impress the teenager, but the sea of sailors in blue uniform that has gathered in his absence does. Such a large scale of human life on the line is simply too much to ignore. D-Day is set for 5 June, and as the countdown turns to single digits towards the end of May, troops are locked in their camps ready for the loading of men on to landing craft to begin. The task is so enormous that five days are set aside just to get everyone on board.

LCH 185 is pulled into one of the dry docks to be degaussed. An electric cable is run along the ship, sending a charge through it in hopes of deterring magnetic mines. This is the second time the craft has gone through the process, the first degaussing having taken place back in the US. The craft then has its 'bottom scraped', as the crew call it. Any barnacles, muck or rust are removed from 185's exterior, before a layer of red lead primer is added and the hull repainted. The telegraphists aren't free from this task, but soon wish they could be. Patrick is told to scrape away at the metal hull vigorously as men above, who are supposed to use the toilet in the harbour, decide instead to do their business in the craft's galley. It is, by Patrick's estimate, a cardinal sin. LCH 185 is in a dry dock. There is nothing beneath the keel but solid concrete. When the men flush the toilet, their waste has no water to drop into. The telegraphists have no choice but to dodge human waste as they work, soundtracked by the polyphonic tune of unbelievably bad language roaring up towards the galley.

Once the final work is done, 185 creaks back out on to the water to join the ever-growing number of vessels in Force S. Readying an assault force with thousands of men and hundreds of ships and landing craft takes a huge amount of planning. Each section has been carefully mapped out across the water. Types of vessels are grouped together in areas for collecting, loading and eventually sailing. LCH 185, as a converted LCI(L), is moved to Line C, Area 27, just outside Portsmouth harbour. Beyond the craft, there is nothing on the horizon but the route to war.

Sword Beach is of utmost importance to the Allied landings. The ultimate objective will be to capture the city of Caen by the time the sun sets on D-Day. It's a huge ask. Caen is 8 miles beyond the beach. The plan of attack is relatively simple: first destroyers, RAF bombers and a number of artillery-equipped landing craft will bombard the German defences. Group One, led by LCH 185, will spearhead the invasion to guide in an array of support craft. Group Two will follow, headed up by LCH 269, ready to land twenty Landing Craft Assault packed to the brim with fighting troops. Both landing groups should hit the beach at roughly the same time. If all goes to plan, the 6th Airborne Division will have been dropped from the sky into areas east of Sword Beach a few hours earlier. These airborne troops will take out German strongholds threatening the success of the amphibious landing. The bridges over the Caen canal and the Orne river need to be taken in order to secure the only eastern passage off Sword towards Caen. The Merville gun battery needs to be neutralised. It is expected that the Germans at Merville have access to 150-mm guns capable of firing a distance of 8 miles, close enough to wage hell on those landing at Sword Beach.

What awaits the Allies is not to be taken lightly. Sword Beach stretches 5 miles from Ouistreham to Lion-sur-Mer, but due to offshore reefs the landings can only take place within a one-mile stretch codenamed Queen. While the US beaches at Omaha and Utah are more rural, the British and Canadian sectors are often visited by tourists. Such is the popularity of the destinations that postcards from pre-war holidays have been used by the military to build intelligence on what the area looks like for the invasion. At Sword there are towns, villages and villas, all of which create a strong opportunity for enemy defence. In the area, waiting with gritted teeth for a fight, are some 600 men of the German 716th Static Infantry Division.

The defences those soldiers occupy are a fortress to be feared. On the coast, there is a deadly combination of metal hedgehogs, mines, sniper posts and wooden stakes, as well as six strong-points consisting of multiple 50-mm anti-tank guns, 155-mm guns, 75-mm guns, mortar positions, machine-gun positions, anti-aircraft batteries and command bunkers. Five hundred men occupying another nine strongpoints await any Allied soldier that somehow makes it off the beach into the Normandy countryside. Further back, but still within dangerously close vicinity to the beach, is the 21st Panzer Division, made up of 16,000 German troops and 120 tanks. The Germans might well be taken by surprise, but that isn't to say they aren't waiting.

The landing at Sword has every chance of descending into a fierce and bloody fight between the two sides. There is a very real expectation that the majority of infantry in the initial landings will lose their lives. So much of the plan relies on skill, strong nerve, immense bravery and a huge helping of luck. Everything must work together for D-Day to be a success. Landing craft have to hit the right stretch of beach at the right time, Duplex Drive tanks need to make it ashore without being overwhelmed by the waves, flail tanks need to successfully take out mines, and the men wading through the surf with rifles in hand need to perform in a horrific and unnatural situation. The groundwork laid hours before by the airborne assault needs to succeed. Men must fall from planes in darkness and find the correct landing zones before successfully taking out enormous, well-defended German fortifications. If any part fails across either of the five landing beaches, it will end, if not in Allied defeat, then at the very least in an unfathomably high loss of human life.

It is important to the invasion that no single craft is filled with an entire unit, or too many men with the same speciality. If a landing craft is sunk and takes with it every beach master, every Royal Navy commando or every engineer, the loss will be detrimental to the success of the invasion. To counter this, units and men will be split across the various craft that make up Force S. Stepping aboard 185 for the crossing to France will be ten men from R RN Beach Commando; one man from Detachment 21 Army Group Movement Control Pool; three men from F RN Beach Commando, including the principal beach master; one man from 'A' Bombardment Troop (a senior bombardment liaison officer); one man from HQ 27 Armoured Brigade; one man from B 13 Beach Signal Section; two men from 27 Armoured Brigade Signal Squadron; three men from 7 Field Regiment RA, Battery Control Party from 9 Field Battery; one man from Detachment 3 Recce Regiment (a traffic control commander); two men from HQ 5th Battalion, the King's (Liverpool) Regiment (HQ 5 Beach Group), including the commander of 5 Beach Group; and two men from

Detachment 21 Army Group Movement Control Pool (attached to 5 Beach Group). This array of troops will walk on to 185 from the South Parade Pier at Portsmouth the day before the invasion and brace themselves for what is to come.

Early on 4 June, Denis Muskett is told to join 185 ready for the scheduled invasion the next morning. He'll be heading across with a team of specialised mechanics whose role will be to salvage and repair any landing craft damaged in the landings. Denis is a hardened naval veteran. In 1941, he was serving on HMS *Barham* in the Mediterranean when a German U-boat fired off four torpedoes. The water column caused by the explosion sent the ship on to its port side, where within four minutes munitions on board exploded and sank the ship completely. The event was devastating, causing the death of 862 men. Denis Muskett knows all too well the risk that comes with being at sea.

Later that morning, D-Day is postponed for twenty-four hours owing to poor weather conditions in the English Channel, which could cause havoc during the crossing. The delay leads to an uneasiness among those waiting to head for France. They are amped up, but now must return to waiting anxiously.

Teddy Gueritz prepares to board 185 on 5 June. Having worked on the planning of the invasion, he has been granted more freedom in the build-up. As a result, he's running late and is one of the last to board the craft. Described as a gentleman, during training in Invergordon, Gueritz had begun as staff officer of operations for the commander of Force S, but was transferred to the role of principal beach master. He had undertaken this role during the landings at Madagascar in 1942, but nothing could prepare Gueritz for Normandy. The new team he joins in this role have landed at both Sicily and Italy. He is inexperienced in comparison and knows it. There are few roles in the invasion in the thick of it as much as the principal beach master. It is his job to keep the landing running smoothly on the beach in the face of enemy fire falling all around. Signs need to be erected, obstacles moved and pathways cleared. Above all, troops need to be kept moving. If the moment overwhelms those running up the beach, causing traffic to build, they'll be sitting ducks ready to be picked off with ease by the Germans. Gueritz has been trained to expect vast amounts of casualties, but he still wants to try and spare as much life as possible.

Alongside his bodyguard, Gueritz stands by the water's edge. The two men are told that they will be with the same group of men they trained with in Invergordon. The set of familiar comrades step aboard 185, where Gueritz heads to find Commander Currey, who is already on the craft. Commander Edmund Neville Vincent Currey is in charge of Group One of Force S. From 185 he will command the first wave of the landing and make critical calls as the fight takes place. Currey is a long-serving naval man whose thick, dark eyebrows crown a stern-looking face. He joined the navy in 1927 and during the war years alone has commanded or deputy commanded five different destroyers.

Brigadier George Erroll Prior-Palmer is a graduate of Sandhurst. He is experienced with war, having been mentioned in dispatches, and is now chief officer of the 27th Armoured Brigade. He will be landing with the men and leading the way. Prior-Palmer is realistic about the chances of survival, perhaps to a fault. Alan King, a radio operator in a Sherman tank, will recall after the war that the brigadier had warned the tank crews in the build-up that they would be the assault wave and wouldn't be coming back.

As more and more servicemen head aboard, by the time the craft heads to France 185 will be filled with men from all across the British Isles assigned to undertake jobs from all corners of the military. They have come together from different levels of British society. Some were born into wealth, even lordships, while others come from poverty, having joined up to find an easier existence and be guaranteed three meals a day. The confines of the landing craft are as much a leveller of British men as the fight on the beach to follow.

With the invasion temporarily stood down due to the weather, the atmosphere is tense. The crew can't leave the craft. Other than some junior officers, most on board are unaware of where exactly they will be heading. At 21:00, forecasters locate a window of somewhat better weather that looks to open up the following day, allowing the invasion to take place. The decision is made at around 03:30 for the crossing to go ahead. Ships begin to set sail within hours. LCH 185 will be approaching the beach at the front of Group One, but will make the crossing in the third sailing group. The first two sailing groups will consist of destroyers and minesweepers.

At 14:40, Sailing Group Three receives orders to move.

LCH 185 groans and creaks as its two banks of diesel engines roar into action. After over two years at sea, this is finally it. The craft turns towards France and heads for the Atlantic Wall. Hitler's Fortress Europe awaits. Men are given Benzedrine tablets – amphetamines – to help them stay awake and alert during the long journey to follow. As the landing craft eases into formation, men aboard other vessels cheer and wave as they go. Cries of good luck echo across the harbour. The crew wave and shout back towards the other ships now gradually waking up and slowly joining the convoy like a snake growing out from its tail. Finally on the move, 185 is behind two Landing Craft Personnels (Large) – but leads a line of eight Landing Craft Tanks.

The crossing is rough. Crews should be used to it from the endless choppy rehearsals in Scotland, but there is still a huge amount of seasickness. Shortly into 185's journey, a man loses control of his stomach. He leans to his side and vomits all over Teddy Gueritz and his bodyguard. Without a fuss the two men head to wash themselves down using whatever bucket of water is available. Having cleaned up as best he can, Gueritz takes the chance to look out from the railings. What he sees is spectacular. In front of him is the largest naval fleet the world has ever seen, a stunning image of landing craft and ships spread as far and as deep as the eye can see. It feels like he could climb the railing and hop across the vessels like stepping stones without ever getting his feet wet. It is a sight unimaginable to anyone not seeing it for themselves.

The seven assault forces have left from different parts of the English coast, but meet up in the Channel in a designated spot named Area Z. From here, the armada gets into position to begin the final push towards France. Conditions at sea don't improve. A constant sway of harsh waves keeps the men at a permanent level of queasiness. Many landing craft are towing smaller ones for the crossing. From the back of the stern, 185 pulls LCP(L) 189 along in its wake. When the twenty-four-hour postponement of D-Day occurred, LCP(L) crews were relieved to be given an unexpected opportunity to have their compasses adjusted for more accuracy and to fix their craft up for the invasion. Frustratingly, this didn't include improving the engine. The savage sea has caused many LCP(L)s to break free of their tows. When 185 and 189 are separated, 189's engine fails to start, leaving it floating silently at the mercy of the Channel. LCS(L) 253 comes to the rescue, fixing a new tow and continuing the hazardous crossing together.

LCH 185 remains behind the destroyers as the armada moves steadily in unison, one giant beast rolling towards its prey. Denis

Muskett feels a swell in the water that causes even more men to run to the railing, hurling their final meals into the sea. The air is chilly and the night dark. Thousands of long white wakes creep like veins from the ships, piercing through shadows in the calm light of the moon. The armada is quiet, almost silent. Thousands of engines rumble in a constant drone that almost disappears into itself. There is little other noise but the whistle of wind as it twists through the decks, enveloping the fearful men like a blanket. Small groups of sailors and soldiers are scattered across the upper deck, speaking in hushed tones. Some play cards, some heat up tea or soup on portable stoves. No one knows when their next hot meal will be. Muskett passes some rum between his team of mechanics for one final sip.

The vessels head through an area of water the military has code-named the Spout, which Allied intelligence knows has been kept free of mines by the enemy. The Germans have been using the gap to reach Britain, but now this opening will be used for the armada's lowering position. The approach to the beaches begins here.

LCH 185 is again tasked with towing the LCP(L). This time, some of the personnel craft's crew cross over to 185, adding to the already bustling landing craft. LCP(L) 189 is piloted by men from the top-secret Combined Operations Pilotage Parties (COPP). Two other men from COPP, Jim Booth and Geoffrey Lyne, are already in Normandy. They are on the seabed aboard the midget submarine X23. The vessel has been there for a number of days with its crew living together within its cramped confines. They have been patiently waiting for a radio signal to confirm that the landing is going ahead. While doing so, peeking towards Normandy, the crew have seen German soldiers swimming in the sea. The enemy is unsuspecting of the incoming attack. At 05:00, with Force S heading in its direction, the submarine raises its 18-foot mast and switches on a green light at the tip to guide in the first wave. The approaching armada soon spots it. The crossing from Portsmouth has taken fourteen hours and thirty-five minutes.

Patrick has, for most of the trip, been deep in the bows. With headphones over his ears and his hands on the telegraphy equipment, he is relaying coded messages across the fleet. As France grows closer, Patrick's shift comes to an end. He heads to the toilet and then up top. While he's been working, France has been spotted. Taking a look, Patrick sees the coast on the port side of the craft. The summer sun is starting to creep up ever so slightly. On the shoreline he spots something. England has been through so many dark years. There have been blackouts, shortages, bombings, poverty, civilian losses and the deaths of friends and family in battles fought on distant lands. In this moment, poking through the fumes and salty mist, are two beautiful French houses glistening in the morning sun. It is one of the most stunning things that Patrick Thomas has ever seen. He takes the moment in as best he can. Jack Barringer sees them too. Those wonderful houses shining back at them. He can make out the spires of a church. France is right there.

The two houses symbolise more than a beautiful moment of peace to those in charge. They announce that Force S is in the right place as it approaches the shore. By now, a route has been cleared through the mines and Group One is moving into position. LCH 185 is at the front. LCP(L) 189 has once again broken free, but is managing to struggle on using its now half-working engine. Fifteen minutes later, 185 speeds from 5 knots to 10 and begins heading for the beach ahead of the group. The craft is out on its own and leading the way in front of the first wave. It's a risky move, one which could easily result in the vessel being knocked out of the invasion before it ever truly starts, but there is no fire from the Germans, no scream of machine guns or screech of rockets. Rather, there is an uneasy silence. LCH 185 peacefully travels parallel to the coastline as Commander Currey assesses the situation. Conditions in the water are better than expected and there is a lack of enemy fire coming from the shore. The craft eases from Ouistreham to Saint-Aubin-sur-Mer 200 yards from the shore. Still, there is nothing from the Germans. It's as if the enemy is yet to wake up.

Once Commander Currey is satisfied with his analysis, 185 manoeuvres back towards Group One to take its place at the front. The craft steadies itself and slows its engine. A call is made to launch the Duplex Drive tanks at 5,000 yards rather than the planned 7,000. There's a need to save fuel and the rough waves further out could easily sink the floating tanks. Telegraphists on 185 send messages to the group of Landing Craft Tank instructing them on the new orders. At sixty minutes until H-Hour – the airborne assault, planned for 06:30, that will precede the landings – the craft anchor in position. Ten are spread across the sea 150 yards apart as tanks teeter down the ramps into the water with a cloud of smoke and fumes. With the vehicles now swimming towards the sand, X23 has done its job. The crew of the midget submarine tie a white sheet to its mast, carefully manoeuvre through the fleet, and head back home to England.

Force S slows down. The atmosphere on the water is peaceful. Jack Barringer notices the stillness in the air. Too still. It can't stay like this. The silence is disturbing. Gueritz stands on the deck. He can't believe his eyes when the naval bombardment rips into action and begins to attack the shoreline. There was no chance to weaken the beach defences before the invasion in case it aroused suspicion, but now the navy is making up for lost time. Enormous guns seem to be making months' worth of attacks in a single moment. The sky looks like every firework display in Great

Britain on bonfire night going off in the same place at the same time. The horizon seems to disconnect and push off into the air with the eruption of destroyers, warships and RAF bombers up above. Gueritz almost feels sorry for the Germans beneath the falling barrage, but he knows it's necessary; soon he'll be on that very beach with the enemy and they need to be bombed into submission. Troops crouched in Landing Craft Assault, ready to run towards machine guns, need every bit of help they can get. Jack Barringer is shocked by the sight. Shells are everywhere. The bombardment shakes everything in its wake: every ship, every grain of sand, and every organ.

'Just about did a little piece,' Jack will write to his brother.

The sound is unbearable. A mix of guttural rumbles and sharp, piercing cracks. Patrick will suffer hearing problems for the rest of his life; the noise is quite literally deafening. When the bombardment dies down, LCP(L) pull off to the side of 185 and prepare to lay out a smoke screen, but they decide to hold off. There is no enemy resistance, and smoke would make the situation more difficult than it's worth. LCP(L) 189 returns to the side of the craft to pick up one of its crew, COPP member Don Amer, who has stayed aboard 185 to help navigate Force S and to make sure he has a good understanding of the approach to the beach. As Amer leaves 185, he takes one last glance at the French coastline, a final lock of the eyes on to enemy defences to give those on aboard 189 at least a fighting chance of survival.

The floating tanks are successfully storming across the waves by 06:00. Despite the call to launch closer to the beach, the swell at sea is still relentless, with waves as high as 6 feet. The tanks make slow progress and are soon overtaken by Landing Craft Tanks determined to launch flail tanks and armoured vehicles on to the beach to clear enemy defences.

It doesn't take long for the Germans to wake up after all. As machine-gun bullets ping and rattle against the hull of 185, Patrick tries to ignore the noise.

'Just keep working,' he tells himself. He's done this countless times before. Patrick puts it to the back of his mind and tries to get the job done. Despite being built for a beach landing, 185 has been ordered to instead embark its troops on to a number of smaller LCA. As a headquarters craft, it is needed to guide in the many waves still to follow and the risk of getting stuck on the sand or destroyed by the enemy is too high. Twenty-seven Royal Navy commandos exit 185 on to LCA from Group Two and head for the beach. Within minutes, the small craft hit the sand and drop their ramps. With orders to move, soldiers of the East Yorks and South Lancs hurtle down into waist-deep water where they are greeted with fierce defence from Germans in unseen positions.

The situation on the beach is carnage. Men are confused, lost in a wall of smoke and explosions. Patrick watches as soldiers run out of the shallow surf. He sees men hurl themselves forward with gusto towards those two beautiful houses and disappear in the smoke. Through the suffocating mist Patrick sees silhouettes of soldiers falling to the ground. They do not get up. The young lad is amazed at their bravery to be at the thick end. Jack sees it too. He's glad to be on the naval side of the invasion and not having to head up the beach towards the enemy like those poor souls.

The Duplex Drive tanks finally reach the sand. In a cloud of black soot and seawater, one by one each vehicle's tracks collide with the beach and rise up from the water like a fierce army of bucking stallions. The floating skirts rip off as intended and within one minute the tanks are firing their rounds at the enemy. Hobart's Funnies, a series of modified tanks designed to take out enemy defences, have been carrying out their objectives with the aid of the Royal Engineers. Routes are now being steadily carved through the sand as soldiers quickly fight their way off the beach. Bolstered by the early launch decided and relayed on board 185, only one tank has been swamped by the sea. An hour earlier, at the western end of Omaha Beach, the same decision was made by Captain Thornton to launch the tanks at 5,000 yards but, having to move sideways against the current to get back on target, they were instantly overcome by 5-foot-high waves. The US infantry land unsupported in the area and suffer a devastatingly high casualty rate. The beach will become known as Bloody Omaha.

The Germans do not take kindly to the landing: 88-mm mortars rain down on the tanks; machine-gun fire is formidable, scything men as they exit the ramps of landing craft. The sight of wounded soldiers desperately dragging themselves away from the ever-encroaching tide is one that stays with the men who survive it for a lifetime.

With the first wave of LCAs turning away from the beach having successfully unloaded their cargo of troops, Commander Currey remarks to Gueritz, with perhaps undue joy, that it's time he heads ashore. Alongside a colonel and their two bodyguards, Gueritz climbs over the side and waits for a passing LCA. The group veto a few for being too filled with casualties, but eventually have no other choice but to climb in alongside the dead and wounded. Manoeuvring around obstacles sticking out of the water, many of which are tipped with German mines, the coxswain successfully beaches. Gueritz and the colonel jump from the ramp into deep water that takes the men by surprise. They are able to swim out, but the same can't be said for the bodyguards, who are short enough to be overwhelmed. Gueritz and the colonel drag the men on to their feet just before they drown beneath the weight of their own equipment.

After steadying themselves, the group look around. The view is chilling. Everything is grey. The air, the smoke, the spray from the sea; it's all so bleak and miserable. On what seems like every spot of sand that meets their eyes a man is dead or dying. Machine-gun bullets are bouncing all around. Mortars burst across the beach. To the left, Gueritz spots two beached tanks that were never designed to be mobile vehicles, but instead were dumped on to the beach to allow extra firing support on the flanks. Both of them are on fire. Gueritz sets about finding the signs needed to establish some sort of order out of the mayhem. They were carried in with the infantry, but have been lost when the troops carrying them were injured or killed. The signs need to be located, and a grim hunt through the wreckage of human lives begins.

As the battle on the beach rages on, 185 turns its bow back towards England. The craft will remain at the forefront of the invasion, where its role is now to locate further landing groups and guide them towards the beach. The first wave has been nothing like the rehearsals. This is real. People are dying. If Invergordon is a world away, Shrewsbury is another life.

Knowing that his job has only just begun, Patrick listens to his headphones, gets his head down, and tries his best to ignore the death and horror unfolding beyond the metal hull of 185.

Chapter Six

9 July 2017

Rushing through the wet roads of Portsmouth, I slam on my brakes and come to a halt at passport control. The staff are clearly annoyed at my tardiness. It becomes clear why as soon as my tyres pass over the ramp, when not a minute later the boat is moving. Crossing the Channel takes longer at night. The ferry deliberately slows down to allow passengers to sleep through the journey and wake up well rested in Normandy. Whether or not people actually sleep is anyone's guess. I certainly don't. The push and pull from the current fails to rock me gently to sleep, instead slowly and surely churning my stomach over. I can't help but think of how 185's crew lived a far worse version of this for close to two years. Eventually giving up trying to get any rest, instead I wander sleeplessly along the corridors for a few hours until we finally near France. I grab my bag and head up top to once again watch Ouistreham appear on the horizon.

Gazing off into the darkness, flickering lights of passing ships and the whistle of wind surround me. To be back in Normandy feels like the true beginning of the search. It's exciting to be here. With swollen eyes I drive on to French soil and immediately pull over at a café. While I sit at an antique wooden chair at a wobbly table out on a beautiful street, people run past me behind lorries heading back towards the ferry port. France and Britain are in the middle of a migrant situation. Having watched it play out on the news each night for months, it's surreal to now be sitting in the middle of it calmly sipping a café au lait. It feels wrong to have accidentally become a spectator to such a desperate situation.

With each passing week of the search, the political landscape of Britain has been changing. Where once I found respectful reflec-tiveness and an understanding of the First and Second World Wars, the memory of the country's war dead is often being swept up into questionable politics and nationalist agendas. Divisive leaders have been taking power across the world, while at home victories in historic wars are increasingly used to justify terrible decisions or to stoke a steadily building undercurrent of anger.

Migrants in Europe are often at the receiving end of that vitriol, with calls to sink their boats casually made by the same people that claim to remember the sacrifices made during the Second World War. I can't fathom why hatred is ever the first place the mind arrives when trying to find an answer. How can those that claim to understand the lessons screaming out from the 1940s be filled with so much anger at people fleeing dangerous situations? It has almost become a second front during the search to see if I can find the wreck before losing all hope that the world isn't moving back towards the very political landscape that 185 had been lost fighting against in the first place.

Driving along the coast, the journey towards Sword Beach takes me right across the iconic Pegasus Bridge. History can be felt in the air immediately upon leaving the ferry. It's easy to get swept up in the excitement of being in such a significant place, but I try to stay focused on the task at hand. It's a scorching hot morning. I can smell my skin burning as I stand outside Ranville cemetery. The place is completely empty as I pace silently along the rows of headstones. Sunlight bounces back from the names carved in stone, a sharp contrast to the melancholy that swells in response to the thought of young lives ended in a world filled with fascism. At military cemeteries, I always find myself picking out headstones to read at random. Many here are teenagers, but Jack was twenty-nine. He would have been considered quite old during the landings. It is really no wonder that, with a ten-year age gap, Patrick looked up to him.

Tall trees hide me in their shadow as I move. Like Patrick, I no longer need to think about where Jack's grave is. I'm drawn to it now as I gradually get to know a man I will never meet with every visit to his final resting place. Standing at the grave, it feels like Patrick and I are the only two people who visit. I hope that isn't the case but, even if it is, it's more than can be said for many of the men at Ranville. Gazing back across the rows of headstones, I wonder how many of these names are completely forgotten. I think of the road ahead, about what it would mean to actually find 185. The craft meant so much to Jack and the crew. Not just those that died in the sinking, but the handful who survived to remember the horror of that day. The families too, those that live with an eternal unknown as to where their loved ones ended up. Above all, 185 still means the world to Patrick, the sole living survivor for whom the discovery could bring great relief. I just hope I can pull this off.

Stu Robertson walks across the grass to meet me. Stu lives in Normandy and is one of the most well-respected historians and battlefield guides in the area. He once met Patrick by pure chance in this very cemetery. Stu was giving a tour of Ranville at the exact moment that Patrick and his family were visiting Jack's headstone.

It was the veteran's first time back to France since the war, and the very first time he had stood at Jack's grave. Stu approached the family to ask about Patrick's time in the war and since that meeting the two have kept in touch. When I contacted Stu a week previously, he was keen to help out, knowing how much it means to our mutual friend.

Although now living permanently in France, he grew up near Manchester and still has traces of the accent of a man born in the shadow of the Haçienda nightclub. In conversations away from the task at hand, we've bonded over our love of the bands and music that came out of the city in the 1980s and 1990s. I explain my plan to Stu as we walk back towards the grave.

'Yes, I know Patrick,' he says with a laugh to imply that I know exactly what's funny. 'From the very first moment we met, you could tell he was a real character. Such an incredible man.'

We both know that if anyone will appreciate the effort being put in on their behalf, it's our friend Patrick. I mention how quickly the Second World War generation is disappearing and how crucial it is to make an effort for the veterans before it's too late.

'When I first arrived,' Stu explains, 'it was just kind of accepted that the veterans were here and you could communicate and learn their stories. Certainly in the last decade we are losing so many of them. Very soon this history will be beyond living memory and the veterans will no longer be around to tell us their own stories in their own words.'

'I made Patrick this crazy promise that I would find his boat and he went, "Absolutely, go for it!" What do you think about that? Do you think it's doable?' I ask.

'You've got your work cut out, I think,' Stu says.

Keen to check my rough search zone, I explain that a man on the Gooseberry harbour had watched 185 go down and how the rescue craft, by Patrick's estimate, went on to be shelled by the guns at Le Havre.

'The wreck of LCH 185 has to be somewhere between the view of the Gooseberry and the firing range of Le Havre,' I say.

Luckily for me, Stu agrees. 'If you imagine Sword Beach is very much the most eastern of the five landing beaches where the Allies came ashore on D-Day, and we have the huge artillery batteries around Le Havre: they are in range and shelling the Allied armada, which was occupying a position off Sword Beach.'

Stu shows me a map of the German batteries and each of their firing ranges. This small piece of information is important because it shows the extent to which the guns could reach along the water. By knowing the very outer limits of where the rounds could have landed, it highlights an even smaller search zone than I previously thought. With Patrick's rescue craft being shelled so soon after being pulled out of the water, it seems unlikely that 185 could have been sunk outside the range of Le Havre's batteries.

Asking Stu what he thinks about my plan to find the wreck, I have no idea what to expect in response. I'm never sure if the people I've been meeting along the way believe in the search as much as I do, or just think it's ridiculous.

'I think to find 185, to find the location, it's going to be difficult. If it was easy, it would have been done before.'

Stu is right. There's a reason why people don't go searching for shipwrecks every day. It is an extremely difficult endeavour, but challenges can be exciting. After all, if it's hard then it must be worth doing. Old tales of exploration enthralled me as a child and steered me towards a career in archaeology as an adult. Those expeditions were never easy endeavours, but that didn't stop the explorers pushing on. I look towards Jack's grave. This headstone, and the name carved into it, are what Patrick associates most deeply with the sinking. This is the spot that, for seventy years, he knew he would need to visit one day. For me, Jack's grave now holds a similar significance. It feels natural to begin and end visits to Normandy here, because standing at the grave seems be the most tangible way of letting 185's crew know that they haven't been forgotten; that their names are spoken, not just by me, but by Patrick and every person that has so far helped me with the search.

At least thirty-five men died when 185 was sunk. Only four bodies were ever recovered and buried beneath a headstone. Jack's grave is 7.5 miles from where the craft was on D-Day. The rest of the crew, those that went to the seabed, have nowhere to be commemorated together. Names are scattered on war memorials across the UK, but I can envision a place where all of the families can pay their respects in one place.

I've been sending off emails in poorly translated French for the last few weeks in an attempt to pin down anyone who might be able to get me in touch with those in positions of authority within Lion-sur-Mer. A few days before arriving in France, I managed to reach the office of the mayor. To my surprise, he agreed to meet me. As I leave Ranville, I have no idea how this will play out. Through the language barrier, I never managed to make it clear exactly why I wanted to meet the mayor. I'm sure, as I drive along the coast, that the man waiting for me is wondering what on earth this Englishman has to say that is seemingly so important that he'd come all the way to France to say it.

It's wonderful to return to the town with a fresh purpose. During my last visit, on the day I made the promise to Patrick, I felt every bit the tourist that I was. In a French town I'd never visited, Lion-sur-Mer felt like a place I was locked out of. I've heard much about the importance of local mayors in France and how much passion and sway they hold. As an Englishman, I'm fully aware of the perception many other countries have of us. The last thing I want is to come across as a typical Brit-abroad bounding into a peaceful town to demand that I build a permanent structure commemorating the British on their beautiful seafront. It's a privilege in itself to simply get a meeting with the mayor. That alone feels like a major milestone in the search, but I half expect to receive a cold reception and a swift 'non' to my request.

Outside the town hall, an elegant stone building with an intricately carved facade, a French flag waves proudly in the wind. It is quite simply a very French scene and the thought of heading inside to speak to the man in charge is unnerving. The future of any memorial to 185 is about to either receive the green light or be knocked down before the idea ever gets off the ground. Walking along the gravel forecourt past perfectly kept flowerbeds, I take a deep breath as I push open the door. Inside, the decor is ageing but still grandiose. I feel like I'm stepping into a world not normally seen by outsiders.

Clambering my way up an awkwardly skinny wooden staircase, I lightly step along the corridor until reaching a large door. It's the most impressive entrance in the building. The mayor's office can't be anywhere but behind it. Pausing to compose myself, I check that my shirt is tucked in, adjust my blazer, and give three loud knocks with my fist. A young man opens the door and motions for me to come inside. He's the mayor's stepson, who will be translating our meeting. The mayor speaks very little English and I regrettably know very little French.

'Bonjour,' I say.

My delivery sounds awfully British. There is no attempt at a French take on the word, just a blunt 'bon-jaw'. I wince as it leaves my mouth. Sitting across from me is Dominique Régeard, a handsome, tanned man in his forties wearing jeans, loafers and a dark-pink shirt with the sleeves rolled up just below the elbows. He is an undeniably fashionable chap who, helped by his intense stare and quiet demeanour, gives off a certain mystique. Dominique is not what I expected to see in a French mayor. He is old neither in age nor in tradition. Undertaking his duties for the town just a few days a week, he works most of the time in Paris, meaning that while here in the town hall Dominique has a huge amount of work to do in a short space of time. I don't have long to convince the mayor of my idea.

As I've done many times before, I attempt to tell the story of Patrick Thomas and 185. I haven't planned or even given much thought as to what to say in the meeting, something that I feel the pressure of immediately. In the moment, with no choice but to speak, I choose to tell Dominique every piece of information I've learned about the landing craft so far. Deliberately leaving no stone unturned, my hope is for the story to resonate with him in some way. It's also incredibly important that the mayor is able to understand how crucial the town is to the story and what this place means to Patrick. From the moment I start to speak, Dominique is silent. He stares intently at the photographs and maps that I've brought along, but I find it impossible to tell whether he's interested, bored, or has simply already decided that I have no chance of convincing him of anything.

My eyes wander around at the room. Dominique's office is covered in gold-lined wood panelling. On every third panel is a carefully painted blue inlay adorned with ancient images. It feels like I'm having a meeting inside a Roman villa. Directly behind my chair is a marble fireplace on which is placed the pristine white bust of a clearly prestigious man. Through a small window to my right I stare out over the English Channel. This room is history in itself, screaming importance from every lick of paint and every piece of oak furniture. My pitch is briefly stifled as a member of staff gently pushes open the door. Trying not to interrupt, a smartly dressed lady enters the room carrying a basket of fresh pastries and a pot of coffee. She places them on a grand table in one corner and motions for me to help myself, which lifts the tension in the room slightly. Lion-sur-Mer seems to be welcoming me in. By the time I wrap up my pitch, I've been speaking for at least ten minutes and still haven't gained any insight from Dominique's body language as to what his response might be.

'His story so definitively features Lion-sur-Mer. In his mind, his spiritual home . . . is here,' I say.

My confidence begins to wane as I get closer to the question. I turn to speak to his stepson directly.

'So . . . I was just hoping . . . if . . . I could get an idea from the mayor . . . about what he would think about putting a memorial in this town.'

Waiting with worry as my words are translated across the table, Dominique nods along firmly. I attempt to read his eyes just as the request reaches his ears, but I can make out nothing. The room goes silent as the mayor leans back in his chair and looks out across the room. He thinks for a while. It seems to last forever as I go over in my head what other options I have once the inevitable negative response arrives. Dominique moves forward with his hands clasped on the desk and opens his mouth to speak. My own hands are shaking with nervous anticipation. The words I hear are uttered in simple but carefully worded English.

'It's a very good idea,' he says.

'Yeah?' I reply.

I don't know what else to say. I'm speaking through a laugh of complete disbelief.

'Yes, yes!' Dominique replies, nodding with a huge smile across his face.

'That's so amazing! It means a lot,' I say.

In French, Dominique continues to speak while his stepson translates.

'To have a memorial for Patrick is an amazing idea and for the town it is really an honour. Would Patrick be able to come to Lion-sur-Mer and meet me?'

'Of course! He would be honoured,' I say.

That is the truth. Patrick will be over the moon to meet the mayor.

I thank Dominique repeatedly as I shake his hand. Before we part ways, I tell him that I'm hoping to find the wreck of 185 somewhere in the English Channel and that there's a chance it could be in sight of this very town hall. The mayor is excited by the idea and gives his blessing for the search. It's not something that I officially need, but it still means a lot to have his support.

As I leave, Dominique looks as happy as I feel. Heading back out into the high afternoon sun, I pull out my phone to video call Patrick, something that never has quite lost its novelty. He answers quickly from his sofa at home in England. Patrick's well-lived face appears on the screen just slightly too close to the camera to see his mouth move.

'Patrick!' I shout. 'I went for a meeting with the mayor of Lion-sur-Mer. He said he'd absolutely love for you to get a memorial. Even better, he said that normally it takes a few years, but he wants to get it there for the D-Day commemorations in June.'

That is just under a year away. I've heard countless tales of the French love of bureaucracy and red tape, so I'm sceptical that this can happen in such a short space of time, but I'm going along with it anyway.

'Crumbs! I think that's great,' he says.

'And even better, he wants you to come and visit him so he can meet you!' I say.

'Wants me to visit him? Does he? Well, that's marvellous.'

Seeing Patrick's face so pleased reminds me how big a moment this truly is. I now have permission from the mayor of the town himself to build a memorial in Lion-sur-Mer. The French are on my side. That means everything. Before today, this was a town that Patrick spoke of often and a place where he would visit to pay respect in his own quiet way, but he has never been officially welcomed. Building a memorial will be spectacular for Patrick, perhaps even life defining. For Dominique to want to recognise what happened to the crew of 185 means the world to him. After all, Patrick knows that the reason the craft was in the English Channel all those years ago was to play its part in liberating towns just like Lion-sur-Mer from Nazi occupation.

'Anyway, have you found my ship yet?' he asks, only half joking.

I explain that no, I haven't, not yet anyway, and then say goodbye.

Walking along the street, a local policeman approaches me near the seafront as I take in the classic surroundings. Pierre is a slim, light-haired young man with a neatly kept beard. He introduces himself and asks what I'm up to. As we chat, his eyes begin to light up. I can tell he's been eagerly waiting for me to finish speaking. Sure enough, as soon as I stop Pierre leaps straight into a story. As it turns out, he was born and raised here in the town and through growing up in such a historically important place has become somewhat of an expert on Sword Beach. Ten or so years ago, Pierre explains, an actual landing craft washed up on the sand right in front of the town hall. I can't believe what I'm hearing. The wreck of a landing craft not only survived on the seabed, but then washed up on the beach decades later. It is nothing short of astounding.

'What happened to the craft?' I ask.

'They cordoned off the beach, made us all step back, and then blew it up,' Pierre says.

Such is the issue with modern conflict archaeology. Do you preserve or destroy? The scale of the Second World War was so vast and widespread that it is impossible to save every remaining piece of it. Over the years, I've watched as the former US airfield where I grew up has slowly disappeared beneath roads and industrial buildings. There are many other airfields in the area, which can at times seem to lessen the loss, but if each of those airfields eventually goes the same way, there will be nothing left. When does something become historic and worth preserving? In the case of the beached landing craft, the likelihood is that it probably still had dangerous munitions on board which needed to be dealt with swiftly. Deadly situations quickly make the decision about preservation for you.

Patrick has told me before that he understands the need to take apart some of the wrecks, knowing that it was done to potentially save lives. If 185 had been a part of that, then so be it. Perhaps that comes from his time spent at sea and an awareness of what perils lurk beneath the surface. What does upset him, occasionally to the point of tears, is that the metal seems to have been subsequently sold on, which he views as equivalent to his comrades' coffins being cracked open to sell the wood and handles to the highest bidder. It's clear that the salvaging operations were not significantly recorded in a way that can determine which vessels, or how many of them, were destroyed. On the contrary, I've seen reports of cranes mounted on boats, dropping down giant arcade-like claws to rip indiscriminately at anything that was beneath.

Whatever happened has certainly caused mass destruction of now important heritage, but it also opened the floodgates to allow the wrecks to be seen as fair game to not just visit, but loot. From the 1980s, trips were organised that took recreational divers out off the landing beaches. As part of the package visitors were allowed to take home any souvenirs that could be found. Slowly but surely the wrecks were disappearing as a result. One of the divers who took part in the salvaging tried to save some of the artefacts found on the wrecks, ultimately bringing up so many objects that he managed to fill his own museum. The grounds of the building are now home to a large number of vehicles and equipment, including a US tank still covered in barnacles. Inside the museum, the cabinets are controversially filled with personal belongings. I haven't told Patrick about that, because to hear of such items on display would hurt him. It highlights that the wrecks were at one point filled with dead servicemen, and there's always a chance that some of those items may have come from his actual friends.

The museum gained brief attention when the owner uncovered love letters written by a soldier named John Glass preserved in sediment beneath the driver's seat of an M7 Priest tank, which were later put on display. It caused a debate around the morality of lifting such items from their final resting place. The finder insisted that he had never taken any items from human remains and that he was merely trying to make a living. Bodies on the seabed wouldn't have lasted long after the sinking, making it difficult to tell whether or not artefacts were ever attached to a person, but they possibly could have been at one point. The trips certainly set a precedent that enabled and encouraged divers to desecrate the wrecks. Even now, it's still possible to buy a book of the locations and blueprints of known Normandy wrecks, complete with examples of artefacts to be found within them. Before coming to France, I watched a video of a diver ripping pieces of wreckage apart just a few years before the search for 185 began. I was shocked to see such a careless attitude shown over something not only historically important, but with the potential to be a war grave.

There is one last stop before heading home. Among the carnage of D-Day, Patrick can recall spotting two beautiful houses glistening in the sun. That short moment of peace, a chance to briefly escape the battle, is still vivid in his memory. I've heard about these houses many times, more so than any other part of the story. Amazingly, upon examining the archives back in Portsmouth with Stephen Fisher, it became clear that because those houses marked the centre point between the Queen Red and Queen White sections of Sword Beach, 185 was expected to head straight for them. As a telegraphist, Patrick probably wouldn't have known that. For him, they simply appeared on the horizon, throwing the French sun back through the gun smoke.

I need to locate them, if only to confirm that 185 had definitely been in the water closest to the town in which I now have permission to build a memorial. In case the houses still exist, I've brought along a copy of the faint pencil drawing used in the landing plans. Driving along the coast, stealing views of the sea down each street, I pass through an unbroken streak of quaint towns and villages. There is a calmness to the places I've visited so far during the search. Here, I find a slower pace of life long since lost back home. As I get closer to the coordinates, I've already entered and exited Lion-sur-Mer. I can't understand why I'm not being told by my GPS to stop in the town that I presumed the houses would be in. The next sign I see reads 'Hermanville-sur-Mer', a name that rings no bells. Turning left off the main road on to a small track covered in a light dusting of sand, I'm now next to the water and heading back the way I came. Soon a wooden barricade prevents me from driving any further. Stepping out on to a grass verge, I see a concrete bunker impressively incorporated into a post-war house. Right along the grass I can make out the faint indent of German trenches dug once upon a time to stop Allied soldiers getting off the beach. There is no doubt at all that this was once the front line.

My phone shows my destination to be just a bit further along the road. Slowly walking with the drawing held out in front of me, I squint my eyes to stare ahead, but all I can see are modern-looking buildings, none old enough to have been here in 1944. I wonder if I'm in the wrong place entirely. Maybe this isn't the right town. Perhaps the location is right, but the houses were destroyed in the fighting. Maybe 185 wasn't ever near here at all. Plans in the archives show what was intended to happen, but that might have gone by the wayside under enemy fire. Walking further and further down the promenade, hot and bothered in a jacket I don't need, hope is fading. Defeated, I sit on a concrete barrier and consider giving up. If the houses exist, they could be anywhere along the coast. I can't keep wandering aimlessly.

Then I spot something in the distance. I see a house that appears older than the rest. Walking closer, it doesn't seem quite what I'm looking for. The shape seems wrong, and it isn't until I walk around the building, peering up and down between the wartime drawing and the structure in front of me, that I realise the truth. From the angle I've halted at, I can make out a perfect match for the house on the left of the drawing. Moving again, the house next door is a dead ringer for the house on the right. In front of me are the very two houses that Patrick saw on D-Day.

At the time of the landings, Lion-sur-Mer's location on the coastline was followed by a stretch of countryside to the east, but set far back from the water was a small village called Hermanville-sur-Mer. As the decades ticked by and Normandy rebuilt itself, Hermanville-sur-Mer was developed right up to the water's edge.

The name travelled alongside the expansion and eventually swept up part of the eastern end of Lion-sur-Mer.

Staring up at the two houses, a realisation appears like a dark cloud out on the water. Behind me is the exact spot 185 had been on D-Day. This is where Patrick Thomas and Jack Barringer were. It is here that the eyes of the crew once stared towards France and hoped to live through the horror. Turning to look out to sea, there's an eerie feeling in the air. The wind is calm. Seagulls are swooping silently above. The distant laughter of children playing on the beach echoes quietly in my direction. It should be impossible for me to picture what happened here on 6 June 1944. To search for moments in history is to search for ghosts. Shadows that go unfound, left quietly alone in their corner of the past. It should be impossible, but it isn't. In my head I see the mirage of 185 out on the waves in front of me. The craft is out there. It's calling out to be found, ready to hand over its secrets if I could just walk out to reach it.

Driving back to Ouistreham, I board the ferry home to England. Reaching the dining hall, I put on a jacket and head to the upper deck where, out in the wind, I walk to the guardrail. Peering over as we leave the harbour, the water below is dark and ominous, but perfectly still, like a frozen lake obscuring all that rests beneath.

It must be down there, I think. *Down there, somewhere.*

Chapter Seven

14 July 2017

Patrick is the last person still alive who can speak of the sinking of LCH 185 first hand. He is a link between the past and present. It is a once-in-a-lifetime moment to have a veteran of his age here and still able to help with the search for his own shipwreck, but I've always been aware that the story is not just Patrick's. He was just one of the men on board 185 back then, one sailor with one part of the story. For the full tale of the craft to be told, the rest of the crew need to be found.

An exact list of those who served on the craft during both the landings and in the weeks that followed is hard to define. As of now, such a thing has never been discovered. LCH 185's crew was from the Royal Navy, most of whom had been on board since picking up the craft in the US. By the time training for D-Day had begun, the vessel was filled with a new group of wireless telegraphists and radio operators. Having been sent to the craft to serve in the invasion, these men were not technically part of the crew.

Patrick was initially hesitant to let me see his service record. The document lists him as being on HMS *Odyssey* during the period when he was supposed to have been in France. Patrick was concerned that I'd think his service record showed him to be telling mistruths or exaggerating his role when I eventually discovered that *Odyssey* was never in Normandy. Like HMS *Royal Arthur*, the naval base where Patrick had begun his training, HMS *Odyssey* was a stone frigate. It wasn't in Normandy because it was a permanent structure located in Ilfracombe, Devon. Patrick never actually stepped foot inside the gates of *Odyssey*, instead being sent straight up to Scotland to Marconi College, and then to the rehearsals at Invergordon. This confusion in the records is not uncommon with men sent on to landing craft owing to their overall purpose of disembarking troops elsewhere, making it difficult to pin down exactly who was on 185 at any one time. To muddy the waters more, during the crossing on D-Day, the craft was filled with troops destined to fight on Sword Beach – men who should have been deep into the French countryside by the time the sinking took place, but were they?

Caruth Main and Eric Fletcher were members of Combined Operations Pilot Parties, in team 9, whose job it was to infiltrate enemy beaches earmarked for Allied landings. Heading towards the coast on submarines or landing craft, COPP teams would then transfer to kayaks in order to avoid enemy detection. One man would remain with the kayaks, while a second would swim to shore to observe enemy defences, collect soil samples to assess the beach's load-bearing capacity, and confirm potential exit routes. Owing to their navigational skills, it wasn't uncommon during the landing itself for COPP members to guide landing craft towards the beach. While a few COPP men did go ashore on D-Day, the majority returned to Britain after their duties had been carried out. Fletcher and Main are listed as having drowned when 185 sunk, raising the question as to why the two men were on a Landing Craft Headquarters weeks after D-Day had ended.

They could have crossed the Channel on 185 during the invasion and stayed on board afterwards. COPP 9 might have returned to France at a later date, or perhaps 185 picked the two men up from elsewhere. A single report on the death of Main and Fletcher simply notes that they were 'on loan' to Force S. It may never be known what the two men were doing on the landing craft. The only certainty is that they died in the sinking and became two more stories lost to the sea.

The list of those that stepped foot aboard 185 was ever-changing. As a headquarters craft, servicemen would often board the vessel from elsewhere to attend meetings, and members of the crew could be expected to leave 185 for the same reason. Engineers would also regularly leave in order to repair other landing craft. Prisoners were briefly held on board, troops were often picked up from the beach, and the crew would rescue survivors of sinking ships. All of these uncertain quantities make pinpointing an accurate amount of men killed difficult. The craft rescued sailors from the sinking of HMS *Swift* shortly before 185 itself was sunk. Survivors of that sinking could have drowned in the second. If there ever was a record kept of who exactly walked the deck of LCH 185, it surely went to the bottom of the English Channel.

There is, however, a list of men known to have died when 185 went down, and it consists of thirty-five names. The first time I read the list, I was shocked to see that fourteen were between the ages of eighteen and twenty-one. To read the ages of people barely old enough to drink or vote was horrifying. Only three were in their thirties, the rest were all in their twenties. The range of military titles of the men lost that day is vast, everything from petty officers to leading wiremen, chief motor mechanics and a ship's cook. Four are listed as being buried in graves in France, having been at least partly recovered from the water or found washed up.

One of the graves is located over 100 miles from Lion-sur-Mer at Dieppe, perhaps owing to the distance the body travelled before being found. Other than those graves, none of which are in the same cemetery, the rest of the men on the list of the deceased are remembered as names on various war memorials spread across Britain. It seems that the only right thing to do is to try and track down as many families of the lost men as I can. With plans to unveil a memorial well underway, I hope that relatives of those seamen with no permanent resting place can come together at the unveiling to remember their loved ones. Whether or not that will ever happen, I don't know, but it seems worth a try.

I face a dilemma. While the sinking of 185 took place over seventy years ago, it still isn't outside living memory. Like Patrick, many Second World War veterans are still alive, which means that some of the brothers, sisters, sons and daughters of those that served are still alive. It's easy to see a sense of finality when hearing of a ship going down and reading a list of those that disappeared with it, but in reality that closure simply doesn't exist. Memories of the men that died live for decades, clawing on through the generations. Distant relatives of the crew will no doubt still be here in the form of great-nephews and nieces, cousins and second cousins, and perhaps even great-grandchildren. They might not know about the wartime death of their relative, but it's a given that they are out there.

When I think of finding the families, I'm worried that I might locate even closer relatives. If someone died in 1944, they likely left behind siblings, even a young son or daughter. Those are relatives that might still remember their loved one. If they do, they will still miss them. Perhaps their voice echoes in the mind with the cherished recollections of days before the conflict ruined it all. No doubt the hurt of losing a father or brother in the war will still ache after all these years.

Aside from the four bodies recovered, every other person that went down with the craft was never seen again. They have no grave and no place to rest. They are still missing, and the loved ones left behind may still be waiting for them to walk back through the front door.

I've little doubt that any relative, close or distant, will be thrilled to hear of my plans to build a memorial, yet I can't help but wonder how they might feel about an attempt to locate the wreck. Wherever it is, the wreck will have been the final resting place of many of those who died in the sinking. Families may not want that found, preferring instead to leave it undisturbed. If that is the case, I'll understand. I wouldn't blame them for feeling that way. I'd probably think the same had it been my grandfather that was lost at sea, but where would that leave the search? Patrick wants it to take place. He wants the wreck discovered. Does the wish of the final living survivor take precedence over the wish of relatives of the deceased, and who am I to decide?

Taking hold of the list of names, I examine what little information there is. If I'd been trying to find relatives of these men in six of the seven decades that have passed, I'd have been standing before a hopeless task. These days, almost everyone is on social media. It still won't be easy, but most towns and villages tend to have online groups dedicated to local history. With that in mind, I take a selection of the thirty-five names and write up posts for sites related to the places they were last known to have lived. A small number of the deceased have hometowns listed. Even fewer have the names of their parents. Mostly, there is nothing to go on but a name and age.

'I have promised my elderly friend Patrick Thomas,' I write, 'that I will find his long-lost Second World War shipwreck. I'm hoping to find families of those who died in the sinking so that I can invite them to the unveiling of a memorial in France.'

The first family I set about trying to find is that of Jack Barringer. It would mean everything to Patrick to speak to them, allowing a chance to pass on the story of what happened to Jack and, in doing so, finally freeing himself of the guilt of it all.

'Both Jack, his wife, his brother, and his parents were from Northampton. The family might still be there. Any leads would be hugely appreciated. Thank you.'

I press send, posting to a group dedicated to Northampton's past, then do the same for locations spread right across Britain. I look for Robert Henley Tucker in Plumstead, Kenneth Simpson in Lancaster, George Casselden in Lewes, Ronald Patterson in Dagenham, Robert Wears in Hendon, John James Rimmer in Kirkdale, William Piper in Ayrshire, and Henry Jeffrey in Enfield.

A friend of mine named Sarah Stewart, who has been following the search for 185 with keen interest, kindly offers up her skills in genealogy. Together, using ancestry websites and family trees, we set out on a separate and much more complicated search for the families of Geoffrey Dunkerley, Alan Maxwell, John Nicholson, David Saunders and Norman Smith.

Twelve men leaves many others out, but with limited time before the memorial is set to be unveiled, it's important initially to search for those with the most information available before continuing to track down the rest as and when we can.

With the net cast, there's little left to do but wait. It's surreal to know that the memories of those names are creaking into life. For so long, they have laid dormant on a list of dead sailors, but are now being teased out of their own personal corner of history. This is just the start. The search for relatives will continue for years to come until every last family has been found.

* * *

My thoughts turn to that of 185's sister ship LCH 269. The two landing craft were launched in the US together and stayed that way until the sinking of 185, so what happened to the sister ship? I have no idea whether or not it survived Normandy and continued to fight. Perhaps it was sunk later on. If the craft did go the distance, perhaps some of the crew are still alive. Better yet, the craft could still be out there. A quick internet search pulls up a page dedicated to the wartime memories of a man named Basil Woolf. Basil was a petty officer in the engine room of 269. In 2005, then aged eighty-three, he had written down everything he remembered about serving on the craft. To have found Basil's account so easily is both astonishing and a frustrating reminder of how elusive information on 185 has been. Reading on, I'm pleased to discover that the sister ship did survive Normandy, managing to avoid a fate to which so many other vessels in the Channel had succumbed.

After the sinking of 185 on 25 June 1944, 269 remains in France until September. The craft then pulls into Poole in Dorset, but its work is far from over. With three campaigns under its belt, the vessel is taken in for some much-needed repair work in preparation for whatever the next operation will be. As he waits to hear where his newest destination is, Basil Woolf has a feeling that they'll soon be on the way to the Pacific to take on the Japanese. Instead, on 28 October, the craft heads back across the English Channel. The crew have only just left Normandy. There isn't any need for them to go back, and Basil is confused. Out at sea the craft turns north to head up the Channel. It then turns again, steering north-east by east. Basil enquires with the coxswain, who replies that he suspects that the destination is Belgium. While 269 continues on, the crew are unsure and uneasy about what awaits them at their mysterious final destination.

After hours on the water, they pull into the harbour at Ostend, a city on the coast of Belgium. The coxswain was right. Despite the crew being on active service, they are given four hours' shore leave. With a warning to avoid the roads, which are still laced with German mines, the sailors head into a once-popular destination long since decimated by war. The men, perplexed to have been allowed off the craft, follow the sounds of distant music to the nearest bar still running and swiftly drink as much wine as can be found. They would have liked beer, but it has all been either taken or consumed by retreating Germans. Basil forgoes the pub, choosing instead to head to one of the only remaining shops in the town. He buys a bottle of Chanel perfume for his fiancée back home. It is one of the only items left in the entire building and kept in an otherwise empty vault.

On 1 November, 269 leaves Ostend to join up with the Support Squadron Eastern Flank (SSEF). Another landing is on the horizon. It will be the craft's fourth, and its second as a headquarters craft. Safely among the array of ships that make up the SSEF, Basil is finally told of his destination. To be heading for Walcheren comes as a surprise to the crew. Most have never heard of the place, but the destination is important to the Allies. Since the successful landings at Normandy, the concrete Mulberry harbours towed over from Britain and the port at Cherbourg have been used to provide vast quantities of troops and supplies to fuel the push across Europe. Now, as the war moves further away from Normandy, new options are needed.

The Scheldt estuary is a waterway running 217 miles through France, Belgium and Holland. At the upper end is the port at Antwerp, which was successfully taken from German hands on 4 September. The approach to the port, along the Scheldt estuary, is still occupied by the enemy. At the mouth of the Scheldt is the former island of Walcheren standing defiantly in the way of the Allies using the port at Antwerp. As well as blocking use of the estuary, the area is being used to launch V-2 rockets towards Britain, making it crucial that the area is taken from the Nazis.

By the time 269 reaches the estuary, Walcheren is the only piece of land yet to fall. Assisted by the British, Canadian troops have been fiercely attempting to take the island since October, but now a frontal assault has been ordered. Walcheren is heavily fortified, occupied by the German 15th Army and guarded with a number of anti-aircraft guns. The island is a final bastion of defence and the Germans have been told they are not to surrender under any circumstance. There remains no outcome but a fight to the end.

The next day, alongside HMS *Warship*, HMS *Erebus*, HMS *Roberts*, two monitors and twenty-six other landing craft, 269 storms towards Walcheren. There has been no air support and the craft are attacking in broad daylight. The Germans are waiting. It doesn't take long for chaos to erupt. Basil Woolf listens from the engine room as batteries begin to launch deadly rounds into the sky. LCF 37 (a Landing Craft Flak is a converted Landing Craft Tank) is the first vessel to be hit when a shell drops towards the bow, causing the craft to explode. LCT(R) 334, a Landing Craft Tank (Rocket) which has 1,200 rockets stored on its deck, manages to fire a few rounds at German defences. They fall short. When the enemy returns fire, 334 is hit and sent off course. The explosion ignites a number of the rockets, which are launched screaming towards the rest of the landing group. To add to the confusion, LCT(R) 457 and 368 fire towards the enemy, but the rounds don't reach their targets, instead landing near four Allied landing craft.

Basil covers his ears with his hands. He has no idea what is happening. The noise is worse than anything he had heard back in Normandy. Sick to the stomach with fear, ears ringing like a whistle, there is nothing to do but wait for the explosions to stop. A minute goes by in what feels like hours. As silence finally falls, Basil heads up a ladder to find out what has gone on. He's horrified by what he sees. The estuary is on fire. Craft are ablaze, some are sinking. Across the water dead men float in the flames. There is life left in the few struggling to stay afloat. The crew of 269 pull bodies, both alive and dead, out of the water. By the time the smoke clears, five landing craft are gone and thirty sailors are wounded.

LCH 269 takes the survivors and burned corpses to a hospital ship nearby before heading back into the fight. Despite the horror, the assault on Walcheren proceeds. Enemy defence on the island is brutal. The support craft are expected to get close to the coastal batteries to draw fire upon themselves in order to allow attack forces an easier landing. It is, in many ways, a suicide mission. Heading through the waves, the craft are hit badly.

When a shell falls close to the stern of 269, the crew are gripped in fear. Shrapnel rapidly arrives in torrents, ripping holes into the thick hull with ease. Estuary water pours in, gradually filling up the engine room. Basil and his shipmates use broken wooden plugs to patch up the holes. It's a temporary fix that lasts only until another direct hit on the bow tosses the men through the air. There is now an empty space like a window in the hull. The crew are shaken, but somehow manage to stuff the jagged hole with a slapdash contraption of plywood and hammock fabric.

After surviving hours at the mercy of the German attack, 269 floats calmly in the estuary. The sea is quiet as dusk rolls in. On board, the crew are unsure if the infantry has taken out the enemy guns, or if the Germans simply think that there is nothing left alive on the water to fire on. A radio message arrives announcing that five enemy targets, possibly E-boats, are heading towards what remains of the fleet. LCH 269 is already battered. The crew are mentally and physically exhausted. Torpedoes will chew them up like sharks on a seal. Determined to go down swinging, exhausted sailors rush to arm themselves with rifles before heading to the deck. After surviving Sicily, Italy, Normandy and now the devastating landing at Walcheren, it looks like the end is near. Basil and his shipmates wait with bated breath for the torpedoes to hit.

Luckily a destroyer cuts the five targets off, tearing the first E-boat to shreds and badly damaging the others. The enemy vessels turn around and limp back to where they came from. LCH 269's crew are relieved, but the peace doesn't last long before another message is received. Midget submarines are thought to be approaching alongside diving units ready to stick magnetic mines on the hulls of the landing craft. There is a deep sense of disbelief among the men. The situation feels unreal. They can't catch a break. It's decided that teams will work through the night to drop depth charges into the water every three minutes to keep the enemy at bay. Through the explosions and the stress, no one gets any sleep. In the morning, Basil awakes to find that only 269 and the hospital ship still float unaided. Walcheren has been catastrophic.

As the craft leaves later that day, Basil swears to never again set eyes on the place in his lifetime, a promise that he never breaks. LCH 269 and the damaged fleet limp carefully back through the water. They have been in a fight, and it shows. Pinned to the hull is a cutting that reads, 'Stop purring. The war isn't won yet!' The irony of the words is not lost on the deflated crew or the injured men that have been taken aboard from other damaged or sunken craft. The weather is terrible, sending the remaining vessels off course into an Allied minefield. Those on board are terrified.

Sailors tiptoe the deck barefoot to stay as silent as possible. Engines are slowed as much as they can be without stalling. Basil watches, a cigarette dangling between his lips, as the hospital ship hits a mine and launches into the sky. It splits in two and sinks. LCH 269 creeps across the water to search for survivors, but none are found.

After eventually manoeuvring out of the minefield, Basil tries to sleep, but the only thing on his mind is the shock and disbelief that he is now on board the only vessel left standing. Walcheren has been like no other battle. Nine ships have been sunk and eleven are so badly damaged that nothing can be done to save them. In their grief, the crew pull together some money in the hopes of building a memorial to the men that have died in the fight, many of whose bodies were pulled on to the craft.

When the craft finally arrives back into Poole harbour, it feels like arriving at an oasis. Basil is given leave. He goes home to see his fiancée, who is so thrilled at the bottle of Chanel perfume that she drops it on the tiled floor.

Basil's memoir ends when he reaches Poole. The craft didn't sink at Walcheren, but it did sustain significant damage. What then happened to LCH 269? After a bit of digging, I find that to my surprise the craft had not only avoided being scrapped at the conclusion of the war, but had lasted for decades afterwards. After the conflict ended, 269 was taken back across the Atlantic Ocean to the States, where it was scheduled to be scrapped in 1947. The landing craft managed to return home to the country it was built in, its life set to end in the same place it once began. Instead of being scrapped, 269 was saved when it was purchased by a private buyer on 28 January 1948. The new owner, a man named Herby Henson, renamed the craft *Quaker City* and docked it on Ohio Avenue, Atlantic City. There was naturally a huge quantity of leftover equipment in the years immediately after the war, and Herby used the vessel as a base to sell military surplus.

In March 1962, a hurricane smashed through the area. *Quaker City* was set loose and carried out on to the water, where it might have reached the ocean had it not first collided with a mudflat. Basil Woolf had believed the craft to have been scrapped, but when his memories were published online, a man local to Atlantic City named Jim Mason wrote to explain how he recalled seeing *Quaker City* used as a surplus store. Recognising it as a landing craft and curious about its history, Jim had backtracked through registries to find out what the landing craft had originally been known as.

Amazingly, writing in 2005, Jim believed that 185's sister ship was still permanently stuck on the mudflat after all these years, remaining as a silent shadow of a hastily disappearing war. Reading the conversation between Jim and Basil, I spot the coordinates of where *Quaker City* supposedly still rests. Pulling up Google Earth to look for myself, sure enough, I see the shape of a landing craft large enough to cover the entire side of what looks like a tiny island. For a moment, I think about booking a flight to the US to visit the site. It would be the closest I could ever come to walking the deck of Patrick's craft. I'd be able to stand in the middle and know that the vessel saw everything that 185 once saw. Sadly, if the wreck I'm looking at is 269, which the information certainly points towards, then it is in a state too poor to make the trip worth it. A craft is there, undoubtedly, but it is no more than an outline. My efforts are better placed pushing harder to find 185. Still, I can't resist setting the date of the satellite image back a few years to watch as the wreck gradually rebuilds itself into 269. In 2002, when I was eleven years old, the craft was barely a wreck at all. It looked almost good enough to take to sea. Once again, it seems, I am just a little too late.

I manage to find Ian Woolf, the son of Basil, and send him a message on 31 July 2017. He replies soon after to inform me that his father had sadly passed away on 1 June. It's hard to take just how close I was to being able to speak to a man who had been alongside 185. Basil had even visited Normandy for the seventieth anniversary of D-Day, the same year that Patrick returned for the first time. If only they had known, they could have met; a sailor from each sister ship shaking hands after all those years. Ian informs me that his father had moved to Florida and taken up painting in his later years. He emails me some of the paintings, one of which is a beautiful interpretation of LCH 269 heading across the water into battle.

Before long, I start to get replies to my posts looking for the families of 185's crew. Most of the time, I'm sent words of encouragement from people who are interested in the story, but every once in a while I get lucky, and gradually a small number of relatives gets in touch. It's astonishing to see the difference in the ages of people that come forward. Some are the elderly children of those who had died on the ship. Others are great-nephews roughly the same age as me. No matter the age, it seems that none of them has forgotten the loss that their family had suffered. The trauma and memory have travelled down the generations. As I read the stories sent to me, the veil of time gradually peels back as the lives of those who died on the craft come to life.

Firstly, there is Alan Haigh Maxwell. I discover Alan not through any family, but through a memorial sheet in the school archive at Sherborne School in Dorset. Maxwell was a sophisticated-looking man with a thin face and slick, neatly combed hair. Alan had come from a privileged background. He was the son of Sir Reginald Maxwell, a civil servant in India, and Lady Mary Lyle Maxwell.

Reginald sat for six portraits, which are now kept in the National Portrait Gallery in London. Alan had flourished at Sherborne, a boarding school, where he had served as not only head of house, but also as a prefect in charge of agriculture, PT instructor, and even editor of the school magazine, the *Shirburnian*. He was a keen artist with a wonderful passion for trains and railways. Alan planned to study medicine at Cambridge University, but felt so strongly that he should do his bit for Britain that he postponed the degree in order to fight. Joining up through the 'Y Scheme', aimed at promoting Royal Navy ratings to officers at a young age, he was soon sent to Combined Operations, but after breaking his wrist was put on softer duties for a short time. During his recovery, Alan would return to his former school, having left quite a legacy, to give talks to the students. After returning to the war, he was just twenty years old when the sinking of 185 ended his life.

Geoffrey Dunkerley had the look of a Hollywood lead. He had first served on HMS *Orchid*, a corvette, from which he sent his Aunt Betty a Christmas card. The card, which still remains in the family, shows the black silhouette of HMS *Orchid* soaring on the ocean waves. Geoffrey had no children, but left behind a devastated fiancée. Geoffrey's cousin Rosemary passes this information to me. Rosemary thinks that she must be the only family member left alive who ever actually met Geoffrey. She endured her own struggles in the war, having been sent from the English countryside, via an Arctic convoy, to Canada, as many British children were at the time. Rosemary had been told of Geoffrey's death through letters from her parents back home. She still remembers the grief felt upon hearing his name read out in her school's chapel as 'killed in action'.

Norman Smith was the eldest son of Norman and Elsie Smith. He had four siblings, Irene, Peggy, John and Wendy. His father was a respected builder who had served in the trenches of the Great War.

The two Normans would work together on construction projects, at one point helping to rebuild Coventry after it was destroyed by German bombing raids. Norman's nephew Steve informs me that Norman's sister Peggy is still alive. It is incredibly moving when a photograph of Norman arrives. I find myself staring at an average-looking boy, cheerful in the face, smiling, but with bags beneath his eyes. It is a photograph of a photograph, taken on a phone. The image I see is badly glared, not through poor photography, but because the original is in a frame. The photograph of Norman still stands proudly on his sister's fireplace. Peggy remembers her brother as a 'lovely, kind, and caring boy'. The two siblings had spent hours making plans for what they would get up to together. Peggy and Norman taking on the world, after this awful war is over. Looking at the photo on her fireplace, which never gathers dust, Peggy still wonders where he is.

'My Norm', she calls him.

At nineteen years old, Kenneth Simpson was one of the youngest to have died in the sinking. He was a teenager who had left school to become a chef. Kenneth took up an apprenticeship at the King's Arms and County Hotels and on occasion would work at the Lansil silk works in Lancaster. In the photo I receive from his family, Kenneth is wearing a shirt and tie. He looks proud. As a result of his trade, Kenneth entered the war as a ship's cook. The last time he saw his niece on the eve of heading to war, he gave her a shoulder ride home, which she still remembers fondly.

David Saunders likely lied about his age to fight in the war. He is listed as having died aged twenty-one, but his family believe him to have actually been twenty. David's parents had divorced, the family was struggling, and life at home was tough. He was keen to get away. Shortly before his death, David posed for a photograph with his aunt. He wears full naval uniform but can't hide how young he looks. His aunt is beaming with pride while her nephew cheekily sticks out his tongue.

George Casselden was twenty-six when he died in the sinking. He left behind a wife and three daughters. George was known as Gus to the crew of 185, but his family knew him as Bay. When George was given two days' leave before the invasion, like many he ignored orders to stay in Portsmouth, instead rushing home to spend time with his family. In his obituary, the photograph of George shows him in naval uniform with a huge smile across his face. Upon his death, the local sports club purchased a new darts cup in his honour. George's wife was left to raise the children, all under five, on her own. It was tough for the family; the devastation of their father's loss left an impact on the daughters for the rest of their lives. George's wife was never keen to remember such a traumatic event and had to be convinced to allow her husband's name to be added to the war memorial in their hometown of Lewes, where one of his daughters still lives. Before her death, the last trip George's wife took was to visit the naval memorial in Portsmouth. Their daughter left her alone, standing beneath George's name.

'Bye bye, Bay,' she said. 'I won't be coming here again.'

It is hard to believe that I have now looked into the eyes of a number of Patrick's shipmates. The search will go on, but in this moment I try to take it all in. I never knew if the men were remembered. For so long, these sailors have been a list of names etched on war memorials, but I finally know that the memories of at least some have never been forgotten. The men still live quietly in postcards and letters home tucked carefully into drawers, their laughter heard in anecdotes told by family members who still wonder what happened, and their faces seen on the mantelpieces of siblings still mourning the loss.

Having seen the faces of some of the crew and learned their stories, an uneasy feeling finds me. I'm unsure if I'm doing the right thing, shaken by the idea of searching for the wreck. If the craft is found, unless it's absolutely necessary to stop myself floating away in an emergency or to take measurements, I won't be moving anything on the wreck. Still, the conclusion to the story of 185 for these relatives has always been that their loved ones are missing in an unknown part of the sea. If I find the wreck, then I find the resting place, and that narrative changes. George Casselden's daughters are still alive. They lost their dad in the sinking and still live with the pain each day. It is so easy to get swept up in the excitement of the search and forget at times that the names on the list were people who had actually lived at one point. I try my best not to, and rarely do stray far from that thought, but it has been hard to discover that daughters of the deceased are alive and contactable by email. The same goes for Norman Smith's elderly sister, who still stares at her brother's photograph in the hope that he may one day return. If, within the small number of families I have been in touch with, there are daughters and sisters, then there are surely other close relatives to be found for the rest of the crew. I'm not sure I have any right to disturb those stories or to churn up such a trauma. I question myself for days until, one morning, I open my computer to a message.

'Hello, I'm Jack Barringer's nephew. I have shared your post to the family. They would like to get in touch.'

I can't believe what I'm reading. Jack Barringer's nephew. The man's name is Timothy Barringer. He explains that he is the son of Keith, Jack's brother. Jack had three brothers: Keith, George and Les. I message Timothy back straightaway. He's excited to hear about the project. I'm over the moon to be speaking to a relative of Jack. Timothy contacts his cousins Dave and Jeff, the sons of Les Barringer, who quickly send over what information they have on their uncle. I find myself looking at a photograph of Jack Barringer for the first time ever. This is the face of a man that Patrick has spent so much of his life remembering. He hasn't seen the eyes of his friend since they disappeared beneath the waves on 25 June 1944. Jack looks so young for a twenty-nine-year-old. His face is round and filled with a mischievous smile. He looks kind. As I look through photographs of Jack and his family, I see one of his wedding day. The image strikes at my heart. I read the original telegraph to Les from their mother, informing him of the sinking.

JACK MISSING. COME IF POSSIBLE = MUM ++

There is a black and white photograph of the original hand-painted wooden cross placed in the ground above Jack's body in France. It's surreal to see, knowing I've stood in that exact same spot with Patrick. To have such a personal look into the life of a man I have never met, but heard so much about, is strange. Jack Barringer is a name that I have experienced through a tragic story that has haunted our mutual friend for so long, but now his life plays out in front of me.

I receive a letter written by Jack, sent home from the deck of 185. It sends shivers through my body. An actual letter, written by the friend Patrick lost from the landing craft I've heard so much about. As I read the handwritten words, Jack speaks of the horror he has seen, how exhausted he is, and how he can't wait to get home. I know that at some point I need to give Patrick a copy. I speak regularly with the Barringer family, telling them of my hope that they can attend the memorial unveiling and meet Patrick. They inform me that the Barringer family has never forgotten Jack and that they visit his grave whenever possible. He was their father's brother. Jack is their uncle. This is not distant history to the family. I know how much it will mean to Patrick to hear that the grave is not forgotten. It means a lot to me as well.

I ask the Barringers what they think about the idea of searching for the wreck. The family is thrilled by it, they say. I ask the same question to the other families I have spoken to. They all believe in the search. I know now that I am doing the right thing. Those men deserve to have an ending to their story, and so do the families that were left behind. The search will not end here.

Walking towards a shed in my back garden, I have the intention of turning it into a severely cramped expedition headquarters. A few years before, I had nailed a plank of wood in one corner to use as a desk, but never put it to use. As I step inside, ducking to not hit my head on the entrance, I'm not entirely convinced that I'll occupy the space this time either. Sitting down, I open up the folder filled with the maps and photographs I presented to Dominique in Lion-sur-Mer. Uncomfortably teetering on a worn-thin garden chair with my elbows resting on the corner of the chipped plank of wood, I peer through the files while dodging drips from the ceiling.

Flattening the creases of a map of the Normandy coastline, I pick up a pen and hover the tip in the air as I pause to think. Then, despite the failing ink, I draw a firm red circle on the spot that seems to be the best bet for 185's location. There are no witnesses to my decision, but I'm making a stand. This is a letter to my future self. If the project gets as far as a dive expedition, if anything is discovered, I will be able to look at this map and know whether I was right or wrong. Removing a rusty drawing pin from an aged British flag attached to the ceiling, I stick the freshly marked map to the plywood wall, walk outside, and padlock the door shut.

My day job in commercial archaeology is still in full swing and I'm straight back to work. My bosses are supportive, kindly offering me a few extra days' leave should a dive expedition ever come to fruition, but my life is beginning to feel divided. There is my normal life, and there is the life I live during the search. The search has begun to drum up a bit of media attention. Newspapers and magazines are picking up on what I'm attempting to do, which lands me a few small appearances on television and radio. It isn't rare for me to be excavating a deep prehistoric pit, only to sit at the bottom to take phone calls about the expedition.

When the idea to search for 185 had first come to me, one man in particular kept popping up again and again in my research. Chris Howlett is an oceanographer who has been mapping the seabed that surrounds Britain for a number of years. Although uncovering shipwrecks is not his full-time job, inevitably he does exactly that as a byproduct of studying the seafloor. Chris is a professional, but also an enthusiast. Outside of work, he tries to establish the identities of wrecks found off the coast of Normandy.

Chris is the most important person for me to locate. Whether or not he will be at all interested in helping me is another thing entirely. From a dusty van one lunch break, I send Chris an email to explain what I'm doing. I expect to hear nothing back, presuming he's too busy to get involved, or that he simply can't take a young archaeologist with a such bold idea seriously. Luckily for me, I'm wrong. In a couple of hours, I have a reply from Chris, asking for the name of Patrick's craft.

With that question, I'm hit with an unexpected problem. Having Chris eager to help is amazing, but I feel reluctant to give out the name of the craft. No one owns 185 and no one owns the right to search for its wreckage: its history belongs to both no one and everyone. Until now I've simply referred to the project as the search for a landing craft, a tactic that has annoyed a few journalists along the way. I hold genuine concerns that if others know the exact vessel I'm attempting to find, it might kick off an unnecessary race to discover the wreck. The world of archaeology can be quite ruthless. There isn't an infinite pool of ideas. Stories such as Patrick's are especially rare, making it crucial, to me at least, to be the one to discover the wreck. I promised Patrick that I would try to locate 185 and, if a stranger discovers it first, it couldn't possibly mean as much to them.

There is little choice, though. I have to loosen my grip because, if I don't, I'll end up trying to undertake the entire project on my own. Not only would that be incredibly difficult, but I'd be doing both myself and Patrick a disservice if the search were to fizzle out beneath the weight of carrying the whole thing alone. Many people will be needed to pull it off, I have always known that. Ultimately, I tell Chris the name of the craft. I need his help.

To my surprise, he is already aware of 185. It's not a wreck he is actively trying to identify, but it has come up repeatedly in the records during research for other wrecks. The craft has been resident at the back of Chris's mind as one that he hopes to get around to investigating properly in the future.

While 185 was known as LCH 501 on D-Day, afterwards it reverted to its original name. Finding information about the craft's role during the invasion has been hard, but it isn't too difficult to uncover reports of the sinking. These are never substantial, more often than not no more than a few lines in various files. Above and below mentions of 185 are almost always accounts of other ships lost off the coast of Normandy, bringing home just how easily the story of Patrick's landing craft was forgotten in the fast-paced horror of the war. One of these reports seems to confirm the eyewitness testimony of Patrick's post-war colleague from the Gooseberry harbour:

> This craft, which was engaged as an HQ Ship in the vicinity
> of Queen Beach, had just taken on supplies of water from a
> water boat anchored in the artificial harbour. The craft had
> been under way for only a few minutes and struck a mine
> and is believed to have sunk within four minutes.

With these words, the story begins to come together. The reason a witness saw the craft sink while standing on the Gooseberry was because 185 had been visiting it shortly before the tragedy unfolded. The craft had manoeuvred itself to the artificial harbour in order to fill up its water supplies and, having been on the return journey for a few minutes, the explosion occurred. LCH 185 could not have moved far in that time. The report continued:

> The rating states that he was thrown into the water and
> picked up later in an unconscious condition; it is not,
> therefore, possible to obtain any definitive information
> as to the number and names of survivors.

There is a reasonable likelihood that with so few survivors of the sinking, the man being questioned was a disorientated Patrick Thomas. He can, after all, remember being interviewed while on the rescue craft. A further report states:

> Where: About one mile from shore in Sword Area.
> Method: Thrown into water by explosion.
> Circumstances: Engaged in controlling Landing Craft
> in the vicinity of Queen Beach on the Normandy Coast.

This backs the theory that the sinking happened in the Queen sector, made up of Queen Green, Queen White and Queen Red. Although it hadn't shown up on Alan Smith's map of hazards back on HMS *Medusa*, according to wartime maps the Gooseberry was located a few miles off the shore between the Queen White and Queen Red sectors. My search zone is getting smaller. Things are looking promising. The prospect of diving in the English Channel is seeming increasingly real.

There is another report, one that makes little sense when compared to the others. It states that 185 sunk close to HMS *Largs*. This report is a cause for concern, because HMS *Largs* was located significantly further out to sea and much further west along the coast. It's hardly surprising to find contrasting reports, but that doesn't make it any less disheartening. Juggling contradictions is how historical research tends to go, and when it comes to something as traumatic and confusing as a ship sinking in the English Channel, it is really no wonder that different accounts don't match up. People recall events differently: these reports were written in the middle of an active war zone.

It is important to note that even first-hand accounts have to be taken with a pinch of salt. Over seventy years passed between the sinking and Patrick telling me his story. How many people remember the exact details of what they were doing on a specific day a couple of weeks ago? And Patrick is in his nineties, trying to remember something seven decades in the past when he was still just a teenager. The wreck might well be next to the Gooseberry, as many sources attest, but it could just as well be miles away in the vicinity of where HMS *Largs* once was.

This isn't the first time Chris has been directly involved with a shipwreck search in Normandy. For the seventieth anniversary of D-Day, there had been a large-scale operation to undertake sonar scans of the entire stretch of Normandy's historic landing beaches. Chris, as an expert oceanographer, was on the expedition. I know that if there's any chance that 185 has already been stumbled upon prior to the beginning of my own search, it would have been during this enormous archaeological project.

The survey was a huge undertaking that covered a vast expanse of seabed, but there were elements that made me doubt whether 185 could have been located. The size and keel depth of the ship used for the expedition meant that the scan had to take place a significant distance from the shore. Plenty of wrecks could have been missed in the shallows. The survey was also done as part of a television documentary to be aired in the United States, understandably giving the expedition a slight US emphasis. The British and Canadian beaches were surveyed, but not as far as their eastern limits. The extreme east of Sword Beach was where 185 seems to have sunk, meaning that there was a chance the search had stopped short of where the craft could be.

The expedition had uncovered around fifty individual wrecks, as well as hundreds of anomalies on the seabed. I need to access that sonar data to see what was found at Sword Beach. If that is not possible, then I'll have no choice but to somehow run my own sonar survey. To do that will be impossibly expensive, likely stopping the search for 185 dead in its tracks. Luckily for me, Chris has access to the data.

We arrange a video call and a few days later speak face to face for the first time, albeit through a computer screen. Looking into the camera from a dimly lit room, I begin to talk.

'Gooseberry 5 is a real key clue in the search for 185. Is any of that still there?' I ask.

'Well, funnily enough, that's a question that has been bugging me for some time,' Chris says. 'Most of the ships are still there in some form or another. Not in very good condition, though, because Normandy has a high tidal range and that erodes steel.'

It's eye-opening to be discussing this sort of thing with a person that has been involved with a sonar survey in the English Channel. The search has just jumped up a level of professionalism, from a pipe dream to a tense reality.

'The idea behind the survey was to scan as far as they could,' Chris continues. 'They found about 650 things on the bottom that were quite identifiable.

Such a high number of sonar hits shows the impressive quantity of ships in the English Channel in 1944, as well as the terrifying rate with which they were sunk by the Germans. I try to imagine the seafloor scattered with enough piles of rusting metal to resemble a vast historic scrapyard. My mind is jolted back to the screen when Chris comes out with something that leaves me cold.

'I think I know where it is.'

I'm not sure I heard that right. 'Really?' I blurt out.

'I think we did cover it,' he says.

On the edge of my seat, I wait for the inevitable 'but'. Except it never arrives. Chris really does mean LCH 185.

'I think there is a record of it. Well, not a record – I think there are the remains of it on the seafloor, off Gooseberry 5.'

I'm floored. This is an enormous moment, a place in time that I never truly expected the search to reach. Chris thinks he knows where the wreck of 185 is. He has seen it in the sonar data. It all seems too good to be true. I'm ecstatic and can't stop smiling. Chris, serious throughout the meeting, can't help but smile either. He knows how much it means not just to me, but to Patrick.

My excitement is soon dampened by a sense of trepidation when I remember that if Chris has seen the wreck of 185, then he has seen the craft on which Patrick and his friends had suffered so terribly. It was on that vessel that, at just nineteen years old, Patrick had been forced to choose whether or not to save his best friend.

Chris clicks a button, instantly throwing the original data from the survey up on to my computer screen. I see a map of the Normandy coastline with a large area of the ocean coloured a reddish brown. Within that block of colour is what look like the lines of the freshly ploughed Suffolk fields of my childhood. They are routes by which the expedition had travelled up and down the water while scanning the seafloor. Sonar is often likened to mowing a lawn. It's a fair comparison. You move the sonar along one line at a time until you reach the end. Then you turn back around, shifting over far enough to cover the next line of the seabed, but still overlapping with the previous. The end result looks like a freshly cut garden.

The areas left unscanned are significant. Any wartime vessel that sank too close to the shoreline will not have been found during the survey. The search extended just a few miles out to sea, and the survey ended with a good size of the eastern end of the area left unscanned. There is no telling what was overlooked.

Soon something catches my eye. Sticking out from the eastern end of the search area is one single line of sonar data stretching slightly further than the rest. Chris explains that on one particular day the expedition had decided to continue a short distance past the usual stopping point. When the data was later checked, a single anomaly had been picked up in the area where the boat had turned back on itself. Had that decision not been made, Chris wouldn't have been able to tell me his next revelation. He thinks that 185 *is* that anomaly.

I'm now staring at a small red circle, known as Target 16, on the map. The target is at high tide around 20 metres below the surface and roughly 3 nautical miles from the shore. As the image of Target 16 loads up, I hold my breath.

Before my eyes is a grainy image of what could well be the wreck of LCH 185. I find myself unable to do anything but laugh in disbelief as I picture Patrick's face knowing how happy he will be if this turns out to be his long-lost shipwreck. The image isn't like a photograph. It is multibeam sonar data, resulting from beams bouncing back from hard surfaces, be it the seabed or a shipwreck. In this case, they have outlined the shape of a wreck on the ocean floor. I'm looking at a collage of computerised shades of red and yellow surrounded by the blue of the seabed. I'm enthralled to be looking at the target, but there is a distinct emotional disconnect. This isn't a true image of the wreck, but something put together using data points on a computer. That seems to create a separation between Patrick's tale and what I'm looking at. This is science over story. Up until this point, perhaps naively, it has been the opposite.

The multibeam data shows the target to be in a disastrous state. I have always expected that any wreck found will be in terrible condition, but I'm not prepared for just how awful the reality was. Target 16 is a mess. A very rough shape of a boat is just about visible but, as I look at Target 16, I wonder whether, without the context, without knowing what I am trying to see, I would even know that the target is anything other than some rubbish on the seabed.

I concentrate and try to make out any obvious points of interest. The outline does at least somewhat resemble the shape of LCH 269 seen on the mudflat in Atlantic City. One end looks possibly to be a stern, giving some sense of layout and direction. Other than a few pieces of debris, there is no sign of a bow. In front of the stern is an area of wreckage that resembles a box, with cage-like lines across the top. Three more lines in the shape of a tripod link the box structure to the possible stern. These pieces seem discernible enough to perhaps allow information to be teased out of them at a later point, but other than that, there is little else to go on. The wreck looks to be riddled with scattered pieces of wreckage, showing up on the multibeam as unidentifiable shapes resting at different heights from the seabed. Overall, the data shows little more than a pile of twisted metal in a vaguely boat-like shape. It is hard to not be disheartened looking at the tangled mess, but I try to remain positive. After all, I am looking at Target 16 because it may well be LCH 185.

Four different ships were sunk in the area of the sonar target. Aside from LCH 185, they were LCG(L) 1062, LCG(L) 831 and LCG(L) 764. Because three of the vessels were Landing Craft Guns (Large) and only one was a Landing Craft Headquarters, it could have been simple to work out if the wreck is 185 or not without needing to dive. LCG(L) were larger, had more artillery guns and had a different stern to an LCH. Owing to the condition of the wreck, it is frustratingly impossible to tell what kind of craft the target is. Having to dive to the bottom of the English Channel is becoming a serious prospect. Going down there will allow me to locate any small details that the sonar couldn't pick up: artefacts, crucial measurements, pieces of radio equipment and any other diagnostic features.

As the reality of the situation hits me, I feel a lump in my throat. I had wanted to dive, but now there is a *need* to dive. Target 16 has to be dived in order to confirm its identity. The best possible outcome of visiting Target 16 will be to return to Patrick and let him know that I have found LCH 185, but if this pile of wreckage can be definitively identified as any of the ships that went down in the area, it will still be a positive outcome. None of the four wrecks that sank close to Target 16 has ever been located or identified in the English Channel. Lives were likely lost on all of those landing craft and each deserves to have its story told.

Mistakes were made in the past when it came to preserving the wrecks off the coast of Normandy, but thankfully times have changed. The French government is now applying to have the landing beaches and related shipwrecks listed as a UNESCO Heritage Site. Officials are keen to gather data and identify as many ships as possible to support the application. My expedition has the potential to add to that, which in turn would grant the beaches and wrecks protection.

There is something else that Chris wants to show me. Because a Landing Craft Headquarters was a converted Landing Craft Infantry (Large), the exterior blueprints are the same for both. On one side of my screen is Target 16, while on the other is a blueprint for an LCI(L). Chris drags the blueprint slowly along, moving gradually across the multibeam image. Time slows to a snail's pace as the hairs on my arms stand up. The two images line up and slot into place. It looks like a perfect match. The cage-like part of Target 16 fits exactly with the freshwater tank found on the blueprint. The two images now appear as one. This wreck really does look like it could be Patrick's landing craft. I'm already wondering how to tell him the news. After thanking Chris for his help, I nervously explain that I need to start hunting for dive schools.

A few days later, I receive an email from Chris. It contains the side-scan sonar results from the same expedition. Side-scanning differs from multibeam in that the equipment is towed behind the boat like a fishing lure. It measures the intensity of the signal bounced back, as opposed to the distance measured by multibeam. A side-scan image looks almost like a sepia photograph of the seafloor. Whereas the multibeam image made Target 16 look barely recognisable, the side-scan shows something else. The wreck looks far more like an actual ship this time. There appear to be large pieces of intact wreckage that could be explored. It fills me back up with the hope I had lost when I first saw the multibeam image. The chance of identifying the target suddenly seems greater.

Armed with both the sonar images, I head for Eastbourne. There isn't much time to sit with Patrick, but it's important to me that I see him. I don't know how long we have left together and, if I find any piece of information that seems important enough to pass on, I always endeavour to do so as quickly as I can in person. Arriving at the house, we have our customary cups of tea and a chat. I explain that I have something he might be interested in seeing. As we sit down in his conservatory, he looks uneasy. It's the first time he has seen me since I went to France. Patrick can sense that my visit has something to do with the wreck of 185. The sun is beaming outside and the glass room has reached an unbearably high temperature. Patrick, perhaps owing to his age, never feels the heat. The warmth in his home at best puts me to sleep and at worst causes me to almost faint.

'What have you been up to then, Pat?'

'Well, just trying to keep the fish safe,' he says, pointing to a pond in the garden. 'The bloody birds keep swooping in and eating them! I saw a crane sat out there the other day, staring back at me. He was laughing at me!'

I picture Patrick's stare-off with a lanky bird as it steals the prized goldfish from right beneath his nose.

'But next time . . . I have this!' he says, brandishing a slingshot.

Patrick looks deadly serious for a second, before letting out a roar of laughter. He is joking, I think.

'The last time I saw you, I said I was going to try to find LCH 185,' I say. Patrick nods. 'It's important to point out that I haven't done that. I haven't found your shipwreck. That's still a long way off, if it happens at all, but I did manage to get in contact with a man named Chris Howlett who was involved with scanning the seabed.'

From a wicker chair, Patrick stares at me but says nothing. He's waiting for the news before reacting.

'And Chris thinks that he may know where 185 is.'

'He does?' Patrick gasps.

'There is a wreck near Sword Beach that looks to align with what we know about 185,' I say. Reaching into a plastic folder, I pull out the two sonar images of Target 16 and hold the papers close to my chest. 'Again, this could be 185. It could also be something else. I won't know that until I dive down there.'

With that, I pass Patrick the multibeam image. He holds it tightly in both hands as he stares down at the paper. Straightaway, I know that he's upset. It's obvious, regardless of age or archaeological experience, that the image shows some sort of destruction. Patrick doesn't immediately acknowledge the state of the wreck, choosing instead to point out the things that he can identify.

'I think that's the stern, so that must be the bow.'

I nod, joining him in looking down at the page.

'It looks like the scrap dealers got to it,' he says.

'I don't know, Patrick. It looks like it, but it could be just the degradation from being on the seabed for so long.'

That is true, but I know full well that it has probably been at least partially salvaged. We move to the same dining table where a few weeks before we had been poring over maps in an attempt to kickstart the search. I place my laptop down and begin the same magical reveal that Chris gave to me. As I drag the blueprint and sonar image together, Patrick's face lights up. It is undeniably a solid match.

'It's amazing, John, that you've managed to find all of this out. I'm thrilled!'

The entire time we have been talking, from the conservatory to the dining table and now the sofa, Patrick has not loosened his grip on the image of Target 16. With wide eyes, he looks to me and asks a question to which there can be only one answer.

'Can I keep this, please? I'll treasure it.'

'Of course you can keep it, Pat! It's yours to put with all your other memories.'

He looks so pleased. I have done very little, merely printing a piece of paper and laminating it, but to Patrick, the image means so much. If Target 16 is 185, then this is the first time that he has seen his former home since leaping from its railings into the unknown in 1944. To get to this point of the search, to be showing Patrick a sonar target, is a dream come true whether it's the craft or not.

I can't help but think of my family. Presenting Patrick with the image of Target 16 reminded me of the missed opportunity to talk to my grandfather about his own wartime experiences. I wish I'd taken him back to his old battlefields, to have helped him bask in the same glow of appreciation that Patrick enjoys in Normandy. Maybe he wouldn't have wanted to. Basil Woolf swore to never visit Walcheren again. My two great-uncles never returned to see the Death Railway. Maybe Grandpa was different. Perhaps he was just waiting for someone to ask what he'd seen.

The situation I now find myself in began with his death. The seeds of the search were sown with the guilt of failing to learn about his war. It pushed me to preserve other stories in order to not make the same mistake again. I've met many veterans since, but only one encounter ever ended up like this. Why did Patrick's and my worlds come together in such a significant way? An archaeologist ready for change and an old sailor with a tale to tell.

I almost cancelled my volunteering trip to Normandy because I'd just started my archaeological job and didn't think I could take the time off so soon, but I went anyway. Patrick took me in and gave me a place to sleep. If we'd met a few years earlier, I wouldn't have been an archaeologist and he wouldn't have been ready to tell his story. A few years from now, Patrick will be too old to be by my side. I don't know if I believe in fate, but maybe we were supposed to cross paths. Maybe our lives were meant to collide, to stop the story of LCH 185 from disappearing.

I wonder what Grandpa would think of it all. He never gave away much of how he felt, but I can recall a particular smile that appeared on his face when he was pleased. I saw it a few weeks before he died, when he walked over to me in the living room to hand me a small cardboard box. Stamped on the front was the address he lived at as a boy. The house is still there to this day, next to the church where we scattered his ashes. Inside were the medals he won fighting in the war. Grandpa didn't say much when he placed the box in my hands. He never did say much.

'I'd like you to have these.'

I smiled, said thank you, and opened the box. The contents were exactly as the day they had arrived in the post shortly after the war. Four ribbons folded in half. Four medals in a pile. The metal was covered in patina, but the ribbons were perfectly straight. Worn only once but always kept safe, just like the dog tags in his bedside drawer, the invasion currency that he never threw out, and the piles of fading photographs from across the world. At the bottom of the box was a tiny piece of paper without any creases, on which was printed a list of the medals received. I carefully placed everything back and slid the box into my jacket pocket. Grandpa and I walked to the kitchen to sit down for breakfast and never spoke of the moment again. I've seen people display their relative's medals framed on walls, and seen descendants wear the medals on remembrance days and in parades. I've still got Grandpa's medals, but I keep them in the box in a drawer, exactly as the day they arrived.

From the moment I leave Patrick's house, the excitement and optimism that have propelled the search forward are replaced with a tension that will only worsen as the months go by. It began as a simple promise rooted in friendship, but quicker than I ever imagined I find myself apprehensively standing on a cliff edge. I've dreamed of locating a target on the seabed. I've sworn to dive there myself and laughed off any warning of how hard it will be, but with Target 16 now resting in my hands, there is an actual wreck for me to reach. Things are suddenly different. The search is real. All that rests before me now is a need to kneel on the bottom of the English Channel.

Chapter Eight

2 September 2017

I sometimes joke with Patrick that perhaps there's a way he could head down to the seabed with me. Maybe he could be manoeuvred into a vintage brass diving helmet and suit and lowered by rope to the bottom. Perhaps I could float him down inside a submarine. He is, after all, an experienced submariner. Sadly, although Patrick is young at heart and undoubtedly wishes he could join me, it would be impossible. Instead, I will be his eyes; the vessel through which Patrick can visit the wreck. Through the link held within our friendship and the promise that dangles between us, when my hand reaches out and touches Target 16, so will Patrick's hands.

Knowing that the search can move no further until I learn to dive, I head for an industrial estate in Ipswich. It's a less-than-glamorous introduction to the underwater world, and I'm unsure of what to expect as I walk, coffee in one hand and pen in the other, through walls of dive gear towards a classroom. Here, each Saturday morning for four weeks, I will be learning the theory of diving from a whiteboard. The instructor, an energetic man named Tom, goes around the room to ask each of the students why they want to learn to dive.

'I'm going to Thailand in a month and want to dive out there,' says one.

'I'm honeymooning in Egypt and we want to dive in the Red Sea,' says another.

Picturing the crystal clear waters and sandy beaches awaiting my fellow students, I'm envious. When my turn comes, it feels ridiculous to say that I'm learning to dive in order to front an international expedition in search of a lost Second World War shipwreck, but the response from the class is one of fascination. The instructors themselves even offer to help in any way they can. I have to eventually veer the conversation back from the wreck of 185 to the task at hand.

As I learn the theory of diving, I'm fascinated. From the time you can spend at certain depths, to the different combinations of gasses in your tank, heading to the seabed is an equation to be solved each time a diver pulls on a wetsuit. It's much more of a science than I ever imagined. I'm slightly worried that I won't get my head around it, but by the time I pass the theory tests, I've gained a fresh perspective on diving. Although I'm now aware that it's a mostly enjoyable pastime, some elements are making me question whether or not I truly want to do this. There are the bends, officially known as decompression sickness, which have the potential to turn my blood into fizzy syrup when heading for the surface without stopping to decompress. There are riptides, invisible currents waiting to send me straight out to sea in an ocean-sized washing machine. Overhead boats are locked and loaded, ready to decapitate me upon my return to the surface. Perhaps worst of all, I could run out of oxygen and suffocate on the seabed. The list of perils is long, but I attempt to put it to the back of my mind, thinking instead of the thousands of people worldwide who dive for leisure every day.

On a cold, damp weekday evening in November 2017, I drive straight from an excavation to my first practical lesson in the Suffolk countryside. I'm still wearing muddy clothes when I step out of my car to gaze up at a vast old building now used as a private school. The pool has been rented out by the dive school for our lessons. By now I've purchased my first mask and snorkel. They're basic and cheap, but I'm proud to have the beginnings of my first set of dive gear. Walking through the rain towards the waiting area I feel nervous, but I'm excited to finally be on the cusp of diving for the first time, if only in an indoor swimming pool.

My feet slap into puddles on the tiled floor as I walk out from the changing room to the poolside. None of the students has any idea what is about to happen, but we've been told to wear T-shirts to stay warm in the pool. In neon-green swimming trunks and a faded band T-shirt, I grab a pair of fins from a box that teeters on the edge of the water. Tom comes bouncing excitably through the back door and with the precision of a soldier passing out supplies, starts to hand out sets of equipment. There is an oxygen tank, a buoyancy control device more commonly known as a BCD, a belt threaded with lead weights and a regulator set, which controls the gas pressure.

We had been given a brief chance to try on the gear in the classroom to get ourselves familiar with how it all works. Now, attempting to not slip on the wet surface, I try my best to remember what I learned, but it feels different now. The process is much more difficult. The water is right there next to me and the pressure of knowing I'm about to jump in is making my hands shake. I fail to recall how each piece of equipment links together but, with some help from Tom, I eventually manage to get my arms through the BCD, link the regulator to the oxygen tank, and get my mouthpiece in. My classmates and I walk to the shallow end of the pool and slowly climb in. Despite wearing heavy equipment and knowing that I'm about to head underwater for the first time, I try my best to relax.

Tom tells us to lean forwards just enough for our faces to enter the water. As instructed, I kick my legs back and push my head down. Now floating on my belly with my face submerged, I paddle carefully. After a few seconds, I realise that I've been breathing underwater without knowing. It is a bizarre sensation. The situation doesn't make sense. Liquid surrounds my body, but oxygen is still entering my lungs and leaving from my nose. This shouldn't be happening. Every corner of my mind is screaming that something is wrong. This is something that humans shouldn't experience, but experiencing it I am. Looking around at my classmates, I see a similar reaction in their eyes. We look like a group of strangers who have just been shown a magic trick underwater.

The dirt and occasional used plaster resting on the floor of the pool are far from the most exotic view through my new mask, but I try to picture what wonders could one day be in front of me.

Our next task is to learn how to jump in. Pumping my BCD full of air to ensure that I float, I carefully step forward, hold the mask to my face and launch into the pool. Jumping in sounded easy, but upon hitting the water I find myself immediately disorientated. A vicious fight between the air-filled buoyancy vest pulling me up and my weight belt pulling me down tosses my body violently around. It's a relief to somehow find the surface, take my regulator out, and breathe fresh air.

Each week for a month I drive to the remote mansion to put on my dive gear and jump into the pool. Hours are spent learning everything from clearing water from masks and crucial hand signals, to the careful balance of buoyancy that keeps a diver floating perfectly between the seabed and the surface. The T-shirt never does keep me warm. Despite the pool being heated, a human body can only stay submerged in water for so long. We spend most of our time kneeling on the bottom of the pool, learning how to deal with emergencies. By the time we finish, I'm always shivering uncontrollably.

My course involves one more lesson than the rest of the class. In order to dive in Normandy, I'll need to wear a drysuit rather than a wetsuit, which requires slightly more training. Wetsuits let water in, which is then trapped to the body and warmed up. As the name suggests, a drysuit keeps you dry. An undersuit, which for me in the pool is an old pair of pyjamas, is worn beneath. Over the top, I squeeze into a bulky rubber suit which can be pumped full of air to control both warmth and buoyancy. I jump into the water and unexpectedly sink straight to the bottom of the pool. Kneeling on the tiles, it soon hits me that I can neither breathe nor rise to the surface. Struggling to wrap my head around what's happening, after a few moments of panic I finally realise that I've jumped into the pool with not only zero air in my BCD, but without the regulator in my mouth. With the extra weight of the suit added to the already heavy weight belt, I've been pinned to the bottom of the pool with no way of getting air into my lungs. I stay still for a moment, trying to remain calm while I attempt to remember everything I've been taught. Pushing my hand behind my back, I rise my arm up in a large circle to catch the regulator. Balancing it carefully across my wrist, I pull my hand forward and put in my mouthpiece. Taking a shallow breath, I quickly fill the BCD with air and float back up to the surface. Sitting on the side of the pool with my feet dangling in the water, I'm as white as a ghost and breathing in as much air as my lungs can hold. I'm in shock at how quickly things can go wrong.

* * *

Having finished the pool sessions, the time has arrived for the final stage of my training. No amount of practice in an indoor swimming pool can ever prepare me for the real thing. I have to undertake four open-water dives. There aren't many places to dive in Britain without getting into the North Sea or the English Channel, so on a freezing-cold December morning I head up to Leicester. Stoney Cove is a disused quarry on the outskirts of the city, now used for diving. I studied archaeology at the University of Leicester. Returning here for my dive training seems fitting. The quarry is bleak in the cold air of a winter morning, but from certain angles there is a beauty to the still water and sheer-faced grey rock that encloses us from above.

Pulling on my drysuit in the car park, I realise that it's covered in tape, which to my horror is clearly covering up a number of holes. Feet first, I wriggle inside like an astronaut donning his spacesuit and pull the oxygen tank on to my back by leaning on the boot of my car. Waiting for the rest of the class to suit up, the gear feels heavier than ever. I've always had problems with my back and, to make matters worse, a few months ago I ruptured a vertebra at work. Standing wearing a metal cylinder against my spine and a belt of lead weights resting on my hips, I feel a warm, gooey agony slowly building up.

Finally, we begin the long waddle through the car park towards the water's edge. Passing by a parade of soaked divers returning to their designated parking spaces, I see that each person is a different shade of frozen blue, but together their faces tell a common story of misery. Carefully teasing my way down the metal staircase, I slip, slide to the bottom, and slam my back into the final step.

At the launch platform, I'm aching badly. I should spend more time preparing and going over the steps in my head, but I'm desperate to get into the water. The weight on my already damaged back is overwhelming. Tom jumps in first, then the rest of the class go one by one, until my time finally comes to step to the edge. Passing a bucket of water, I spit on to the inside my mask to prevent it clouding up, wash it in the bucket, then pull the rubber strap over the back of my head. I then do what I've been taught. I pump my BCD full of air, cover my mouthpiece and mask with one hand, wrap my other arm around my waist and take one giant leap forward.

In a split second I'm underwater. All I see is darkness and thousands of tiny white bubbles speeding past my eyes. I can't work out which way is up. In the confusion, I struggle to breathe. As soon as I enter the water, the buoyancy of my BCD rights my body and pushes my head back through the surface. I throw up my hand with a signal to announce that I'm fine, before leaning my face into the water. Staring down, I can see the bottom. We're on a ledge that runs around the edge of the quarry. The base is only 10 or so metres below, but this is the first time I've been in the water in full gear without being able to touch the floor. I'm dangling weightlessly over the great void of an unfamiliar world. It's incredibly exciting. With a nervousness in my stomach, I lie back to enjoy the relaxation that comes with finally floating in the water. There really is no feeling like the relief of suddenly losing all of the pain after becoming weightless. It is a moment of bliss rarely found during the search for 185.

After some instruction from Tom, it's time to head below. The others descend without a hitch, but my BCD won't deflate. I'm left floating on the surface desperately squeezing my arms into my body in an attempt to sink, when suddenly it works. I'm sent crashing down through the water, smashing into the bottom of the ledge with a muted thud and a cloud of silt. When the view clears, I slowly peer around. Fish dart past my face in a flash of silver. Crayfish scuttle by my knees. For the first time in my life, I'm now part of an underwater environment. It's beautiful to be within nature instead of looking at it from afar.

I pump some air into my drysuit to try and warm up. It doesn't work. The cold and damp mount with each passing minute until, despite being in the warmest suit in the group, I can't feel my legs. My body shakes as we practise the manoeuvres and emergency drills we learned in the pool sessions, before heading off for a trip around the quarry. The journey is an epiphany. I'm finally diving, and diving well. It seems to come naturally. From the delicate dance with each breath that controls my buoyancy, to the need for rhythmic breathing to keep my oxygen intake down, I'm hypnotised by the nuanced process. It is liberating to find myself underwater and away from the reality of life on land. No phones. No emails. No way for anyone to bother me. Keeping alive beneath the surface is so all-consuming that my head is void of anything other than what plays out in that moment. It is a thoughtless luxury that I've not experienced since childhood. I breathe, kick my legs, pump air into my drysuit, check oxygen levels in the tank, and check the depth. There is no space for the worries of the real world, no room for the anxiety or stress of normal life. I feel free down here. Kicking my feet over the edge of the deepest part of the quarry, I stare into the eyes of a confused pike.

Swimming peacefully through the water, I feel something slipping down my waist. I look to see that my weight belt has come loose and is now cascading down my legs. For a first-time diver like myself, it seems like a life-or-death situation. I am surely going to be sent hurtling towards the surface with no decompression stop. They'll have to helicopter me to a hospital with a decompression chamber. I won't survive. I signal to Tom that I have a problem, and he immediately goes to work. My classmates look on in fear, realising that an underwater emergency is taking place. Tom pins me to the bottom, sending silt up into the air. We disappear from view. Others jump in to hold me down. I feel like the flailing corpse of an antelope smothered beneath a pack of hungry lions. Within seconds, there's a tight pull on my waist and the belt is back on. Tom gives me the thumbs up and I give one back. We swim on, crisis thankfully averted.

After half an hour we start to ascend. I float a few metres from the surface as I wait for my dive computer to give the all-clear. My first-ever decompression stop feels significant. It is the end of my first successful underwater mission. Climbing out of the quarry, I'm animated by the thrill of becoming a real diver, but quickly understand the grimaces I saw on returning faces earlier. My body has frozen over from the cold. The tank on my back is still there, but the feeling of floating weightlessly on a cloud has vanished. The gear feels unimaginably heavier and the want to get out of the equipment as quickly as possible has become a need.

With each of the dives I complete at Stoney Cove my confidence grows, feeling myself steadily turning into a strong diver. I soon learn that the weight-belt emergency from my first dive was less life or death, more of a quick fix, and feel slightly silly that I'd needed help at all. I'm taking the training very seriously. Perhaps it's knowing that I have to be good in order to dive in the English Channel. Out there, there will be no room for error and no second chances. By the fifth and final dive, I'm ready to head home. The underwater chill has become worse each time. My drysuit has been steadily leaking, filling up with ice-cold quarry water and locking my body into a frozen hell. Still, what's another half hour of shaking? I do the final dive anyway. Down below, we head along the old quarry road, following it around as we descend. At some point, I'll be reaching the depth at which Target 16 sits. My eyes keep a constant fix on the dive computer on my wrist.

14 metres. 15 metres. 16 metres.

Sunlight from the surface is barely visible. The water gets colder as we descend.

17 metres. 18 metres. 19 metres.

It's pitch black now. We switch on our torches. I can see nothing but yellow, misty beams swinging like searchlights ahead of me, illuminating glimpses of fins a few inches from my nose.

20 metres.

I am here. This is the same depth as Target 16.

Digging my knees into the trackway, I steady myself and gaze up to the surface. Expecting to see the overhead sun cutting through the depths, I see nothing. Utter darkness consumes everything around me. It's no longer clear which way is up and which way is down. There is simply a void. I feel vulnerable. My chest tightens. This is a depth that demands respect from even the most experienced divers. Doubts begin to creep in as to how I'm even down here at all. Humans are not meant to be 20 metres below, cradled by the pressure of thousands of tonnes of water. I remember that the only thing keeping me alive, the only piece of gear allowing me to continue to exist, is a battered yellow tank on my back which has been filled with oxygen by a stranger to whom I blindly handed my trust.

Reaching the surface, I'm now a qualified diver and will soon have a card in my wallet to prove it. I'm proud to know that I've carried an idea from a miserable building site on an eroding cliff edge to a point where I can stand among other divers across the world and hold my own in both conversation and skill. But I still need to gain more qualifications to guarantee that I can dive on my own expedition.

* * *

With that in mind, I board a plane destined for the Mediterranean. Malta is a small island between North Africa and Sicily. It's tiny compared to both, but was hugely important during the Second World War. It was said that whoever controlled Malta controlled the Mediterranean. Located in the middle of the sea, it's easy to see why. Any ships wanting to travel through the central Mediterranean have to pass by. In Allied hands, that made Malta an ideal embarkation point for the invasion of Sicily in 1943.

I land with a small suitcase and a large, blue duffel bag. Inside is my dive gear, which has been slowly accumulating over the last few months. I now have my own fins, shoes, gloves, computer, a knife, a torch and a BCD. I've also replaced my cheap mask with a retro-looking black one with a single glass front. I feel more like a diver now.

Walking through the dusty streets, I admire the Arabic architecture and wonder if the crew of 185 ever trod past the same enchanting doors that I'm craving to peek behind. Perhaps my grandfather did too. He was here during the build-up to Operation Husky and had once told me about travelling from Malta on a landing craft to disembark onto the beach at Sicily. As I turn down every sun-drenched street of the island, I'm subconsciously searching for answers.

It's hard to not feel like James Bond as I slam my bag down on the table in my hotel room and stare out of the window at the Mediterranean Sea. The water looks rough, and I'm nervous knowing that I'll be jumping in. An hour later, a white van pulls up to the hotel entrance with a slam of its squeaking breaks. The vehicle is covered in rust. This is a van that has been beaten by sea air every day. It's perfect. Hopping in, I introduce myself to Kevin, an instructor from England who owns a dive shop on the island. After an impromptu tour of Malta, including a dangerously fast drive along an old Second World War runway, we pull up at a spot near Wied iż-Żurrieq named the Blue Grotto. The place is stunning. Steep volcanic walls climb out of the water and small brightly painted wooden boats are floating on the waves. On the opposite side, I can see a wartime pillbox made out of local rock blending so perfectly with its surroundings that the structure is almost invisible.

In the back of the van I find a large plastic container filled with the dive gear I don't yet own. I suit up as best as I can on the hot concrete before stepping forward towards the water. Climbing backwards down a metal ladder barely hanging on to the rock, the sensation that comes with launching into the sea is instantly different to what I'm used to. Being a quarry, Stoney Cove had no current at all. At the mercy of the Mediterranean, I'm now being thrown around like a rodeo rider. It isn't a strong current, by any means, but the difference to Leicester is huge. Kevin and I check our gear and descend.

What greets me is nothing short of spectacular. The water is a breathtaking glacial blue, its views crystal clear. Shoals of fish crowd around us. It's difficult to fathom how something so spectacular can be right there beyond the glass of my mask. I am existing within a painting. Kevin takes the lead, pointing out the beauty of the natural world as we pass. Everything from lionfish and parrot fish to rainbow wrasse are all swimming by my side. We slowly explore the edge of the island, creeping through archways and deep caves carved by time. I'm flying through a weightless wonderland that I never want to leave. I finally realise, after months of swimming pools and miserable quarries, just what diving is.

On our journey back to the shore, Kevin waves his hands frantically with excitement. I lower my head to see a flying gurnard.

With its neon-blue-tipped fins spread wide, the fish soars gently through the current like an awoken pterodactyl. Though silent, I can still hear the deep thud of its 'wings' as it moves in slow motion beneath me.

The rest of the week is spent diving each morning and exploring wartime sites each afternoon. One afternoon, I locate the airfield where my grandfather was stationed in the build-up to the Sicily invasion. It's the first time I've ever knowingly trod in his wartime footsteps. Standing outside crumbling buildings earmarked for demolition, I can almost see him passing through the streets.

With my thoughts occupied with 185, I imagine each dive as a Normandy rehearsal. With that in mind, for my final descent I request a specific site that I've read about. It's the closest I can get to the conditions I'll face in France. The wreck of HMS *Maori* rests just outside of Fort Saint Elmo, a short distance from the city of Valletta. A Tribal-class destroyer, the ship was sunk by German aircraft on 12 February 1942. At 16 metres, *Maori* is only four metres shallower than Target 16, and is in a relatively similar condition. That is to say, not a good one, but the vessel is also a bona fide Second World War shipwreck which suffered loss of life when it sunk.

Alongside Kevin and his wife, a fellow instructor named Lindsay, I lie on my back to kick through the water. We're heading through a tiny fishermen's bay. The gentle waves are filled with bits of broken netting and fish innards. Floating through the thick soup, staring up at the fort walls, I think of all of the history that this island has witnessed. There has been much turmoil and change here over the centuries. Phoenicians, Romans, Arabs, Normans, Ottomans. This tiny rock in the Med has seen it all. The harbour would have been one of the last visions of safety for both 185 and my own grandfather before heading towards the enemy. I wish I had more time here. I'd love to have followed in the wake of the craft towards Sicily.

We descend and begin a long swim underwater towards the wreck. As a tiny island, Malta is at the mercy of any passing storms. This is evident immediately from not just the wheelie bins standing upright on the seabed, but from the car that has either been blown in by the wind or pulled in by waves. The power of nature is right before my eyes as an ominous reminder of the risk a diver takes whenever they give themselves to the grasp of the sea.

It isn't long before the faint image of a ship slowly appears, as HMS *Maori* leans through the distant haze. First, I see a ghostly mirage, then small pieces of debris appear on the floor, until finally I see the awe-inspiring hull of a warship. The vessel looms over me, as if questioning my reason for visiting. I feel insignificant in its shadow. There were a few wrecks at the bottom of Stoney Cove, but they were deliberately sunk for divers. Some have a history, but none that relate to their final resting place. After being attacked, the badly damaged *Maori* was towed from the harbour to where it now remains. The stern was lost along the way in the deep blue, but the wreck is still the real deal and in a legitimate context.

This is the first Second World War shipwreck I have seen. As I explore the rapidly corroding exterior, my throat is tense with emotion. I've come so far to reach this point, to now be swimming in the shadows of a ship sunk in the same conflict as 185. Descending to the bottom of the wreck, I find myself face to face with the strangely familiar expression of an octopus peering out of its home in the sand. The creature seems almost as curious towards me as I am towards it. This is the first time I've ever seen an octopus in the wild. I'm fixated by its human-like eyes. Our brief encounter shows me that long after the echoes of sailors' voices have left the seabed, life continues on.

Turning at the tip of the wreck, I reach a section that has collapsed outwards. Something is shining in the debris. It looks like gold. My archaeologist's heart is racing, but as I get closer I realise that I'm actually staring at a piece of brass. These are brass shells, live rounds left over from the ship's enormous guns. I carefully move as close as I can safely get while knowing how volatile old explosives are. Kevin, who has dived the wreck countless times before, quickly darts ahead and starts to dust sand from the base of the shells. With a perplexed shrug of my shoulders, I head towards them. I can read '1942' as clear as the day it was stamped on the base of the shells, and the arrow marking confirms these as British military manufactured.

I'm shocked to be so close to such dangerous artefacts that still remain in their original location. Since the day these shells were loaded on to the ship they have never left; here I am, over seventy years later, staring at explosives on the seabed. As an archaeologist working on land I rarely, if ever, see archaeological remains sat on the surface exactly where they were left. I can't imagine turning up to an excavation and seeing everything just resting on the soil, but down on the seabed that is often the case. The underwater world is one giant archaeological horizon.

Swimming up to the top the hull, I head through an intact section of the wreck. For the first time, there's a ceiling above me and a floor below. The men that lived and worked on the ship enter my thoughts. The devastation felt when their home was destroyed must have been immense. These enormous metal beasts weren't just places to do your job. I took that for granted before meeting Patrick, but now it is never far from my mind. I know that a sailor died in the sinking of this ship. Thinking about him, a twinge of sadness hits me as the excitement of diving my first historic wreck fades away. No matter how fun or fascinating visiting here is, it still remains a place where a tragedy occurred. A man died on this ship. That sailor was someone's son. The wreck, although incredible to visit, deserves to be explored with respect.

Looking down at the island through the window of a plane, I think about what Target 16 really represents. The wreck of 185 will be nothing less than the grave of roughly thirty-five men. As a diver, I'm ready to visit but, as Malta disappears into the clouds, I wonder if I'm ready in myself.

Back in England, I turn the key and duck into the garden shed. Looking at the initial search area circled on the map, I know that to move the search forward once again, I need some help. My time in Malta earned me the qualification of Advanced Open Water diver, allowing me to go as deep as 30 metres, but there is no way that a newly qualified diver like myself can run an underwater archaeological survey on their own. It's time to put a team together.

Stephen Fisher has already helped me in the archives and Chris Howlett has provided his experiences with sonar, but I need experienced divers. During our meeting, Chris mentioned a dive club that he has previously worked with, who seem like my best bet. Within a few days I'm on the phone to Alison Mayor and Martin Davies, a married couple who are both part of the Southsea Sub-Aqua Club. I've heard of the group before through the role they played in the discovery of the wreck of the *Mary Rose*, one of Henry VIII's warships. Martin is a respected underwater photographer and a dab hand at photogrammetry. Alison is a diver well versed in maritime archaeology.

The club is based in Portsmouth and run by a team of volunteers. They organise projects to preserve and record Britain and France's underwater heritage and once led a similar project to mine, centred on LCT 427, a landing craft that had sunk 4 miles from Portsmouth on its return from Normandy. Volunteers from the club unveiled a memorial and managed to track down family members of some of the crew. I can tell Alison and Martin are passionate about what they have achieved, and it's clear that the club can bring a lot to the search for 185. When I mention that I've gone from no diving experience to Advanced Open Water in such a short space of time, Alison and Martin look concerned.

'How hard can it be? You just put on the gear and swim to the seabed, right?' I jokingly ask.

I know that it will be incredibly difficult. But as serious as all this is, the search is still an adventure for everyone involved, including Patrick. If we aren't going to at least partly enjoy doing it, then there's little point. Nonetheless, Alison and Martin are quick to inform me that diving is in fact incredibly dangerous and needs to be taken seriously. We agree to begin working on the scheduling and preparation for the expedition. The club knows from experience that April will be the best window to head to Normandy for the dive expedition. That time of year has the best potential for a combination of good visibility and relatively warm water for the English Channel. We will, unfortunately, have just a few days for the expedition. The entire team, including myself, are volunteers. Funding is tight, schedules are busy, and ideal water conditions are rarest of all. I feel relieved to have pencilled in a date, but with it comes a new frustration. I've been driving the project forward on my own without a pause, but now momentum will slow as I settle in for a nine-month countdown until my very own D-Day can take place.

Chapter Nine

22 April 2018

The wait passes quickly and I soon find myself back in Portsmouth. Parking up, I walk across Southsea Common beside picnickers and jackets-for-goalposts football games. I came to this very common for the seventieth anniversary of D-Day a few years before. At the closing of those events, I'd stood beneath the enormous naval memorial on the promenade and read from the thousands of names engraved on its walls as I pondered what it had been like to witness the embarkation in 1944. I never could have predicted back then that some of those names would one day become such an important part of my life.

Standing at the memorial, I pull out a piece of paper from the pocket of my jeans and unfold it. On the page are twelve names that I scrawled down months ago. Carefully searching, I pause as each sailor seems to jump out at me from across the plaques. These are twelve men who died in the sinking of 185. Twelve men who drowned alongside Jack Barringer. Twelve men that Patrick knew. I read the names out loud, wondering how long it's been since they were last spoken. Perhaps I unknowingly read these names when I was here before.

* * *

The more times I board the ferry the more the journey to France takes on a symbolic meaning. It's the beginning of a trip with a purpose, a leaving behind of normality to cross towards the grandiose. Back in France, as I travel my usual route over Pegasus Bridge towards the landing beaches, it feels like coming home. After a short drive along country lanes lined with the same notorious Normandy hedgerows that were once so feared by Allied soldiers, I reach a crossroads. To my left is an extravagant French château. To my right is a driveway leading into the woods. I slowly drive along the winding gravel road until I see a more modest house start to appear through the trees. This building will be the headquarters of our dive expedition. It has room to sleep the entire team and a swimming pool to test-dive equipment. Pulling up to the house, which looks like a cross between a farmhouse and a cabin, I spot someone walking inside. I step across the gravel towards an orange dive rib on top of a trailer. Ropes are spread out by my feet as I place my hand on one side of the rib, knowing that this is the very boat that will take me out to Target 16.

Inside, I find the dive team scattered around the house. I'm greeted by Alison and Martin. It's the first time we've met in real life, though it doesn't seem like it. I wander around the rooms to introduce myself to whoever I stumble across. Aside from Alison and Martin, the dive team is made up of Doug Carter, Tom Templeton and Jim Fuller. There is also Richard Rowley, who I warm to the most. Richard is the coxswain of the rib. He is thorough, very professional, but still good fun to speak to. Stephen Fisher is here too, having pedalled his bicycle on to the ferry and ridden to our headquarters. The commitment from everyone is impressive. As I look around at the team I've put together, I am pleased to have an excellent group of people helping me.

We're finally all together, but I can tell something is off. The divers seem agitated. I'm not sure if I've done something wrong, but it's certainly an odd experience to walk into my own expedition headquarters with a tense atmosphere already hanging in the air. Wanting to get out of the way, I grab my suitcase and dive gear from the car and head up to my bedroom in the converted attic. It's been a long day and I'm tired. Perhaps the others are too. After a short rest, I walk down two flights of old wooden stairs and head back out to the rib. There I find the whole team chatting among themselves. The plan had been for everything to be set up before my arrival and for divers to have been in the water that morning. They were going to be in France a day early and the idea was for the team to locate Target 16 and place a buoy on it. With that out of the way, it would allow the expedition to hit the water the next day and for us to get straight to surveying the wreck.

'How was today? All good?' I ask.

Alison looks worried. 'Er . . . could have been better. We've had a little incident.'

My heart sinks. Our schedule is already so tight. We have just five days to get everything completed, but even that is a push. Any hiccups at all will throw the entire expedition up in the air.

'You'll notice the engine cover is off,' Alison says.

Sure enough, I look up and see that the plastic lid of the outboard engine has been removed.

'We have a problem with the engine. It's been making very funny noises. Quite concerning. It sounded like a bag of stones rattling along. We're going to have to go to the marina tomorrow to see if we can get that fixed.'

I'm nodding in agreement, but it must be obvious to everyone here that I'm not happy. I've worked so hard to get to this moment, only to hear that the boat broke before I'd even stepped off the ferry. The expedition has stumbled at the very first hurdle. It's hard to believe that this is really happening.

'So you managed to get the buoy out?' I ask, although I already know the answer.

'No,' Alison says, joined by a chorus of mumbled confirmations coming from the rest of the team. 'We've still got that job to do.'

'These things happen,' I reply in a half-hearted attempt to make light of the situation.

'Welcome to the world of diving. It's disappointing, because we're all set and ready to go,' Alison says.

Disappointing is an understatement. In reality, the team had barely made it back to shore, crawling home with a failed engine. I've been at the expedition headquarters for less than twenty minutes and already we're a day behind schedule. To make matters worse, the broken engine isn't the only blow to be dished out. The Department of Underwater and Submarine Archaeological Research, known as DRASSM, is a governmental organisation that documents, preserves and attempts to identify France's underwater heritage. Anyone can recreationally dive the Normandy wrecks, but to undertake an archaeological survey requires permission from authorities, including DRASSM, because surveying counts as commercial work. The fact that we are all volunteers matters little. So far each challenge thrown my way has been approached methodically and taken in my stride. That mindset has got me right to the point of being in France ready to dive, but now DRASSM has other ideas.

At the eleventh hour, we are informed that I'm no longer permitted to take part in the archaeological surveying. In order to do anything but simply dive the wreck, I now need commercial dive training. That will mean undertaking a huge number of dives and the type of qualifications most commonly given out to those that dive for a living. I won't be permitted to do so much as lift a tape measure on the wreck without those certificates. Members of the team are qualified to this level, but I'll never be able to reach that standard in such a short amount of time.

I'm already here. It's too late. The news is both heart-breaking and infuriating, leaving me to wonder if this is the end of the line. The point of locating 185 was for me to reach the wreck on behalf of Patrick, but I've instead just been told that the only people permitted to visit Target 16 are the dive team. They are generous, knowledgeable people and I'm grateful for their help, but this is the first time we've ever met. They have never met or even spoken to Patrick. The human connection to the wreck is slipping away, destined to be lost completely if I don't see Target 16 for myself. Patrick and my bond is what started the search. My promise is what drove it forward. I can't let my friend down, not this far in.

After a restless night, I meet the dive team in the living room. With wooden panelling on every wall and antique French furniture everywhere I look, the space feels like the inside of a grand ship. It's the perfect place to establish the expedition's control room. Martin has already set up a computer to run photogrammetry at the end of each dive, and I spend some time pinning sonar images and landing-craft blueprints to the walls. After breakfast, we discuss how to push the expedition forward. We're all here. I'm ready to dive. We can't let this be the end. It's certain that I can't take part in the surveying. I've had to reluctantly accept that, and while it's hard to take, there is really no other choice. We can't risk having me take part unofficially and get caught. Not only could we be arrested, fined and have our equipment seized, but it would delegitimise any results we ultimately do come up with. Plus, if Dominique Régeard in Lion-sur-Mer thinks that we're a group of Brits trying to pull a fast one over the French, the memorial plans could crumble.

I still need to get down to Target 16. To me, the project will be a failure if I don't see the wreck for myself. For now, it is decided that I'll run the expedition topside while the dive team survey the wreck, bringing back data for us to analyse together. Then, on the very last day of the expedition, I will finally dive to the target. While I'm not allowed to take part in the survey, it is as simple as removing a few tape measures from the wreck. After that, my presence down there is completely fine. It seems silly, but rules are rules, and I'm grateful to be allowed to dive at all after the curveball I've been thrown. This does mean, however, that time is now even more limited. The expedition is scheduled for five days, with only four days to dive. That should have been just enough time originally, but we've already lost a day to a broken boat that still hasn't been fixed. That now leaves just two days for surveying and one day for me to dive. To survey and hopefully identify a heavily damaged shipwreck within four dives is optimistic at best. Everyone in the control room knows it. The atmosphere, which should be one of excitement, is one of concern.

We gather creaking chairs in a circle and make a plan. If the boat can be fixed, and that is a big if, then there should be two dives tomorrow morning. The first will be used to locate the wreck and establish a buoy and shot line, with the second used to undertake an initial survey. The next day will see two more dives take place, during which photogrammetry will be carried out. Martin will take thousands of overlapping photographs to create 3D models of any potentially diagnostic parts of the wreck. On the third and final day, I will dive once in the morning and once more in the afternoon. By then, we should have undertaken enough observation, measurements, drawings and photography to know what we're looking at. The sole benefit to only being permitted to dive the wreck at the end of the expedition is that there's a chance that, by the time I hit the water, Target 16 will have been identified as LCH 185.

Next, we begin to use the sonar images and landing craft blueprints to create a plan of action for the surveying and photogrammetry. Initially, the length and width of the wreck will be measured. The team will emphasise locating the bow area. Three LCG(L) and one LCH were sunk in the vicinity of Target 16. LCG(L) had a flat, ramp-like bow to allow tanks to exit, while LCH had a more typically pointed bow. Although the bow of Target 16 looks to be non-existent on the multibeam, the side-scan results indicate a slightly better chance that at least some of it remains. There is also an area that looks to be the shape of an anti-aircraft gun. These were located in specific positions depending on the type of landing craft, making it a point of interest for potential identification. The cage-like structure seen on the multibeam, which seems an almost perfect match for the freshwater tank on an LCH, will be another area of crucial importance to the survey. If we can confirm what that is, then there's a chance that the target can be identified once and for all.

There are also things not seen on either sonar image that if located could be a smoking gun. Landing Craft Headquarters had a large tripod foremast not found on any other landing craft in Normandy. The vessels were also filled with a vast amount of telegraphy and radio equipment. Although we aren't permitted to move or lift anything from the wreck, there's still potential to find personal artefacts belonging to the crew resting on the sand. None of us will know what the condition of Target 16 is until we get down to it. French salvage efforts may have destroyed any hope of ever identifying the wreck. The original German attack might have made it unrecognisable. Treasure hunters, souvenir-taking recreational divers or overzealous fishermen may have caused untold damage. The only real guarantee is that the wreck will have been degraded to a devastating level by the passing of time and the brutal push and pull of relentless tides.

We'll know soon enough what is waiting down there. Everything now falls to chance. That's archaeology. I'm used to it and so are the dive team. The unknown of the wreck is exactly why we do what we do. A person doesn't become an archaeologist to become rich. It's often a thankless life of unpredictability and insecurity. A person becomes an archaeologist to add to their knowledge of history and for the excitement that comes with discovering an artefact that was last touched by a person long forgotten. We are pushed by what could be around the corner or beneath the soil of the next site. It's that exact 'what if?' that drives us.

That evening the dive team leave for the marina to find some way of fixing the boat. Alone for a while, I pin photographs of the crew to the wall of the control room. Faces of those who lived and died on 185 will be looking down as we work, serving as a reminder of why exactly we've all come together here in Normandy. Stepping down from an unsteady stool, I look out of the window at the stacks of dive gear by the front door. This really is it. There is nothing left to do now but visit the wreck. I'm beginning to believe that I might actually pull this off.

During the Battle of Normandy, the house we are renting was used as an aid station. There is a wall in a barn in the garden on which British paratroopers are supposed to have pencilled their names. The door is locked, so I visit a shed in the corner of the garden instead. The owner of the house has been metal detecting his land and has filled the shed with rifles, helmets and other military artefacts. On the floor, in a pile of crumbling rust, is an entire US Willys Jeep pulled out of the ground.

Walking behind the house to drink a cup of tea and watch the sunset, I move to stand in a spot overlooking the stunning Normandy countryside. My feet are sinking into the grass. The ground is strangely soft where I'm standing. A short distance ahead I can see an old monument. As I get closer, I realise that the stone once marked the grave of a single British soldier killed in the fighting. His body had been moved after the war, but the headstone remains. I sink into the ground with each step as I head back into the house. In the hall I notice a photograph on the wall. It's a black and white image of the garden. Where I've just been standing, there were once rows of crosses sticking out from freshly dug graves. The garden had been a hastily put-together field cemetery for over thirty men. They were moved to official military cemeteries later, but the empty graves remain. I feel uneasy knowing where I've just been walking. Everywhere I look is a battlefield.

The dive rib can't be fixed at the marina. The situation is getting desperate and concern is growing rapidly. We need a new boat, but the chance of finding one at such short notice is beyond slim. I consider cancelling the expedition, but there's little hope that if we go back to England we'll ever have the chance to try again. In a last-ditch effort, the dive team tracks down a place that rents out fishing boats. We blindly book whatever is available on their website and hope for the best.

At midnight, a car pulls into the drive towing a small trailer. Looking at what we've booked, it's hard not to laugh. It's not a fishing boat, but a fishing rib. It's a dinghy. Like the one the team had brought over from England, but much, much smaller. The original wasn't large to begin with, but this bright blue-coloured replacement is barely bigger than the blow-up dinghies I'd take to the seaside as a child. We all doubt that this thing will even stay afloat, let alone survive the expedition. The dive team is used to diving from their own rib. They are well versed in how their own onboard sonar equipment works. We are all uncomfortable with the unfamiliar set-up, but this is all we have. Locating a replacement at all is a minor miracle. This second-rate dinghy will have to do.

Early the next morning, I head outside to see off the dive team. There's a stillness in the damp mornings of a Normandy sunrise like no other I've felt across the world. It normally sets the tone for the day ahead, but this morning will not be so calm. Every minute of the expedition is now more urgent than ever. Armed with the new rib, a convoy of cars leaves our compound to head for the water. The task for the initial dive is to locate the wreck. We've seen sonar imagery, we have the coordinates, but we still have to find it on the seabed. Even the smallest patch of ocean is unimaginably large when trying to locate anything at all.

I wait tensely in and around the house, settling into a long day filled with laps of the garden and nervous nail biting. After an anxious few hours, I hear car tyres rolling over the gravel. Peeking out from the kitchen window I see the dive team looking stern-faced, cold and fed up. It isn't the joy and celebration I was expecting to see. Yet again, my heart sinks realising something that isn't right.

'Hey, John!' Alison calls out from the driveway.

'Yeah?' I say, stepping out of the front door.

Alison lets out a sigh. 'We didn't find it,' she says.

For the second time, standing outside the expedition headquarters, Alison is telling me extremely disappointing news.

'You didn't find it?' I ask, politely missing off *What do you mean . . .* from the start of my question.

'We spent two hours trying. We can't find it.'

'So, what's the plan now?'

'Try again, as ever. We don't give in.'

Alison is right. The dive team have been huddled together in the tiny boat for two straight hours at sea, mowing up and down the rough English Channel to try and locate the target. The odds were not in their favour. While the weather was lovely, the conditions at sea were far from it. The rib was thrown around, tossing the soaking-wet team up from their seats, letting in a dangerous amount of water through a leak. The onboard sonar equipment is not only one that the divers are unfamiliar with, but it's also in French. Rather than locating the wreck, the sonar was instead recording the waves, skewing the image of what was beneath.

The dive team move inside to get warm and call up anyone they know that might have a clue as to how the equipment works. I climb up into the old broken dive rib to get a feel for what lies ahead of me. Until now I've never dived from a boat, instead always reaching the water by stepping off from a ledge or swimming from the shore. Diving from a boat is entirely different. That my first time will be in the middle of the English Channel has been worrying me for months.

Seeing that I'm sitting in the rib alone, Richard walks over and climbs up. I tell him about my concern. In response, he tells me to sit on the edge of the boat. Out on the water, the distance between the rib and the waves is only a few inches, but perched high up on a trailer, it's a sheer drop to the hard gravel below. Trying not to tip out of the rib, I try to pay attention as Richard explains how to roll back into the sea. I slowly lean back as much as I can without falling, teetering just far enough to feel uncomfortable. It's a strange feeling to know that soon I'll be doing this above the dark of the deep blue sea. I'm also aware that getting into the water will be one thing, but climbing out again will be much harder.

After leaving Target 16, I have to swim back to the rib and remove most of my equipment with nothing beneath me but the seabed. When I think about getting back into the boat, it seems awful, but I have no chance to practise. I'll just have to wing it.

That afternoon I join the dive team at the marina. This is the first time I've been to where the expedition launches into the water. Ouistreham is where the cross-Channel ferry comes into France. I've been here many times before, but I never in my wildest dreams expected to be back here for a shipwreck search. I pass across a narrow bridge to the other side of the water, heading towards an array of fishing boats and private vessels. In among the mismatched armada is our new dive rib, looking tiny next to even the smallest fishing boat as it rolls on the waves.

'Do you suffer from seasickness?' Martin asks with a glint in his eye.

'We'll find out, I suppose!' I reply.

I pass some equipment down into the boat before the engine roars into life and the dive team head out to sea. They wave to me and I wave back with a shout of 'Au revoir!' I watch as the rib leaves the harbour, my eyes glued to the boat until it disappears on the horizon. Target 16 *needs* to be located on this dive. Tomorrow is our only full day of surveying. It *has* to be found today. There is no other choice. In order for me to dive the wreck, we've promised DRASSM that all archaeology will be finished before I hit the water. If anything else goes wrong, if the surveying has to be extended into my dive time, I won't be able to visit Target 16.

With the team at sea, I set about finalising plans for the memorial. I've got verbal permission from Dominique, but owing to his position as mayor and another job in Paris, he's a very busy man. We've exchanged a few emails about the general idea for the memorial, but nothing has been decided. We are a worryingly long way away from making it happen. It's April now, and the unveiling is scheduled for June. I've had the town's blessing to build the memorial for almost a year, but I still have no inscription, no design, no one to construct it, and nowhere to put it. I had a feeling that this would happen, and doubt that the memorial will ever exist, but I head to meet Dominique and hope for the best.

Outside the town hall, he comes bounding out on to the street looking as smart as ever in his trademark fitted suit. Dominique is a man of few words, but those words always seem to deliver something special. Straightaway he announces that he has something to show me. We walk towards the seafront and turn right on the promenade until we're standing on the very same patch of grass that I had first thought of putting a monument a year ago.

'You can put the memorial here,' Dominique says, smiling.

I have been left speechless a number of times since the search began, but this time I'm really taken by surprise. It is stunning to be told that such a perfect spot on the promenade will be designated for a tribute to 185. The spot is located just inches from the sand of Sword Beach, pointing towards England with a backdrop of the sea. In front of the triangle of grass stand two of the oldest and grandest houses in the town and a path frequented by hundreds of people a day. This is the main route along the beach. Countless people will see whatever I put there. A small corner of France has now officially been set aside to honour Patrick's forgotten shipmates forever. It's an honour for which I will never be able to repay Dominique and Lion-sur-Mer. The mayor explains that the memorial will need to be unveiled on 6 June as part of the town's D-Day commemorations. Our unveiling will start off proceedings before the annual walk to each memorial in the town begins. I tell Dominique that I'll get it sorted, thank him even more times than I did back when I first got his approval, and ring Patrick to tell him the news.

'. . . And there will be a band and everything!' I say.

'Crumbs!' Patrick can do nothing but laugh. He's as speechless as I am.

I'm over the moon, but I know that I now have less than seven weeks to get the memorial designed, planned and built in a country that I don't live in. The pressure to achieve everything I set out to do is beginning to mount up.

Later that day the dive team return. We gather in the control room to discuss the day's events.

'Good to get us back together. You must be pretty tired. Does someone want to run me through what happened?' I ask.

I can tell from the smiles on their faces that, to my enormous relief, they have successfully located the target.

'I had the privilege of being the first one down,' Jim says. 'We went along and at about the distance that we expected to find the bow, we found a winch.'

'That's good . . . right?' I ask, unsure of the answer.

'Yeah!' Alison beams.

Landing Craft Infantry (Large), from which 185 was converted, were known to have winches in the bow of the vessel. These were used to lower and raise the two ladders that came out from the bow on to the beach in order for troops to disembark.

Martin loads up the footage that he has captured on to the computer screen. I now find myself staring at the wreck. This is actually Target 16. It's a moment I never thought I'd reach. I can feel my lips wobbling with emotion until I notice the condition of the wreck. Target 16 is barely recognisable as a ship at all. As the camera moves through the wreckage, all I see is a pile of twisted carnage. Although I expected as much, it's still difficult to accept. Target 16 has been destroyed. That is the cold hard truth I now face. I immediately wonder what Patrick's reaction will be. He, after all, has the greatest attachment to the wreck and the most invested in the search for 185.

We discuss what was seen during the dive. The bow, which we had hoped to discover, is gone, which severely limits our chances of identifying what type of landing craft this wreck is. But there is still hope. The team have located what seems to be the stern, as well as a capstan used to wind up rope. In the situation we find ourselves, with minimal time and a decimated wreck, any identifiable object is a good result. We now know what we have to work with tomorrow and what parts of the wreck to pay attention to during the final two surveying dives. The expedition has come down to the wire, but at least we're finally making some progress. For the first time on the trip, there is laughter and excitement in the control room.

The dive team are out on the water before I awake the next morning. I spend a few hours repeatedly throwing myself backwards from the rolled-up swimming-pool cover. In an attempt to rehearse for my entry into the English Channel, I fall a few feet before hitting the water with a vicious slap. It seems ridiculous, and I wonder what someone would think if they saw what I'm up to without context. My idea seems to work, though, and rolling back into the sea seems less scary with every smack into the pool.

The dive team return at lunchtime. I head to meet them outside. They are smiling again. As Jim and Doug set about refilling empty oxygen tanks, everyone seems in a good mood. The day's first dive has gone well, thankfully. I join Alison and Martin, who are still in their undersuits, in the garden.

'How did the measuring go?' I ask.

'We went down to the stern today. It's definitely upside down. You can see the shape of the stern itself. Some of the plating has gone, but you can still see the outline. We went up to the winch and did a bit of photogrammetry, so I'll run the pictures when we're out.'

'It's exciting for you guys to come back and tell me these things,' I say.

'It's all these little clues,' Martin replies. 'There's no real big stuff, but some of the smaller stuff . . . when we actually do piece it together, sometimes that will be the final . . . "it could only be this".'

A substantial amount of measuring has been undertaken. To make up for the dives we have lost, Martin began photogrammetry early while the rest of the team surveyed. He thinks that the winch might be connected to an engine and possibly a generator. I ask the question that none of us wants to address.

'Is Target 16 the wreck of LCH 185?'

Martin hesitates before stating that he's 90 per cent certain the wreck is the one we are hoping to discover. The winch and engines seem to be in the right location and the stern resembles that of a Landing Craft Headquarters. The width and length of the ship seem to be roughly correct. Everything is looking positive.

There is one more dive left. After a short rest, the team load up and head back out to sea. This is the final chance for any archaeological work to be done. Anything left to be discovered needs to be discovered now. The plan is for the team to measure the stern and what looks to be the freshwater tank. I'm dying to get into the water. That moment is now less than twenty-four hours away. My thoughts are bouncing between one of the most important days of my life tomorrow, and knowing that Patrick is currently crossing the Channel to join the expedition tonight.

While the team are out at sea, I head for Hermanville cemetery. I meet my parents there, who have come over to witness my dives. Until now, I've only ever visited Jack Barringer's grave at Ranville; the other three graves of the crew are in separate cemeteries. John James Rimmer, who had signed up on his eighteenth birthday, lost his life at the age of twenty. In that short time, he had managed to survive the landings at Sicily, Italy and Normandy. I feel compelled to visit the young sailor on the eve of me reaching what could well be the site where he was killed. John is not just a name on a long list of dead men. He is not just a statistic. John James Rimmer was real. He missed out on growing up, on getting married and having kids. He never got to know that people appreciated what he did in the war, because the war ended his life. Instead, he left behind a mum and dad in Liverpool who must have been beside themselves with grief.

Kneeling down to place a paper poppy by his headstone, I gently push aside a flower to read the inscription written by his family all those years ago.

Till we meet again, au revoir.

The words weigh heavily on my heart. Tomorrow is for him. Tomorrow is for John's parents, Margaret and James, and for his sister. It is for the crew of LCH 185 and the countless family members that they left behind. Walking through the gate of the cemetery, I feel an urge to look back. As I do, I see that a single black crow has landed on John's headstone.

The ferry arrives late at night. I phone to tell Patrick to head to his hotel, but he insists that he will comes straight to the headquarters to meet the team. Escorted by his grandson Paul, Patrick eventually arrives at 2 a.m. We meet outside in the kind of darkness you only find deep in the countryside. A star-laden sky blinks above us. It feels special to have him here in the expedition headquarters. Stepping into the kitchen, despite the time, Patrick pours a large glass of red wine.

'Here he is then, the man of the hour!' I call out as we enter the control room. Each diver stands up to introduce themselves.

'This is my friend Patrick,' I announce, proudly.

As our special guest makes his way along the procession in a manner not too dissimilar to the Queen, he shakes hands with Jim, Martin, Doug, Tom and Richard, before giving Alison a kiss on the cheek. Everyone is thrilled finally to meet the man that they have heard so much about. He is the reason that we're all here. It feels like the expedition team is finally together properly.

'It's jolly nice this wine, isn't it? It's very moreish!' Patrick says, sinking back into a worn-out leather chair. We all laugh.

'These are all of the sonar images,' I say as I point up at the wall. Patrick turns to look, locking eyes with a photograph of himself as a teenager in his naval uniform.

'Oh, crumbs!' he says, remembering what it felt like to be so young.

'We found something,' I say. It's late and I want to cut to the chase.

'You did?' Patrick replies. He looks alarmed. It's one thing to be told that someone is looking for his wreck, but now that the team has actually visited the seabed, it all seems very real.

'It's a bit more complicated than we thought it would be,' I say, before Alison explains to Patrick that the wreck is upside down.

'When she was turning!' Patrick replies without hesitation. I nod.

'We've also found some particular parts of the ship that we think match LCH 185, but there were other parts that maybe don't fit,' Alison says.

On the previous dive, assessing Target 16 had become more complicated than it had initially seemed. Some of the measurements match, but others do not. There is a number of factors that might play into this, most prominently the erosion and damage the wreck has suffered. Wrecks fall apart and parts come off. They can even expand from rust and corrosion. Because of this, we're all understandably hesitant to tell Patrick whether what we have found is or isn't his wreck. We can't make that decision until we've properly gone over the data, which we simply haven't had time to do, but nonetheless I ask Patrick if he wants to see footage of the wreck.

'At my age, John, if I don't do things now, I might never do them,' he says.

Martin loads up the screen as we turn our chairs to face it. I've been so swept up in the excitement and stress of the expedition that the weight of this moment hasn't really crossed my mind. In many ways, this is the pinnacle of the expedition. Patrick Thomas, the last survivor of the sinking of LCH 185, is to see a shipwreck that could well be the landing craft on which he had lost so many friends. As his eyes stay fixated on the screen, the camera moves through grainy footage of dark, emerald water. Fish pass by as Martin explains to Patrick what he is seeing.

'We think this is part of the stern area.'

'That's right!' Patrick replies. 'That's what I would have said.'

'It's quite narrow, but you can still see some shape,' Martin says.

The stern is one of the most intact parts of the wreck. The camera glides above to begin the slow journey towards where the bow would have been located. Patrick goes quiet. Martin continues his commentary, but Patrick drifts away. There are tears in the eyes of my old friend. The room is silent and the air is thick. His eyes don't move from the wreck. I begin to cry.

'It's been so badly destroyed . . . you can hardly recognise what it is,' Patrick says.

His words break up as they leave his mouth. As he lifts his hand to wipe the away the tears, I try to imagine how it feels. Patrick sees the wreck in a way I never can. This is a view he never expected to experience.

'But I think it's so kind of you, that you've all done this for me. Well, I feel it's for me, and for my shipmates,' Patrick says, changing the subject to stop the hurt.

Martin presents the photogrammetry he captured earlier in the day. Looking at a 3D image of what we think is a winch, engine and generator, Patrick is impressed and finds the technology fascinating. I point out the faces of his shipmates on the wall. He hasn't seen them since the day 185 disappeared. It doesn't upset him. He's happy to see his old friends again.

'You remember that tomorrow I'm going to dive, Patrick? Are you going to get up nice and early to see me down at the marina?' I ask.

'Yes! Now you good folk want to go to bed, surely, don't you? I'm going to let you go. And I'll see you all again!'

With that, Patrick downs the rest of his wine in one go and heads for the front door.

Chapter Ten

6 June 1944

LCH 185 storms back towards Sword Beach, leading groups of landing craft ashore. Hesitant soldiers are beginning to cause a jam on the beach, while corpses and casualties are piling up in the shallows, putting fresh waves of troops at risk of becoming sitting ducks the moment they land. Teddy Gueritz and his men have successfully located the beach signs and are busy establishing some order. If the landing halts, the situation could turn into a massacre. There is no time to waste. But Gueritz isn't fearful; he's relieved to finally be here, dropped in at the deep end and holding his own after spending so long training for this moment. Gueritz had his fears in the build-up to the invasion; that he wouldn't be ready when the moment came, or that he'd crumble when the Germans started firing back. As the soldier looks across the sand, bodies spread across the beach, spent rounds slapping against his wet uniform, Teddy Gueritz is delighted to have made it this far, thrilled to be standing in the face of the enemy, proud to be playing his part in the big day. He will not see the commander he landed with or their two bodyguards until their bodies are discovered later that evening, having been killed by a mortar.

The battle is not easy, but soon it begins to appear that the Allies might fight their way off the beach. Inland, paratroopers have successfully taken Merville battery, preventing it from firing upon the landing. The bridges over Ouistreham canal and Orne river have been fought out of German hands. Batteries at Le Havre have been tied up in a firefight with offshore battleships for most of the morning. The infantry assault has been overwhelming in numbers and relentless in its commitment to push forward. Wave upon wave of landing groups are pouring troops, vehicles and equipment on to the beach, gradually pushing the battle towards a tipping point. The endless rehearsals are paying off, and within an hour of Allied feet first hitting Sword Beach, the initial German defences have been reached and attacked. By 09:30, soldiers are beginning to queue at exits leading inland. Sword Beach is in Allied hands; the landing has been a success.

A counterattack by the 21st Panzers later in the day manages to reach the beach at Lion-sur-Mer, but by the time night finally falls on 6 June 1944 just under 29,000 men have passed through Sword Beach from the decks of landing craft. Initial success has come at a cost, with at least 683 men having been killed in the Sword area on D-Day. Across all five landing beaches, where 156,000 men have landed, losses reach 4,400 dead and over 9,000 wounded or missing. The beach may have been won, but the fight is far from over; troops fighting through the Normandy countryside now face some of the most severe violence of the war.

As the sun slowly sets, 185's crew gaze up at the gliders flying overhead. The flock looks so dense that the gliders appear as one single blackbird flying silently above. They float peacefully and with grace, down and around into the countryside, ready to reinforce troops fighting at Caen. Lit by fading sunlight, a telegraphist on LCH 269 can make out one, perhaps two gliders being shot out of the sky by what seems to be their own side. With D-Day over, the navy will not be returning home. For those at sea, where thousands of ships still float on the waves, their battle is only just beginning, just as it is for those fighting through towns and hedgerows. The sea off Sword Beach is still immensely dangerous. The Luftwaffe has long since lost control of the skies above the English Channel, but the Germans still occupy Western Europe and the enemy is more than capable of sending planes towards the Allies. With the five landing beaches now taken from the enemy, the beaches are to become the mouth of a supply chain necessary to keep the Allies moving forward. Ships and landing craft remain a target. There is little they can do about it. So high is the expectation of attack from above that when Teddy Gueritz and his bodyguard had landed on D-Day, they did so with a pair of shotguns to detonate any butterfly bombs dropping from German planes.

Utah, Gold and Juno beaches are in a somewhat safer position by virtue of being sandwiched between the two extreme ends of the five beaches. Geographically, once past Omaha Beach on the most western flank, the water eventually reaches the Channel Islands, which are still occupied by the Nazis. Sword, as the most eastern, is even more exposed. Once past Le Havre the coast opens up to Europe. France leads to Belgium, then to Holland, Germany, Denmark and finally Norway. All of these countries still remain in German hands and will stay that way until each grip slowly loosens beneath the weight of Allied pressure. This means that, to the dismay of the thousands of men working tirelessly on vessels spread across the English Channel, the German navy can and will come for them.

It begins almost immediately. At 01:00 on 7 June, less than twenty-four hours since the invasion began, a German fighter plane screeches its way overhead, soaring low above the decks of the landing craft. It's a huge risk for the pilot, like running across hot coals. The combined fire power below could tear the plane to pieces with ease. Even 185 has two anti-aircraft guns on its deck, and it takes no time at all for the plane to come hurtling out of the sky, smashing into the water beside Patrick and his shipmates. The pilot is injured, but alive. He is pulled out of the water, most likely on to 185 itself, before being transferred to another craft.

With this attack the floodgates have opened. Enemy planes begin to arrive daily, carving fear and panic into the hearts and minds of those still at sea. Crews are forced to watch as machine guns and bombs churn up the beach, launching clouds of sand and water high into the sky. These initial attacks don't cause much damage, but that won't last for long.

The plan for D-Day had naturally included ways by which to try to prevent enemy attacks after the initial landings. The English Channel needs to be as safe as possible to allow the influx of troops and equipment to continue for as long as is necessary. Giant concrete harbours, the Mulberrys, are towed over from England. There are two such harbours, one at Omaha Beach and another at Gold. The Normandy coastline becomes a place to unload a near endless run of supplies that will keep the war machine rumbling towards Berlin. It is extremely important that this set-up is not destroyed by the enemy, because without it the Allies could be starved into defeat.

With D-Day over, Force S is grouped together across the water by type of vessel. Other areas are designated for discharging or waiting, while further out are places for ships to be repaired, refuelled and restocked with water. The anchorage becomes a floating city on which men live and work twenty-four hours a day. At the farthest eastern point of the anchorage is the Trout Line.

This defensive strategy is important. There is a constant threat from E-boats, submarines, manned torpedoes, R-boats and Linsen explosive motorboats, all of which are capable of creeping down from the east to launch devastating attacks on the thousands of Allied vessels still in the area. The Trout Line is commanded by Captain A. F. Pugsley, and is formed of Force S, Force J and Force G. It consists of a mass of landing craft linked up as a double line of defence spaced roughly one-tenth of a nautical mile apart. At every half mile, minesweepers are positioned on each side of the line. Craft are periodically moved in and out of position depending on the roles they are needed for throughout each day. Often, nights are spent with the crews on alert for enemy attack. During the daylight hours men catch up on sleep or make repairs to their vessels. LCH 185 and 269 are a part of the Trout Line and will remain so until Force S heads back to England in the future.

On the evening of 7 June, 185 touches French soil for the first time. The craft had unloaded its troops on to smaller LCA on D-Day, but now with the beach occupied by the British, the craft powers through the water, sliding to a stop in the sand. After attaching a tow to a stranded landing craft, 185 heads back out to sea, pulling the vessel with it. Once back into position, 185 finds itself in the thick of numerous German dive-bomb attacks. To those on board, it seems that the enemy is putting into action a relentless onslaught to take out those that had dared to take the fight to them.

'Bombed to hell,' Jack Barringer writes home, 'managed to escape it, touch wood.'

The immediate role of 185 after D-Day is to undertake ship-to-shore communications with those fighting through Normandy. For this to take place, equipment needs to be set up inland. This was rehearsed in Scotland, but those that took part back then will soon learn that the practice run was a walk in the park when measured against the real thing. Crew members draw straws to see who will head inland. Patrick will never be able to recall who drew the short straw, but he never forgets the relief felt when it wasn't him. When Jack Barringer writes to his brother Les from the deck of the craft, he speaks of the trip into France: 'We had a narrow escape yesterday . . . we went inshore, and was nearly dropped by snipers. Phew, we got them though. George revenged. I don't think there was much left of them.'

George, the third of the Barringer brothers, had already been killed in the war. He drowned when the German submarine U-575 sunk HMS *Asphodel* off Cape Finisterre on the west coast of Spain in March 1944.

As telegraphists, Patrick and his colleagues receive and relay messages from units often under intense enemy fire. The emotional pull that comes with receiving first-hand news of both Allied victory and loss weighs heavily. The fighting in Normandy is some of the most notorious of the war, noted for its viciousness and large loss of life. The infamous hedgerows of the area, enormous in their height and sturdy in their construction, play a part in many situations in which the Allies find themselves heading straight towards German machine guns. The telegraphists and radio operators are some of the first people to hear about these moments.

Denis Muskett, having reached France on board 185, is busy keeping a diary of what happens each day as he sets about repairing damaged landing craft. His role means that he steps on and off 185 repeatedly depending on what needs fixing on any given day. On 8 June, two brutal raids take place. As dive bombers cause havoc on the anchorage, it seems as if no Allied planes are anywhere to be seen. The crews in the water feel strung out and helpless from attack. The next night, three searchlights are installed in the anchorage. With better vision, the sailors are more easily able to make out a Messerschmitt Bf 109 fighter plane being shot down by anti-aircraft guns firing angrily into the night sky.

Next, Muskett heads aboard HMS *Albatross*, where he finds the deck in a terrible state. The number of bombs dropped over the past few days has almost caused the ship to sink. Fixing what he can, he then heads to LCT(L) 750, where the engine room is riddled with bullet holes. An enemy shell has ripped an enormous hole through the steel hull, causing the room to flood each time high tide rolls in.

Two days later, batteries at Le Havre relentlessly fire upon the anchorage. The warships of Force S are too tied up to help, busy firing inland to provide support for the ever-advancing fight for Normandy.

LCT(L) 1023 is struck by an acoustic mine, causing a huge amount of damage to the deck. Muskett heads aboard to make repairs, and afterwards decides to spend a night in the engine room rather than risk travelling on the open sea back to 185. Slinging up a hammock dangling precariously over cold seawater that has poured into the room, he tries to get a good night's sleep for the first time since D-Day. As Muskett sways from side to side, the terrifying sound of shrapnel landing in the sea beyond the landing craft keeps him wide awake. The metal is hot and gives off a sizzle as it slices through the waves with a smack before gently hissing towards the seabed.

LCT(L) 1023 is just one of many landing craft to fall victim to acoustic mines. The weapon is an ever-present threat that hangs like a dark cloud over the exhausted crews. Sailors fear mines; they are a modern navy's worst enemy. Germany has taken years to expertly develop and evolve its mining technology, and now, in Normandy, the enemy is ready to put its latest development into action.

Acoustic mines have been in use since 1940, when they first aroused suspicion as a new weapon of war when Allied sailors began to notice that German planes seemed to be cutting their engines dead shortly before dropping something from their fuselage. Faster ships were getting hit, thought to be owing to their louder engines. There was no way to deal with acoustic mines in the early days. Ships were ordered simply to slow down in an attempt to not set the deadly contraptions off through noise or vibration. By 1941, posters were printed with diagrams of acoustic mines beneath the title 'The Acoustic Mine – A New Terror of the Under-Sea War'. On 9 September that year, Winston Churchill said in a speech that the Germans had developed a new mine that had already been littered across the North Sea. It was causing an immense nuisance to the navy, but British mine experts were busy working away to develop a means to counter the new weapon, Churchill explained.

Contact is not necessary for a vessel to set off an acoustic mine. They are a difficult threat to tackle, and a fresh fear for men at sea. For years, mine laying on both sides has consisted of a cat-and-mouse game. New, innovative mines are placed into the water. The weapon causes immense havoc and death until the other side can safely capture one to be used to study and develop an effective way of safe detonation. As such a range of means to tackle acoustic mines has been developed, from placing a hammer against the hull of a minesweeper, to creating loud noises and vibrations under-water with bundles of hand grenades, or simply smashing loose metal piping together to set the mines off. None of these methods is ever that successful. Acoustic mines have somewhat been held back by the Germans, ready for the inevitable landings in France.

This proves to be a remarkable strategy. In the months that follow, the contraption will be one of the most effective means the enemy has in its arsenal to attack the Royal Navy. Each night, enemy planes fly across the water, dropping mines into the sea. While many of the vessels have been degaussed in anticipation of magnetic mines, this does nothing to stop the acoustic variant. In the dark, it is incredibly difficult to know where the weapons have been dropped. When the sun rises, efforts are hastily made to detonate whatever can be located before any Allied vessels can be destroyed.

The strain of life in a war zone soon begins to take a toll on the minds of those living it. Enemy attack is heavy. The fear of being killed never goes away. British naval artillery is a key element of the Allied plan in the Battle of Normandy, and the seemingly endless blasts of enormous Allied guns chip away at the nerves of the crew. No peace is granted by either side.

On 12 June, the guns open up once more to fire towards Caen. The city was planned to have been taken on D-Day but, almost a week later, the fighting is still raging. Allied bombers cruise over the anchorage towards the beaches escorted by fighter planes. Two are shot out of the sky by a German anti-aircraft gun. The naval guns are deafening, rattling the insides of men for miles. It causes immediate chaos for the Germans, but leaves a lasting impact on many of those nearby for a lifetime.

That night, after the dust seems to have briefly settled, E-boats disturb the Trout Line as German dive bombers once again hurtle their way across the anchorage. Men are not sleeping, gripped by a combination of fear and adrenaline that keeps minds on high alert and hearts constantly racing. LCH 185 itself has not been damaged by the enemy, but the stress of each day is seriously impacting the mental health of those on board. The attacks continue, becoming more deadly and ever frequent. Some mornings the crews of 185 and 269 awake to find German prisoners on board who are swiftly sent to other landing craft in order to be taken to prison camps in Britain. As the days turn into weeks, shelling from German positions inland intensifies as the amount of enemy aircraft attacking overhead increases. Denis Muskett is almost hit on several occasions while moving between the different landing craft he needs to repair. Crews regularly find themselves watching in disbelief as they hastily retreat from an area of enemy shelling only to witness a direct hit on the position where they had been just seconds earlier. Close calls are everywhere. Dying seems inevitable. Shells now drop so close to vessels that a man on board HMS *Albatross* is struck and killed by a piece of shrapnel from an explosion in the air away from the ship. The Gooseberry harbour takes a direct hit. It is now a case not of if, but when, your time will be up.

A storm rolls in on 20 June and stays for a number of days. It is strong enough to destroy the Mulberry harbour in the US sector, and with access to the shore cut off, 185 is in higher demand than ever for assignments. At this point, daily reports and war diaries are rarely without casualties or sunken ships. Those who manage to survive each day get closer to breaking point. With landing craft now unable to head to the shore, the dropping off of supplies slows down. LCH 185 takes various trips around the Trout Line and anchorage. Like every other vessel, it is struggling to dodge not only the endless artillery shelling and Luftwaffe attacks, but the frightening amount of acoustic mines now floating all around them. The water off Sword Beach is a death trap.

On 24 June, HMS *Swift* is rapidly sinking nearby as desperate men cry out for help in the water. After being built in 1941, the S-class destroyer took part in the Russian convoys before being assigned to Force S. On D-Day, the ship shelled the coast, then remained in the area to provide artillery support. When *Svenner*, a Royal Navy ship lent to the Royal Norwegian Navy, was struck by a torpedo on D-Day to become the only Allied ship sunk by German naval forces on 6 June, *Swift* was tasked with rescuing survivors. Having now returned from England, where it had been replenished just a day earlier, HMS *Swift* has been hit by an acoustic mine. The ship is splitting in two and about to head to the seabed. LCH 185 hurtles towards the chaos in an attempt to rescue any survivors.

A short distance away, MV *Derrycunihy* rocks back and forth on the morning waves. *Derrycunihy* is a cargo ship launched in November 1943 that was quickly requisitioned by the military, who added number of guns, stripped it out, and sent the ship to war. It had arrived in Normandy on 20 June 1944 with the intention of unloading its cargo at Sword Beach, but the storm, as well as heavy shelling from the enemy, has been preventing *Derrycunihy* from docking. Instead, the ship has been forced to wait out at sea for a few days. On board, among supplies and equipment, are the A and C Squadrons of the 43rd (Wessex) Reconnaissance Regiment, who are needed at Caen. After three days on the water it is decided to attempt to disembark the men at Juno Beach instead. As 185 moves towards the desperate situation at HMS *Swift*, MV *Derrycunihy* starts its engines.

Patrick watches in stunned silence as *Derrycunihy* lights up in a hellish ball of fire. An acoustic mine has detonated beneath the keel of the ship, severing it in two. The stern is filled with soldiers. One man wakes up in the air, tossed with ease by the explosion towards the ceiling, before landing back down in his hammock. An ammunition lorry is pouring oil on to the water, and the fuel is set ablaze and causing the sea to burn. The crew of 185 have just unknowingly witnessed a moment that will go down in history as the largest loss of Allied life in the English Channel during the invasion. Two hundred and eight men are killed in the sinking. As the crew watch on they feel desperate to help. A sailor never turns away another man in need of help at sea, but they have orders: 185 must head to *Swift* and save whoever is left. There is not enough room for survivors from both ships. When 185 finally reaches *Swift*, the stern and bow have been completely separated. Sixteen lives are lost.

The next morning is one like any other: 25 June is not an extraordinary day. It is just as difficult as any other day in the waters off Normandy. In the American sectors of Omaha and Utah, four ships have taken direct hits from the enemy. Further east, HMS *Glasgow* has been taken out. The Allies report sinking a U-boat. None of this is special. Every day has been a dance with the enemy for weeks, but the events of yesterday have shaken the crew of 185 more than anything that has come before, and many are taking the opportunity to try to get some well-earned rest; a chance to close their eyes is a chance to momentarily leave the conflict. Sleep is almost impossible with the constant noise, but they need to try.

Earlier that morning, Denis Muskett returned to the craft from a motor launch boat, which is still tied to the side. Around the same time, a small group of men, including a Welshman named Eyon Davies, left the craft to attend a meeting on another vessel nearby. Having worked through the night, Patrick has headed for the deck on his break. He looks into the sky and spots a German plane flying across the anchorage, which is quickly shot down. The sight isn't unusual. Patrick pushes the image from his mind as he unrolls a camp bed beneath the high afternoon sun. The teenager is soon fast asleep as 185 and 269 start their engines and begin to move across the English Channel. The crafts dock at the Gooseberry harbour to refill their freshwater tanks before heading back to the Trout Line.

LCH 185 started off as a landing craft. It was a machine made for war that rolled off a shipyard conveyor belt in New Jersey. When the crew joined, it became something more. It became home to a group of young men a long way from their own beds. Together, they have crossed the Atlantic, touching down in Bermuda, before heading to North Africa and then Malta. The bond on board has grown with each day and each brush with death. By the time Patrick Thomas and Jack Barringer stepped aboard for the first time, the deck they walked across had already headed towards the enemy at Sicily and mainland Italy and pulled drowning men from the water in the Bay of Biscay. Up in Scotland, when more men joined and the crew rehearsed again, and again, and again, in the rough Scottish seas, they became a family; British lads from every corner of the country and every level of society living and working together as one. They were scared, of course they were, but they were excited too. It was an adventure, a chance to leave their mark on the world, to play a part in ridding the world of fascism. D-Day was the big push, the beginning of the end. LCH 185 wasn't just there, it led the way, guiding each wave towards Sword Beach. The craft then joined the Trout Line night after night to defend the anchorage. LCH 185 has been shelled relentlessly ever since. The men on board have laughed and smiled in the short moments when death didn't pour from the skies, but they are tired, unshaved, unclean. Patrick and Jack and the rest of those that call the craft home are rattled. They are scared and fixated on survival. They are fighters who have survived everything so far. Just a few more weeks and they'll be back in England.

'I hope to see you soon,' Jack Barringer writes home, 'I will be on the old train just as soon as my feet will let me, don't you worry!'

On board 269, a telegraphist is hard at work when a brutal explosion shakes the craft violently. He turns his seat slowly, knowing full well what horrific sight will greet him. The man peeks up from the stern of the landing craft. He looks out, then silently swings his chair back around. He looks to Peter Dwyer, a fellow telegraphist, and tells him what he too already knows.

'It's 185. She's bought it.'

The crew of LCH 269 can do nothing but watch their sister ship burst into flames. They have orders. LCH 185 and their friends on board disappear from memory with every inch that the hull sinks beneath the waves. Inside the craft, young men desperately try to fight their way out into the open sea, but it is no use. The crew of 269 discuss the sinking in the hours that follow, but no one will ever recall what was said. A numbness fills the air, a stunned silence of men beaten into submission by grief, shock, and the ever-creaking key of deteriorating minds.

After four minutes, LCH 185 is gone forever. A handful of the men are saved, but the vast majority drown. As tales of the explosion spread along the military grapevine, Maida Murphy, the fiancée of Eyon Davies, collapses, unaware that Eyon left the craft that morning.

When news of the sinking reaches England, Patrick is listed as missing and presumed dead. In fact, he had survived the explosion, hurled himself into the sea and been rescued. In France, it's decided that he should be taken home. The handful of survivors arrives at Portsmouth harbour. Dockyard workers cheer in support as they limp past. The group feel a sorry sight. Patrick and the rest of the walking wounded board a train for London and see a man so badly hurt that other injured servicemen are helping him use the toilet. There is a Canadian nurse handing out packets of cigarettes at the station. Patrick, who is now dressed in army khakis, takes one.

'Hey soldier, do you think you're old enough to smoke?' the young lady asks. If she only knew what he had gone through.

The wounded men are kept out of sight of the public, loaded into army ambulances and sent to a hospital in Chesterfield for a week. One afternoon, Patrick strolls out of the grounds with two wounded men from the 8th Army. As they wander through a shop, a homeless woman approaches and gives the men a sixpence each. It is a fortune to her. The three servicemen are moved by the generosity, but saddened by the pity given them by someone in her situation.

With the war still raging and rockets flying above the London skyline, Patrick waits for a train at Waterloo station. Standing patiently, keeping himself to himself, he notices a man coming through the crowd. Patrick recognises him. It is Stan Jennings, the man whose watch had stopped at the exact moment he launched into the water. It is as if he is witnessing a ghost of that day on the English Channel. There is little time to talk. Both survivors have trains to catch and new corners of the war to head towards. Patrick and Stan don't speak about the sinking, but what happened is scorched into both their memories.

Patrick heads to Portsmouth to collect the diary he had kept in the build-up to the invasion. He was made to hand it over, in case he was captured by the enemy in possession of crucial information about the landings. He is given a fresh naval uniform and allowed back to Shrewsbury for a week. They call it 'survivor's leave'. He goes straight home to see his mother and father. Patrick opens a drawer from his childhood and puts away the diary. He then removes his military belt, still covered in blood and grey paint, and puts that away too. It is here that the two artefacts of Patrick's brush with death will remain for years.

Everyone he meets in his hometown reacts as if they're seeing a ghost, and they are. They all thought he was dead. The local newspaper printed his obituary. He is a revenant. Patrick gets hold of a copy, reads it once, then gently folds the piece of paper and places it in his wallet.

After taking a short but well-earned rest, the wounded sailor learns that he has been reassigned for service on submarines. He is first sent to HMS *Dolphin* in Gosport, then HMS *Elfin* in Blyth. Here, he is taught how to work and live underwater. After a few weeks, Patrick is made to face the trauma he experienced in Normandy head on. The teenager is put at the bottom of a 30-foot concrete tower and made to escape a mock-up of a sunken submarine. Unbeknown to Patrick, as he trains his father is sending a handwritten letter to the navy in an attempt to try and halt the assignment.

'Put him on surface craft,' John Raymond Thomas pleads.

The sinking of LCH 185 has shaken his son and, although the nineteen-year-old has not specifically expressed as much, it is clear to a father's eyes that it is too soon after the tragedy for a confined life in a metal tube beneath the waves. Patrick's new commander sends back a typewritten reply. Telegraphists are desperately needed on submarines, he explains. Besides, his father's letter has arrived too late. Patrick is already on his way to serve in the Far East. The commander reassures John Thomas that he has spoken to the boy, who insisted that while he would prefer serving on a surface craft, he feels no effect from the sinking of 185.

'The lad is endowed with intelligence, youth and spirit which I am sure will mean not only his enjoyment of the life, but that he will be a great asset to us.'

With that, Patrick Thomas is a submariner. Thoughts of 185 are suppressed, emotions pushed down as far as they will go. He gets on with the new job and tries to forget what happened. That's all he can do. Life on the submarines isn't so bad. It is unbearably hot at times, but the crew rarely meet the enemy and get more time on leave than in Europe.

No matter how much a person may wish the past could fade, it can never be forgotten. Memories creep up in the dead of night, grabbing hold in quiet moments alone. Images of scared faces, screams of desperation, thoughts wandering to where the bodies ended up. Who made it out? Who got dragged to the bottom? Eventually, the past arrives for Patrick in the form of a crumpled yellowed envelope that has chased him across the world for months. He carefully tears it open and unfolds the three pieces of paper inside.

Hello Pat,

I hope this comes as a pleasant surprise to you and that you [don't] mind my writing, you see we went into [REDACTED] a little time ago and of course I went along to see the gang at mother's. Edith, Emma and so on. Edith said you were still OK. Well I believed you killed as Jack has been reported killed as no doubt you know, I thought if I wrote to you, you wouldn't mind telling me anything what did happen to Jack, as all we or I should say Mum had was saying he was missing then after a telegraph saying he was killed, how or where it never said. If you could enlighten me in anyway, I would be very grateful to you as you could guess it shook me up well, but mum and his wife were much worse than I.

I hope you are in good health and so on, myself passable. Pleased when this lot is all over and finished so we can all get home again, what's say?

Well Pat, I'm afraid I haven't much else just now but if you could tell me what happened out there I sure would be grateful to you for the information as mum still hopes that it will turn out for the best.

So please write when you can spare a few moments if it's just a few lines.

So until next time I'll say cheerio and keep smiling.

Your Pal,

Les.

P.S I hope you don't mind my writing.

Patrick thinks for a while, taking his young mind reluctantly back to 25 June 1944 and the moment he was forced to choose which man to save and which to leave to certain death. He has hoped never to return to that day, but now there is no choice. Patrick pulls out a pen and paper and begins to explain to Les Barringer that, unlike himself, his brother Jack will not be turning up alive. The letter is the hardest thing he will ever have to write. Patrick almost immediately forgets the words he puts on the page. Perhaps he chooses to forget, perhaps the stress of it all has wiped his memory.

The letter he received from Les stays in his safekeeping for the rest of the war in tattered coat pockets and military haversacks. In the year that follows, Patrick serves on HMS *Thule*, HMS *Totem* and HMS *Taurus*. He visits everywhere from Geelong to Hong Kong and Australia. The letter is kept safe the entire time before finding a permanent spot in a drawer in the post-war years. Patrick struggles to settle down after the highs and lows he went through at such a young age, but the letter is never far away; never revisited but never forgotten.

Being unable to help LCH 185 will haunt the crew of 269 until none is left. They try to forget, as Patrick tries to forget, but they

212

never can and never will. The faces of those who lived, worked and died on the craft never exit the minds of those that knew them. The story gradually fades into history. Of the few that survive the sinking, even fewer ever speak about it. It is too painful. Those that bore witness to the tragedy never cease to wonder what happened. Drifting minds in the early hours, wandering down to the seabed. Names and memories are sometimes mentioned in whispered tales and on paper in letters between those few who live old enough to speak to those who will listen. Sometimes Patrick receives a letter from a person who witnessed the sinking. They are always thrilled to know that at least one man survived that day. As the decades disappear, the few that remain move on with their lives as best they can. They die, as we all will die, and the memory of 185 is buried with them, forgotten entirely but for the stories passed down to children and grandchildren, and the memory of one old man still living alone on England's south coast.

Chapter Eleven

27 April 2018

The dive expedition has taken its toll on all of us. We've been working from 6 a.m. to 2 a.m. each night. I'm exhausted, but as I smash the snooze button on my phone, I remember that my moment has arrived. Dragging myself down the stairs, I begin to throw my dive gear into the car. I'm loaded up and ready to go before the dive team are out of bed. Sitting at the kitchen table shaking my leg anxiously, I'm thirsty, but I'll be out at sea soon, locked in a drysuit for three hours with nowhere to relieve myself.

The weather forecast has been bad for today and there has been talk of my dives being cancelled. I'm supposed to visit Target 16 twice, but the decision is made at the last minute to pull the second dive in order to avoid an incoming storm. The expedition has already been squeezed down to its absolute bare minimum and now my time on the wreck has gone the same way. The pressure is greater than ever before. I have just one dive, one single moment on Target 16. If anything prevents that dive from going ahead, it's all over. I'm less bothered by the news than I expect; by now, what should be a major blow is just one of many sent my way during the expedition.

The dive team check the rib, load the van and put on their undersuits. Martin pulls me aside to warn that fishing boats have heard the radio call put out to announce that divers will be in the water. Fish often inhabit wrecks, and our buoy tied on Target 16 has guided the fishermen straight to it. In the process, they have lost an abundance of large commercial fishing hooks, which are now sticking out of our descent line.

'Be careful,' Martin warns.

The atmosphere has darkened. The dive team have been dreading this part of the expedition. They have never seen me dive but are about to let me throw myself into the middle of the English Channel from a tiny fishing dinghy that they have barely used. I'm not worried, though. I know I'm ready.

The drive to the harbour seems to go on forever. Our convoy of vehicles slowly moves in a row. The tip of the rib is visible a few cars in front. It looks like a funeral procession. At Ouistreham, we back the rib into the water. As fishermen go about their work, I roll my drysuit out on to the cracked concrete. My parents pull up alongside me. They look nervous, even scared. My nerves are building too, but beneath the tension there's an undeniable buzz of excitement in the air. With my undersuit on, I put my feet into the drysuit and pull the tight seals over my head and wrists. Patrick and his grandson Paul arrive at the water's edge. Walking over, Patrick is taken aback to see me decked out in such a bizarre costume for the first time.

'This is it. This is the big moment!' I say as I pat him on the shoulder.

'At last, we've made it,' Patrick replies. He is pensive, clearly saddened by the fact that this could be the end of the search and the end of our adventure together.

'It's not too late to get you suited up and come down, Patrick!'

'You betcha . . . My Lord!' he says.

We both roar with laughter. Patrick and I walk to the jetty to take a few photographs together in the knowledge that this moment will never occur again. I think back to just under a year ago when we were standing outside Arromanches town hall as I promised to find the wreck. I was wearing a blazer then. How different I look now. Turning to Patrick, I look into his eyes and think about how much this means to him. I hope he knows how much it means to me too.

'I'll see you when I get back,' I say.

As I walk away, I can hear Patrick speaking to himself. 'Crumbs,' he says. My friend is lost for words.

Wading into the water, I throw my bag and fins into the back of the boat. I hug Alison on the way past and thank her for the dive team's help. Pressing my hands down on to the side of the rib, I throw myself up and over to get on board. Settled by the engine, I look to the shore as we pull into the water and rumble down the canal. My parents are waving me off. To their right, Patrick is standing with his arm in the air. His hand calmly morphs from a wave to a thumbs up as an uncontrollable smile tears across my face. We've come such a long way.

'You're going to love it,' Martin says as we coax along.

Passing through the canal entrance, I gaze at the horizon. There's a storm coming towards us. Everyone sees it, but no one says a word. This dive has to happen. There's no going back. Richard grips the steering wheel and shouts for us to hold on tight. As he opens up the throttle, the rib begins to roar across the tops of waves, bouncing violently up and down. I turn to watch the Normandy coastline grow wider and wonder how it must have felt to be nineteen and heading towards France on D-Day. War is for the young, for boys who have yet to think of death. It takes green minds and fresh faces and sends them towards machine guns. So many lives wasted, time and time again.

We're at sea for twenty minutes before Martin shouts over the noise that he can see the buoy. We've overshot the site by a few metres and begin to ease our way back. With our speed at a minimum, the rib, which is quickly filling with water, becomes a weightless leaf at the mercy of the waves. Like trying to break a wild horse, Richard wrestles and twists the dinghy into position. We inch closer and closer to the line, before throwing the engine in reverse to hold firm against the current. The engine is almost silent now.

We have arrived. The feeling stops me dead in my tracks. Everything is suddenly quiet. There's a feeling in the air as if the wreck has been expecting us. The buoy rolls on the waves as we try to kit up in the tiny amount of space in the boat. Fumbling over and around each other, we pass gear between our frozen hands and search for lost equipment in damp bags. Jim is ready first. Richard has been relatively quiet since we first met but now, like a drill sergeant, he snaps into action. The coxswain is in charge out here.

'Divers ready!' he screams. 'Five, four, three, two, one . . . Go! Go! Go! Get in the water!'

Jim launches himself backwards with an enormous splash.

'Go! Go! Get to the buoy!' Richard shouts at Jim.

I lose sight of the buoy in the excitement and confusion. By the time I lock eyes with it again, Jim is already gone and heading to the wreck. Finally, it's my turn. After all the planning and training, this is it. I pat the pocket of my BCD to feel my knife and check that my dive watch is fastened tightly over my gloves. Turning on my computer, I look up to see Tom sitting opposite me. We'll be diving together. With a deep breath, I take one last look at the dry sanctuary of the rib before Richard suddenly comes to life once again.

'Divers ready!'

I pull my mask strap tight across the back of my head and put in my mouthpiece.

At the end of the countdown, which sounds more like a battle cry, I toss myself backwards into the water. In a flash my vision is engulfed by a thick coat of green. Wrestling to find the surface, I think of Patrick jumping from the rails of the craft into the same body of water that I now find myself in. My head bursts up through the surf and I'm instantly battered by the terrifying waves of the English Channel. It's worse than I ever imagined. If someone had asked me in my normal life if I'd be willing to be dropped into the middle of the sea, I would have laughed, but through a series of decisions I now find myself desperately throwing my head around in search of a bright orange buoy. I spot it dancing in and out from behind the mountainous waves, then spot Tom by its side. Paddling through the water, the short journey is exhausting. By the time I reach Tom, I'm struggling to catch a breath. My perspective has been completely thrown. What seems an arm's length away is much further in the water. I reach below the buoy, but can't find the rope. This is so far removed from my comfort zone. I'm beginning to panic. Tom reaches down, grabs the line and thrusts it into my hands.

'Breathe! Calm down,' he says, taking out his mouthpiece to speak.

We look at each other with our heads barely poking out above the water as Tom slowly reaches his arm into the air. He points his thumb to the sky and then, as if to sentence me to death, flips it back down towards the seabed. I've never descended a line at sea before. This is another unknown. I grip the rope tight and look below the waves, but all I see is a dark nothingness. It strikes me that the line is heading down to the wreck diagonally. The rope I trained on in the quarry headed straight down because the water there was like a millpond, but this line is being pulled away from the wreck by a fierce current. Hand over hand, I firmly pull myself down. Beyond my mask is nothing but air bubbles and a mysterious void. At the first set of vicious fish hooks, I carefully pass my hands over each sharp end sticking out from the rope and curve my body around those still hanging down menacingly. Pulling my body towards the seabed, I can feel the sun fading away above me. The water turns black and the temperature drops as I enter a world of darkness. Attached to the second lot of hooks is a web of tangled fishing line that I have no wish to get caught up in.

I am climbing a mountain in reverse. My emotions jump from excitement to apprehension. The third trap of hooks is less of a threat. Instead, I find myself startled by two glowing yellow eyes staring back at me. As I get closer, curiously heading towards whatever sea monster awaits, the two eyes turn to three. My mind searches for an answer until I remember the dive torches we are all carrying. The lights are silently calling me to the deep. I continue to pull myself down, when suddenly I feel my knees land with a deep thud. Silt rises up high, entombing me in a grey cloud. I'm confused. I couldn't have reached the bottom already. It went by in an instant.

Pausing in the silt, I realise that it's true. I am here. I am kneeling on the bottom of the English Channel. I think of all the work I've put in, all the effort that has gone into reaching this moment and the weight of the promise I have sworn to keep. I gather my thoughts, calm myself down and run through a mental check list. I can breathe. I can rise up off the seabed and float. On the bottom, the visibility has opened up slightly and I can see a few metres in front of me. I'm good to go. It's time to bring this story to a close. I turn my head hesitantly, knowing that I'll see something, but not knowing what it will be.

My eyes meet a huge piece of rusting metal. Target 16 is right there, looming over me like a vast moonlit beast. In front of me is what could actually be LCH 185. This might be Patrick Thomas's long-lost shipwreck. I can see the cage-like piece that had matched so perfectly with the freshwater tank on the blueprint. It's huge. Bigger than I ever envisioned. Reaching out a hand in the darkness, I wrap my gloved fingers around a steel beam. On my wrist is the same dive watch I'd stare down at on the clifftop back in England. Beyond the watch face I can see the long expanse of a shipwreck. I've done it. I'm on the seabed between England and France with my hand gripped on Target 16. This is a lost landing craft, a forgotten story. I'm in its presence and it is in mine.

After pumping a short burst of air into my drysuit, I lift off the seabed. Throwing my head forwards and kicking my legs back, I'm now lying horizontally. With my buoyancy right, I float perfectly beside the wreck. I feel at ease. For the first time ever, I don't need to think about how to dive, I just do it. Swimming forward, I gaze out across the wreck as it stretches before me. I know where I am. I've spent so many hours staring at the sonar and blueprints that it almost feels like I've been here before. Pushing on through the tangle of metal beams, I see fish everywhere. Every inch of metal is covered in seagrass that sways in the current. Living things exist wherever my gaze lands.

Within seconds I find myself above the gun turret. It's so much bigger than I expected. It is clearly upside down, and the thought of what lies hidden beneath will haunt me for years to come. If I could just see beneath the sand, I could find the answer. Inside the circular trap of the turret are razor shells and a crab. Hovering above, I lift the creature out and set it free. Tom's feet disappear in front of me. The visibility is better than we'd expected, but it is still not ideal. Tom's torch beam is just about recognisable. I'm not the only person on Target 16, but I am alone.

I slowly pass over the middle of the wreck as I peek under each piece of metal for any information. Maybe I'll find a clue. Maybe I'll shut the book. As I shine my torch beneath an unidentifiable rod, a conger eel stands to attention, guarding the wreck. My eyes traverse the piles of rust. Copper wire is sprawled everywhere. Perhaps it's from Patrick's radio equipment. Heading straight down the middle of the wreck, the width of the ship is impressive as I scan for its foggy perimeters. Target 16 is only 8 metres wide, but with each edge fading off into the darkness, it seems to go on eternally. I'm small and insignificant, a minuscule man in a mass of sea. I imagine reaching the end of the wreck, continuing on and disappearing. To my left is a huge, rectangular piece of metal, free of life and sloping up from the sand. Everywhere else is a mess, but this solid block looks to be from the hull. There's an almost perfectly spherical hole in the metal. My heart beats faster. It could be a porthole.

The piece is just out of reach from the rope we are following, but I swear that I will reach it on the way back. I continue on, peeking behind every bit of wreckage for a puzzle piece to complete the tale. Nothing can be taken, nothing may be moved, but everything can be found. I reach where the bow should have been. The pieces that Martin has studied begin to appear in the distance. I push with my fins to glide above and stare into the mighty pistons of an engine blown out from the force of its collision with the seabed. Up and over the generator, I'm hovering above the winch, an enormous circle with spokes sitting peacefully like the wheel of a great ship.

I turn to face forward and look out from the missing bow. Ahead of me is a haunting debris field fading in and out of obscurity with the dark current of the sea. I want so badly to head out into it, away from the bulk of the wreck, forwards into the mystery ahead. The dive team haven't been there. No one has. Something could be out in the mist. The bow, a radio, even Patrick's boots buried in the sand. Our time on the wreck is slipping away. We're pulling the rope up as we go, removing any trace that we were ever down here at all, allowing the ship to once again return to its deep sleep. Facing the stern, I kick off to head back. Martin passes overhead with the bright lights of his photogrammetry camera. I look back to find that I've lost Tom. As I try to work out which torch beam belongs to who, all three of my fellow divers have disappeared from view.

Swimming across the wreck, staring into a rusty crevice, I can make out two large brass cogs. I can't resist. I have to pick one up. As I twist the object around in my hand, I'm naively hoping to see 'HM LCH 185' stamped on the base. I see nothing, and gently place the piece back exactly as I found it. A few metres along, a flash of blue sticks out of the sand. I'm moving too fast to stop, but throw my head down to peer back between my legs. I hold sight of the object as I swim above it. Turning around, I move to get a straight line back but when I arrive, it has vanished. What I saw could have been nothing, but it could have been everything.

Temporarily lost but aware of my surroundings, I take the opportunity to head for the bulk of metal I spotted earlier. Getting closer, I can see that the circular hole seems to have a lip around it. I put my hands on the ridge and gently pull myself forward to stick my face to the hole. Just before I stare through the potential porthole, I feel for a moment that I'm sharing a horizon with the missing men to whom I've become so attached. On the other side, the view couldn't be further from that once shared by the crew of 185. All that awaits me is a bleak debris field. My world falls out from under me in the short time it takes to look out. The sounds of the ship as it once was float over the wreck. There is laughter and chatter and metal cutlery bouncing off plates. Looking back at the wreck, I remember exactly where I am. This is a grave. A war grave. People died here. If Target 16 is 185, this is where Patrick lost his friends and where so many families lost their loved ones. This wreck is haunted not by ghosts, but by memories of the living.

Perhaps I have no right to even be down here. I've been acutely tuned in over the last year to the fact that I'm telling the story of a tragedy, but in the excitement of being on the seabed I momentarily forgot why I am where I am. The swim back to the stern is slower. I'm floating through a graveyard now. Instead of the dirt of a graveside, there is sand; the birds are fish and the grass is fishing nets, but this is a cemetery.

Reaching what we think is the freshwater tank, I swim above. Looking down into the shadows, I can make out what look like ladders hanging down from the top of the structure. If I'm right, these are parts of the ship that human feet once stepped upon. I'm tempted to swim inside and feel a roof above and walls around me, but those very facets can just as easily trap me into the same fate as so many of those held within the craft in 1944.

Gliding over the stern, I see that beneath the rust it's still largely intact. The image is one I'm familiar with from the walls of our control room. This is where, had the sea not done its work, I could well have seen '185' written in paint. I'm staring at the markings of the ship, but they are gone, just like the wreck will be one day.

Moving slowly towards the winch once more, pieces of wreckage are bent inwards, a sure sign of explosion. Martin swoops above again, his lights momentarily startling me. The whole time the team has been on the wreck, we've never really acknowledged each other. I turn and begin one final journey across Target 16. With a glide of my hand, I check the air in my tank: 120 bar. Plenty left. Looking across the wreckage, knowing the ascent line awaits, the thought hits me that it is almost over. It's unlikely that I'll ever return. I will probably never swim in the shadow of this wreck again.

I move my gloved hand up and down a piece of the target. I am as close to history as anyone can ever be, but I feel uneasy, wondering if I've disturbed the peace and quiet that the crew deserve in death. The bodies are gone. They returned to the sea soon after the sinking, yet I see remains wherever I look. Close to each piece of wreckage is where a young man once lay lifelessly on the seabed. It isn't macabre. I've got to know the crew of 185. Each time my mind sees a sailor in the wreckage, it sees not a fallen man, but someone at rest. Most of the crew went down with the craft against their will. For a short while, they were at least together in death. Perhaps they are still here; I'm not sure I should be among them.

With one final swim the end is in sight. I move towards the ascent line to regroup with Tom. We check our air before signalling our thumbs to head up. Like returning to a footprint on the moon, I kick off the seabed from where my knees had first landed. Beginning a slow ascent, I gently roll my fingers one by one up the rope. After climbing a short while, I turn back to see the wreck one final time. Expecting to see a hazy image in the distance, instead I find the craft is still clearly visible. Focusing towards Target 16, I wonder if this will be the very last time I ever see it. After climbing the line again, I turn back once more. I expect to still see the wreck, but this time it's gone for good. There is no fading into the darkness. It was there, and now it isn't.

Tom goes ahead, pulls out a knife and begins to cut the fishing lines as we push back from the rope to avoid getting caught. I watch as the hooks gently drift into the darkness below like raindrops. With the skylight of the surface appearing above my head, I start to feel sick. Seasickness had not got hold of me on the rib, but the current has subtly become more and more powerful towards the end of the dive. I had to fight to stay on the wreck. Now the sea is rocking me as I hold the line for a safety stop. The minutes count down on my computer. It feels like hours as my sickness builds. I concentrate through the dizziness, trying to hold back, not wanting to block my regulator with vomit. Our screens finally clear and we head slowly for the surface.

The instant my head pierces out of the water, I'm back in the hands of the English Channel. The storm has rolled further in, the sky is dark, and the sanctuary of the seabed seems long ago. The sea throws me around at will. I can't hold it in any longer. Tossing my regulator to the side I vomit into the waves, quickly moving my head to avoid it on the current. Suddenly feeling on top of the world, I grab the line and begin to fight the water as it pulls me away. I remove my regulator once more to ask Tom for instructions and instantly receive a forceful punch of saltwater down my windpipe. Turning away in a coughing fit, I see the boat speeding towards us with Richard at its helm. He has his arm to the left side to guide us in.

The boat comes closer. Tom shouts for me to swim. I have never been through any of this before and I'm doubting every move I make. Pushing myself off the buoy, I battle desperately through the water towards the side of the rib. As I reach up and grab on to a handle, Jim and Tom are both giving me instructions at the same time. I can't process it. The current pulls me away. I instinctively kick back with my fins, trying hopelessly to save myself from drifting out to sea, but Richard has been holding on to me from the rib the entire time. He instructs me to dunk my face down into the water to undo my weight belt. The angle my head is tilted at makes breathing difficult. I'm feeling nauseous again, but fumble my way through removing the belt. Carefully carrying it around my body, trying not to drop the heavy lead to the seabed, I pass the belt up to Richard. Leaning back, I unclip the straps around my waist to remove my BCD. I'm now floating on the surface with nothing but my fins and a drysuit. I feel naked and vulnerable.

As the waves fight against us, Richard runs me through the steps to get me into the rib. I throw my hands on to the side and kick my legs as hard as I can. It feels like my body weighs a tonne as I push myself up and launch my right leg over the side. Jim pulls my fin off as I drag the other leg in. I remove the second fin and roll over onto a pile of abandoned gear. Richard orders me to sit by the engine as he chucks across a bottle of water.

Sat at the back of the overloaded boat, I start to cry. The weight of the promise, seeing the wreck, the stress of reaching safety, the seasickness; it's all too much. Tears pour from my eyes as I look to the buoy and try to mentally to put myself back down on to Target 16. Martin surfaces and swims towards the rib, throwing himself in effortlessly. We pull the plug out to empty the rib of water, before opening the throttle with a spin back towards Ouistreham. Our moods lift. The stress and worry on everyone's minds have gone.

I've dived Target 16 and lived to tell the tale. The seasickness has worn off and as I sit on the side of the rib, hurtling through the wind with saltwater curling my hair, I laugh over the sound of the engine, knowing that I've somehow pulled this off. Martin turns to ask me how it went. I reach my arm out, still wearing my gloves, to shake his hand.

'Thank you, Martin. It was amazing. Absolutely amazing.'

'I'm glad. I knew it would be,' he says.

We both turn to face England and laugh as the tiny rib bounces across the surface of the sea.

'Smooth ride home please, Captain!' Martin calls out.

We pass an enormous metal buoy. Martin points out that it marks an unknown wreck still filled with explosives. The journey back seems to pass in seconds. Before I know it, I'm being told to get in the front of the rib. Tightroping my way along the side as we fly across the Channel, I try my best to not fall into the water. Crouching down, the dive team joke that a hero's welcome awaits me. To my left, I try to picture the long line of craft forming the Trout Line and the acoustic mines sinking them one by one. It's so hard to envision the carnage that had once decimated the horizon.

At the canal entrance, Richard slows down the engine. I look up and see my parents waving from the very end of the pier and throw my arms into the air to wave back. Patrick is waving to us and grinning. We pull up to the jetty and throw Alison the rope. She wraps it around and drags us in. My feet are finally back on dry land as I step uneasily across the jetty. Patrick is standing at the top of the walkway. I slowly walk up, aware of the weight of the moment I am living in as I reach Patrick and pat him on the shoulder.

'I did it, Patrick.'

'You did it!' he says, smiling ear to ear.

'I was quite taken aback by how much like a boat it actually is. You can still travel down it. It's big. The images don't really do justice to how big it is.'

Patrick is nodding as he takes it all in. I'm struggling to find the right words to express visiting where his friends may have died.

'It's peaceful down there,' I say.

Taking my friend by the arm, we slowly cross the car park to a small patch of grass overlooking the water.

'It makes me so sad to know that the scrap dealers took her apart. I'd understand if it was a shipping hazard and needed to be done, but to send in the dealers afterwards is unforgivable,' he says. Patrick must have been thinking about the condition of the wreck ever since we showed him footage of it last night.

I ask if this is a sort of closure for him.

'It is, in that sense. I never thought this sort of thing would ever happen. Not to me. I never thought I'd react like this.'

Patrick reaches into his pocket to pull out a piece of crumpled paper. On it, gripped tightly in his weathered hand, is a poem he planned to read. It's a poem that he has often returned to and once read aloud after receiving his Légion d'honneur. I had no idea that he had planned to read it after the dive.

Patrick goes to utter the first word, but can't speak. His face closes up tightly as tears begin to tumble from his wrinkled eyes. I have never seen him this upset before. It is a different kind of upset, like his oxygen has been taken away. Standing for a moment as he tries to stop himself from getting overwhelmed, Patrick suddenly walks away. He's moving faster than normal, trying to escape the situation. Patrick is devastated. His grandson Paul follows, throwing his arm over his grandfather's shoulders.

Just like that, I am left alone. Tears stream down my sunburnt cheeks as the sound of the English Channel beating against the shoreline echoes by my side. I don't know if I've done the right thing. The end goal is to bring closure to this story, to settle a seven-decade-old trauma for Patrick. In doing so, have I dragged too much hurt back to the surface? Have I brought scars back from the seabed with me? Patrick is feeling emotions he has long since suppressed. Whether or not it's a positive thing to finally let them out is not for me to decide but, good or bad, Patrick is now crying in a car park, and that is my doing. I face the sea in search of answers, but find nothing. I can't talk through the tears, drowning in the guilt of causing my friend such upset. Suddenly, I feel arms wrap around me from behind.

'It's OK, John. You did the right thing.'

I peer back over my shoulder and see my mum with tears in her eyes.

'I just don't know,' I reply through shallow breaths. 'I see Patrick like that and I wonder if I should have done any of this. Maybe I should have just let it all lie.'

'No,' she says. 'Patrick is happy you did it. It's just a lot to take in.'

My dad appears. He is crying too. I can count on one hand the number of times I have seen my parents cry in my lifetime.

'You did it, John,' he says, patting me on the back.

I look over and see Patrick speaking to his grandson.

'After all these years, it's brought it all to the surface, I think,' Patrick says. He turns to face me. 'I'm so pleased you've done this! It's great to think that all these people have taken such an interest. I never thought they would.'

Wiping the tears from my eyes, I walk over and shake Patrick's hand. We've done it, together, and I have taken my promise to find LCH 185 as far as I possibly can. It's an honour to have Patrick there by my side, experiencing this moment with me. Whatever the outcome of the survey, however the story ends, neither of us will ever forget this.

Chapter Twelve

28 April 2018

The adrenaline from the dive and the turmoil of Patrick's horrendous upset stops me from getting any sleep after visiting the wreck. Instead, I toss and turn, wondering whether or not it had been the right thing to do. In the morning, I walk into the control room. The curtains are closed, the room is dimly lit, and the eyes of 185's crew stare down at me from the walls. I look across the young faces and wish that they could know what happened yesterday.

The entire team is exhausted from a tremendously tough week, but today, with Patrick by our side, we'll be heading out to sea one final time. Driving to the harbour, I pull over at a local flower shop and buy dozens of small red roses. Once I arrive at the water, Patrick and Paul pull up in their car. I open the passenger door and pass a poppy wreath into Patrick's hands.

'This is for you to put on the waves. Do you want to write anything on it, Pat?' I ask as I hand over a pen.

He nods and without saying a word shuts the door. A few minutes later, Patrick passes me the wreath. I squint my eyes to read the fragile handwriting.

To all my shipmates who lost their lives when LCH 185 was sunk by an acoustic mine on 25 June 1944.

Rest in peace.

You will never be forgotten.

Looking down at my dive watch, I see that we're running half an hour late. We are supposed to be boarding a boat, but there's no sign of it anywhere. I'm beginning to worry, until two unassuming men in hoodies walk over and shake our hands. Philippe introduces himself as the captain who will be taking us out that day. I look to the water to see that the boats closest to where we are standing are tiny fishing boats. We're supposed to be going out on something much bigger. Philippe and his partner walk towards the water as the dive team, Patrick and I move further down the harbour. Suddenly, an enormous orange lifeboat soars down the canal, cutting through the water like a knife. The other three crew members jump off in unison. Wearing matching orange jumpsuits, they toss ropes around moorings and pull in sequence as Philippe calls out orders to the well-oiled machine. As quickly as the crew begin, they finish without breaking a sweat. All five men casually turn to face us as if it was nothing, formally introducing themselves as Captain Philippe Capdeville, Bertrand Desvallee, Christian Dubois, Nicolas Jesep and François Rabineau. We're all standing in awe of the effortlessly cool Frenchmen.

A feeling of pride sweeps over me as I look to Patrick. He stands by my side, an unassuming man, a 'squirt' in his words, staring up at the enormous boat. All of this is for him. The Société Nationale de Sauvetage en Mer (SNSM) is a volunteer lifeboat organisation, whose members have not only offered to take us all out, but have arranged for another lifeboat to travel from a different part of the coast to cover for them. The generosity and kindness of everyone I've met along the way never fails to move me.

Patrick and I stand silently. He holds the wreath in his hands while I grip the roses in mine. Neither of us has anything to say. As we walk down towards the water on the same ramp on which I walked after returning from Target 16, local families are gathering to watch. They must know from the sight of an old, white-bearded man in a Submariners Association windbreaker that something special is occurring. As we reach the boat, the crew are incredibly welcoming. Such is the size of the vessel that Patrick almost has to be lifted onboard. We zip up lifejackets and take our seats. I give Philippe the thumbs up to take us out to sea.

The journey is exciting and a sense of occasion hangs in the air. The lifeboat is going at such a high speed that we barely bounce, instead skimming the very tips of waves. Patrick is still quiet as he holds the wreath tightly to his chest and stares out of the steamed up window. I leave him to his thoughts, keeping my eyes glued to the lifeboat's GPS system. A miniature graphic of the boat is heading across the screen towards a small, yellow circle marking our destination. The blip gets closer as we near the site. I lean over to Patrick and explain what the circle represents. Arriving in the vicinity, the engine slows down as we begin to inch towards the right spot.

The atmosphere suddenly switches when the only noise left is the rumble of the lifeboat manoeuvring between gears to steady itself. Everything else is silent. The moment feels unreal, like we're all living in a mirage. The same feeling had drifted over the dive rib the previous morning as I'd arrived above Target 16, as if an invisible mist had swept down on us. Perhaps a place of great tragedy still holds the pain and suffering within it forever. The captain switches on the on-board sonar equipment. I'd imagined that we would simply stop at the rough coordinates and announce our arrival, but the crew want to make sure it's exactly right.

Patrick begins to rise up. I reach my hand under his arm to help him from his seat. We carefully walk towards the screen as the lifeboat rocks from side to side. Patrick holds the seat with his right hand to steady himself as I take hold of his left and reach up to grab a bar on the ceiling. Together we watch the seabed move across the screen. Everyone else is silent until the crew begin to speak back and forth in hushed French. We don't understand, but I know from the tone that they are discussing the best way to get over the wreck.

'Keep watching,' I tell Patrick. 'The brown line is the seabed. Look for a lump to appear.'

We watch and wait. No one speaks. There is nothing to be heard but the sea as it slaps the hull of the lifeboat and the low murmur of the engine. Then, like a surfacing whale, the shape of a landing craft slowly appears in front of us.

'That's it, Patrick. That's the wreck! You're here.'

Patrick says nothing but keeps his eyes glued to the screen. This shipwreck could well be LCH 185, and he knows it. If Target 16 is Patrick's craft, then he could now be floating on the same area of water that he launched himself desperately into as a nineteen-year-old. This could be same spot where Jack Barringer disappeared beneath the waves; the place where so many men had their last glimpse of the sky before they never saw light again. The seabed below our gently rocking feet could be where Patrick might have ended up had he not slept in the sun that day.

We turn to walk towards the outside deck. Patrick and I hobble through the door. He eases along the railings until reaching the edge of the lifeboat. I follow behind and take a spot on his left. Paul crouches down by his grandfather's side to keep him from falling overboard. The dive team and lifeboat crew form a crescent around us. I've grown so used to the monotonous murmur of the engine that, when the captain flicks the switch to turn it off, the world suddenly feels completely different. All I can hear now are seagulls flying overhead.

The lifeboat constantly moves, sometimes in a vicious swipe and other times as a steady sway. I look around to take it all in. Whether this is 185 or not, this is certainly the general area where it went down. This is where the story occurred. Looking across the waves, I try to picture Patrick with his shirt off helplessly trying to untie his leather boots. I look to the railings and see a younger version of my friend throwing himself into the water below. Somewhere near here, Patrick had to choose between the lives of two men. I look up to the clouds and imagine the blue sky as my final view on earth.

Patrick pulls out the same piece of folded paper that he'd been unable to read yesterday. It's more crumpled than before, and he gently unfolds the page. He steadies himself, lets out a sigh, and starts to read.

> There are no roses on a sailor's grave,
> Nor wreaths upon the storm tossed waves.
> No heartbroken words carved in stone,
> Just shipmates lying there alone.
> The only tributes are the seagulls' sweeps,
> and the teardrops when a loved one weeps.

He pauses and lowers his head as tears drop from his clenched eyes. I too begin to cry. Patrick turns to face the sea. With a sharp jolt of his weak arms, he tosses the wreath overboard. The poppies ride the waves for a moment, before giving themselves up to the power of the sea. The wreath slowly floats towards the seabed, down to Target 16. Patrick looks back at the paper, pulling it tight to fight against the harsh wind.

'Rest in peace all those shipmates who have no other grave than the sea off Normandy. You are not forgotten.'

The faces of those who died that day come to me. The final journey of the wreath matches that of so many of the men I've come to know. I try to say a few words, but I can do nothing but sob. Instead, I step forward to the railings and look down at the roses in my hand. There is one flower for each man known to be lost. With a quick throw the bouquet travels through the air and lands on the water. The current quickly drifts the roses apart. Watching as each flower begins its own silent journey, I turn away and lift my hands to hide my tear-soaked face.

'Look, you can see them!' one of the dive team calls out.

I raise my head to look back at the water. The roses were pulled beneath the lifeboat and have reappeared on the opposite side. One after the other, they float by the hull, carving a perfect parade below the shadow of a French flag waving in the wind.

We stand again silently in a shared moment of reflection. My hand is on Patrick's shoulder, as through the tears I try to tell my friend exactly how I feel.

'You said LCH 185 was your home and the crew your family. Today we brought you home. Finally, after all these years, we have put roses on those sailors' graves.'

Patrick nods. It's premature of me. I still don't know the true identity of Target 16. Patrick knows that, but still for him this is coming home. This may be the last chance he will ever get, one final journey to where his young life was defined so long ago. As everyone heads back inside the lifeboat, I stand alone in the wind. Target 16 is a short distance below us. The only thing separating Patrick from the wreck is the water.

The weight of taking Patrick out here is heavy. I'm proud to have done all of this, and proud to have given my friend some closure, but it's upsetting to know that it should never have been this way. Those young men should have lived. Whenever I've visited battlefields or war cemeteries, there has always been a voice running through my head apologising to each name that I pass. I always have a feeling of melancholy in places of conflict and a sense that we let down those that we send to war.

Patrick is more cheerful on the trip back to shore. Once settled back into his seat, he's like a new man. Having the chance to return at such an advanced age is something that few of his peers ever got. Patrick knows that he'll never come back here again. I could see it in his eyes. Out on the deck alone, I pull a red beanie hat out of my pocket, drag it back over my hair and lean against the railing. As I watch Target 16 fade out of view for good, I think of the silence that surrounds the wreck. Life goes on for all of us, ever changing and moving with the tides, but, down there, the wreck sleeps as the world moves on.

Back on land, I'm not sure how Patrick will fare after such an emotional couple of days, but it feels like we should visit Jack's grave. After a quiet drive together, both lost in our own thoughts, we head to the gate of the cemetery. I was standing here with Patrick the very first time that I ever heard the story of Jack Barringer, and this is the first time we've ever been back together. The walk along the headstones is different with Patrick by my side. Passing row upon row of young men, it feels more like a funeral. When I've walked here on my own in the past, I normally reflect on how men my age, sometimes much younger, lost their lives fighting for my freedom. As Patrick looks at those same names, he knows that the men buried beneath our feet could easily have been him.

I'm holding a small wreath in my hands, in the middle of which I've glued a photograph of Jack. Patrick has never seen a photograph of his friend. The last time he saw his face was just before Jack drowned. As we pass the centre of the cemetery, I hand the wreath to Patrick. He lets out a loud gasp of genuine shock.

'Is that . . . Jack?' he asks sheepishly, eyes wide in complete disbelief.

I nod.

'Where did you find this?'

Coincidentally, on the lifeboat earlier that day, Patrick had asked if I'd ever considered tracking down the families of 185's crew. I told him that I'd thought about it, but that it would probably be too hard. A small lie didn't seem too bad. He is unaware that I've been trying to find the families in case I can get any of them to the memorial unveiling. I want that to be a surprise on the day, but showing Jack's photograph to Patrick now feels like the right thing to do. He grips the wreath with both hands and stares down at his friend's smiling face.

'I tracked down Jack's family. They gave me this photo to show you.'

He's speechless and struggling to find his breath.

'Jack's brother Les, who wrote to you asking about Jack, had two sons,' I say. 'They're still alive and want me to send you their regards. They still come to Ranville to see Jack. They named one of their sons after him. They never did forget him, Patrick.'

He doesn't respond, but I know that he's speaking through his silence. Patrick hugs the wreath close as we calmly walk towards Jack's grave. Standing with our shoulders touching, we bow our heads as Patrick reads the words on the headstone:

HIS MEMORY
WE SHALL ALWAYS TREASURE
IN OUR HEARTS
HE WILL LIVE FOREVER

Kneeling down, I brush away wild flowers from the next headstone along and read the inscription:

HE BELIEVED IN ENGLAND AND HE LOVED
HER FAITHFULLY.

The words hit me in the gut. He believed in England. Maybe the man beneath the headstone had more of a chance to believe in something: that generation shared a collective moment, coming together in a way not seen since, to fight for something worth fighting for. I read a quote in a book once, long since lost, that said that men like Patrick Thomas and Jack Barringer only exist in the context of the Second World War. The bravery, fear and loss of that calibre only exist in relation to the situations that arise in a brutal conflict. To me, it is only the young versions of soldiers that live only within the context of the Second World War. The old men, if they're lucky, live and bleed into further generations. Patrick is still here, living the war every day. His story hasn't ended. Standing at Jack's grave, I think about how many things have come together over the last seven decades to bring the two of us to this one place, side by side, right now.

Patrick not only survived D-Day and the sinking of 185 two weeks later, but he also survived serving on submarines in the Far East. Post-war, he lived for another seven decades, getting through all of normal life's ups and downs. After surviving everything, the old man who was a teenager in the war has made it back to be with me on the search for his own shipwreck. Had he not made it this far, the story of 185 would have been lost. Jack Barringer and the other victims of the sinking would have vanished into forgotten history. I reach into my pocket and pull out something that I've been unsure about giving to Patrick, but the moment has taken me.

'I want you to have this. It's a letter written from the deck of LCH 185. It's from Jack to his brother Les ten days before the ship sank. Don't read it now. Take it away and read it when you have some time to yourself and can take it all in alone.'

The past two days have been emotionally draining for all of us, but especially Patrick. Having him read a letter from Jack above his grave seems too much to put him through.

'How did you get this?' he asks.

Patrick is visibly shaking. It must feel like receiving a letter from an apparition; a message from a past that he never expected to revisit. We turn away from the headstone and walk solemnly towards the memorial cross in the middle of the grass. He turns to me before we reach our destination and puts out his hand. I grab it, and we shake hands vigorously.

'Thank you, John, for everything you've done for me.'

'You don't need to thank me, Patrick. It's the least I could do.'

I'm fighting hard not to cry. I didn't expect this at all.

'For seventy-four years LCH 185 was a thing of great sadness, but now being here with you, visiting the wreck, the memorial being unveiled soon and hearing that the families of my shipmates know that they are being remembered, knowing that I'm still alive and that I'm helping to tell their story, LCH 185 is almost a happy thing for me now, in a strange way,' Patrick says.

We reach the stone sphere that curves around the cross. Patrick puts his arm against my chest to stop us walking any further. He's never taken this sort of control of a situation before, but this is important to him. Patrick stamps his foot, slams his walking stick into the ground, puffs out his chest and raises his head high. He is standing to attention. Patrick has never done this in my presence. To me, he's always been a gentle, elderly man that doesn't ever show the rigidness of his former life in the navy, but now he's snapping back into military mode to pay respect to his fallen comrade. The hairs are standing up on the back of my neck as the old sailor orders me to walk forward by his side. We place the wreath in the centre of the cross with Jack's face gazing up to the clouds, then take three careful steps backwards. Patrick once more pushes his head up high, puffs his chest out and hits his walking stick on the stone. I raise my head as we stand for an impromptu moment of silence. I should be thinking of Patrick's shipmates, but having Patrick act like this, seeing him so proud, has reduced me to tears.

That evening we drive the short distance from the expedition headquarters to Lion-sur-Mer. It's the first time that Patrick and I have been here together, despite speaking for hours about how much the town means to him. When I first stepped foot in the town hall to ask Dominique for permission to build a memorial, he'd asked if Patrick would be willing to come and meet him. The use of the word willing made me laugh because Patrick wouldn't just be willing, he would be honoured.

Dominique, ever true to his word, has asked to meet us on the final night of the expedition. Our rendezvous is at a small restaurant on the seafront. It's relatively empty, but there's no doubt that, being the mayor, Dominique could have got us the best table had it been full. I help Patrick out of the car, holding his arm as we move through the streets. The sun is setting over the water. I still have salt in my hair, my face dried out and red from the sun and sea. Walking through the door, we're escorted to our table by a waitress. Dominique spots us and stands up to wave.

'You must be Patrick!' he says in his thick French accent.

I'm thrilled to see Dominique again, but I decide to take a back seat in the conversation, knowing how much this means to Patrick.

To be welcomed with open arms into Lion-sur-Mer by the mayor is something he never imagined would happen. Sitting down for dinner, we're short of a translator, but the conversation still flows. I sit back in my chair and admire the scene, thinking how different this experience of the town is for Patrick compared to how it had been on D-Day and the weeks that followed.

After finishing our meals, we stick around for a few drinks. Patrick takes the opportunity, slowly and firmly, to tell Dominique his story. He runs through each minute, from leaving Portsmouth to seeing the beautiful houses of Lion-sur-Mer and the final tragedy that occurred off the coast. Dominique heard the same tale from me at our initial meeting, but to hear it from the man himself is a completely different experience. He listens carefully with a sympathetic look in his eyes. This is Patrick's moment, finally. He has waited over seven decades to tell his story in this little French town within sight of which he lost so many friends. Patrick doesn't want gratitude or praise. He just wants the townspeople to know what happened.

Before leaving, Dominique pulls his phone from the inside pocket of his suit jacket and asks Patrick for a selfie. Patrick and the mayor let out a huge laugh as they take the photo. I can't help but smile at a selfie taken of the lone survivor of a historic shipwreck, now in his nineties, and the mayor of the town he'd headed for on D-Day. It is a bizarre image, but a perfect one.

I return home the next day and get straight to work on the memorial, knowing how much there is to get done in such a short space of time. The tribute needs to be able to stand the test of time, because it will be within metres of the English Channel. There is no guide book to building a war memorial and I truly have no idea where to begin. My first move is to email every funeral parlour in my area. It's morbid, but seems a safe bet as a starting point in my attempts to find something that might look like a monument. I take a visit to the closest one to my house, a decades-old, family-run business. Inside, it is dusty and spooky. I can tell the second I step through the door that this isn't the right route to take.

Graphic designers, sign makers and plaque engravers are next on the list, but they don't work out either. Everything is either hugely expensive, or made of materials that won't last long and will need replacing every ten years. Brass needs polishing, so that goes out of the window straightaway. I don't wish to head to France, build a memorial and return to England, leaving the residents of Lion-sur-Mer with the burden of upkeep, but I can't change the simple truth that I won't be in France to look after it. The worry and restless nights grow.

No idea seems to work, and the days quickly disappear. Initially, I'd accepted that I would most likely have to unveil a plaque on a cloth-covered easel on the beach with a promise to install a permanent memorial later, but when Dominique gave me an official spot on which to put the memorial, he handed me a huge opportunity to complete the task in one go, and I don't want to fail.

At my desk, I sit and draw a rough sketch of a stone with a small plaque in the middle. It needs to be put together in a few weeks, so the memorial has to be simple. I email the drawing to Dominique to approve the design. Next, I have to solve the problem of the inscription itself. There's no way that it can be anything less than perfect. Patrick is keen to have the wording in both French and English, and to include the 'No Roses On a Sailor's Grave' poem in both languages. There won't be space for both, so instead I have the poem translated to be read out at the unveiling. A poem changed into a different language won't rhyme, but by chance my cousin has just married a French translator named François, who kindly rewrites the poem in French to rhyme beautifully. Patrick and I exchange countless emails about the inscription. Tiny details are sweated over for hours. An entire day is set aside to discuss whether the craft's name will be written as LCH 185, LCH-185, HMLCH-185 or H.M.L.C.H. 185, having seen it as each on different graves, records and letters. It's clear that this memorial needs to be perfect. The wording will be read by thousands and all involved need to be proud of whatever we put on the ground.

Lacking any design software, I create the plaque on a PowerPoint slide and place the order. Two days later, it arrives in the post. The box sits on my dining table for hours. I'm terrified to open it, knowing that so much as a single wrongly placed comma could ruin the entire thing, but eventually I have to face it. Unwrapping the mound of bubble wrap, I'm relieved to be greeted with a perfectly worded tribute to Patrick's lost comrades. The plaque is real and in my hands. It's tangible, at last. Holding the metal on the sides so as to not cover it in fingerprints, I wrap the plaque back up, change the address and take it straight to the Post Office. Like Patrick in 1944, and like I have so many times during the search, the plaque will now cross the English Channel to Lion-sur-Mer, and onwards to the desk of Dominique Régeard.

Trying to find a contractor to build the memorial proves impossible. There's no way I can afford to take a British team over to France, and there are very few stonemasons or builders in the area. The small number that I manage to contact can't speak English. I can't speak French. It's one thing to get by in France reading road signs and making small talk, but the intricate conversation needed to build something to specific measurements and a particular design is just too much.

The plaque arrives in France safely. During my search for a stonemason, Dominique has insisted multiple times that he can sort it out. I'm reluctant to let the mayor himself take the responsibility of getting the memorial in place. Being allowed to construct it is an honour he has granted me and I feel compelled to make sure I don't burden anyone. Still, each time we speak, Dominique insists and assures me not to worry. It will all work out, he insists. I truly hope he's right.

Chapter Thirteen

4 June 2018

The expedition doesn't quickly fade into the distance. I'm back at work, but while I excavate prehistoric ditches and pits, my mind is elsewhere. All I can think about is what has transpired. The feeling of diving Target 16 remains so vivid. I think about it constantly, replaying my journey through the wreck again and again. In many ways, I'm still down there. Every piece of savagely twisted metal has found a place in my head that doesn't seem temporary.

On the final surveying dive some measurements had been brought back up that made all of us uneasy. We'd told Patrick before showing him footage of the wreck that some of what we were discovering added up to what we needed to see but, strangely, other measurements didn't look quite right. As an archaeologist, I'm used to that feeling. Excavations are so often revealed slowly, unravelling the truth bit by bit. New features and artefacts can take theories one way, only for the direction to change completely with the very next piece of information uncovered. I can recall excitedly working on what looked to be a Roman road, but by the time we'd excavated, cleaned and recorded everything, it had turned out to be a relatively modern farm track. That sort of thing occurs often in my line of work but I don't recall ever being disappointed by it because, on the other hand, I've been excavating what initially appeared to be a modern rubbish pit, only to discover that it was in fact an Anglo-Saxon burial. That's just how it is. Sometimes it goes your way, and other times it goes the other way. If archaeologists already know what they are going to uncover, there would be little point to doing what we do. That's the thrill of it, after all.

Archaeology can also be incredibly difficult. When news broke that the University of Leicester had discovered the skeleton of Richard III, I was about to start my degree and the story gripped me like it did so many across the world. During a television interview, one of the team mentioned that archaeologists don't tend to go looking for named people, because the chance of finding one single person from history is incredibly slim. In maritime archaeology, it isn't unusual to go searching for one particular vessel, but there are far fewer shipwrecks on the seabed than there are people buried beneath the soil. Ships are immeasurably larger than a human skeleton, but it doesn't make the odds of discovering one any higher. If it was easy, then everyone would be doing it.

All of my free time is once again spent researching LCH 185. My evenings are filled with going over the hours of footage we recorded of the wreck. I stare intently like an investigator watches CCTV footage, trying to spot any clue that might reveal Target 16 as the craft we all want it to be. I compare measurements we took on the wreck with any type of landing craft I can find the blueprints for. The dive team is back in Portsmouth doing the same. We're all as determined as ever to find a way to be able to confidently tell Patrick what he wants to hear. Every person involved with the search is hoping for the same, and that moment isn't far away.

After a couple of months, I'm packing my suitcase once again. Driving over the Dartford bridge and through the same winding villages, it's exciting to know I'll be seeing Patrick at the end of the journey. Tomorrow morning, I will be heading to France, but tonight I have a meeting to attend.

After settling in at the hotel, I drive to meet the dive team at their headquarters. Portsmouth is a strange town. Parts make you wish you could live peacefully by the sea, while in other areas you can almost picture smugglers and sailors of yesteryear rocking up and throwing a bottle of rum at you. My journey to the meeting steers through both versions. The roads get longer and quieter. I begin to see hills and cliffs appear on the horizon as the old fort that the dive team calls home suddenly pops into view.

Parking to overlook the sea, I spend a while taking in the scene. The sun is setting and a light pink glow fills the sky, reflecting off the ripples of the Channel. Throughout the search, the sea has never lost its charm. Wherever the project has taken me, be it Patrick's living room or the mayor's office, the water has only ever been a short walk away. Sounds of seagulls are always close by and the smell of sea air is ever present. I know that when this is all over, I'll miss it. Britain is an island, but we never seem to see ourselves as being islanders. I grew up a forty-minute drive from the coast, but that to us isn't close at all. Soon I'll go back inland, but I'll always be happiest by the water.

As I stand and look out to sea, with the fort bearing down over my shoulder, my relationship to the waves feels different. This is the first time I've seen the Channel since I dived on Target 16 and then went with Patrick to the site, a moment that already feels like another life. The expedition and the dive itself have been so consuming. It has taken over my entire life and, during the brief time I was on the wreck, my entire being. Every thought and every movement carefully considered, every breath taken for

Target 16. When it was over, I walked back on to dry land and put the underwater world away. The wreck is a place I once occupied, another part of life left behind. That's something that has been hard to deal with. There was so much momentum heading towards the expedition. For close to a year it was the great milestone on the horizon and the big adventure I was pushing towards. Then, suddenly, it was over. The expedition is gone, occupying the same past that holds the story of 185 and everything that has ever happened. It's history now. The Channel was filled with wonder before I went down, but I've knelt on the bottom, surrounded by a cloud of sand. I've seen the rust of a wreck and come face to face with life down there. The water feels different to me. The sea and I hold a bond that only those that have traipsed through its shadowy depths can understand.

The flaking iron gate of the fort creaks as I pull it open to walk through the courtyard past turrets and towers. Fort Widley, built in the late 1800s to defend Portsmouth, is ominous in its size. The dilapidated red-brick exterior seems like an unlikely place for a meeting, but perfectly fitting at the same time. I have never stepped foot in the fort before, and I'm not sure where I'm heading as I travel through the vast expanse of courtyard and small buildings behind the walls. Following the signs, I take a left turn across a bridge that balances over a sheer drop to an empty moat below, eventually finding a large wooden door adorned with a single brass plaque:

Southsea Sub-Aqua Club: The club that found the Mary Rose

After knocking loudly, I stand while I wonder what awaits me on the other side. Alison opens the door and leads me into the clubhouse. Stepping into a room filled with Chesterfield sofas, exposed beams and a brass dive helmet, it feels like I've gone back in time. There's even a piece of a Roman amphora, which the team recently discovered, displayed in a glass case. In one corner of the room is a wooden bar, but only coffee is on offer today, although I imagine that isn't always the case. In the middle of the room is a large table with the same computer Martin had brought to France at one end.

The team and I hug, shake hands, chat and make jokes about the expedition. I still barely know them, having only spent a few days with them in France. All other contact has been by email, but there is still a bond here seen in slight grins passed to each other with the silent sharing of memories. We've worked together in the search for Patrick's wreck. That's an experience few people can claim.

Taking a seat at the table, the rest of the dive team join me as we are each handed a stack of papers by Martin. As the divers settle down, I disappear into my own thoughts. This may well be the end of our journey together. The outcome of this meeting is either going to be a joyous success or a crushing disappointment. Nobody has a higher stake in this search than Patrick and me, and he more than anyone. This is his story. LCH 185 is his landing craft. Patrick's trauma is real, and the closure of a tragic memory dangles on the archaeological results about to be revealed.

If it wasn't for my promise to Patrick, we wouldn't be sitting here now. Along the way, through the ups and downs of the search, both Patrick and I have been through so many emotions. He has experienced memories brought back to the surface. I know that none of those tears would have been shed had I not brought him along with me. Archaeology so often centres on people from thousands of years ago and the discovery of remains from societies with no living relatives, no memories of names or faces to recall.

Archaeology of the Second World War appeals to me for the exact opposite reason. It is, for a short while longer at least, within living memory. It matters to people still alive today. As I think of Patrick, a living survivor of the sinking of 185, and the relatives of his shipmates who are waiting patiently for news of the search, I wonder if that is such a good thing after all.

I'm apprehensive. Both the dive team and I have been living separate lives and undertaking separate research to try and find the same result. Now, it's finally time to come together. We first discuss the photograph of 185 that Patrick had shown me at the beginning of the search. I filed it away back then and didn't look at it again until after the expedition was over. What I saw the second time round, with the benefit of everything I'd learned since, revealed the truth of the image. Patrick has believed for decades that he has in his possession a photograph of his own landing craft powering towards the beach on D-Day. When he first showed me the image, I knew very little of landing craft and believed what my friend believed. It's clear now that the vessel shown isn't a Landing Craft Headquarters at all. There is no tripod foremast, the smoking gun for that type of vessel. Instead, the photograph shows a Landing Craft Infantry (Large). After much inner debate, I'd told Patrick over the phone. He didn't seem to mind, or even really want to hear it. In his eyes the photograph shows LCH 185, as it always has.

I haven't had a chance to tell the team that since the expedition I've uncovered an actual video of 185 in the archives. It stopped me in my tracks. We had all been working to find images of the craft leading up to the dive trip, but always came up short. The video shows 185 preparing for the invasion of Italy. Patrick wasn't involved with the craft at that point, but many of the shipmates he would later join were. Seeing the video was an emotional moment. I'd wondered what the craft looked like for almost two years.

It was easy enough to see photographs of other Landing Craft Headquarters, but that isn't the same. I'd always tried to imagine what 185 was like as a vessel bursting with life and activity, but actually seeing it had never seemed realistic. Hardly any specific landing craft from the Second World War exist on video but, in an unbelievable stroke of luck, I discovered exactly that for 185. I've watched it countless times since. The short clip is silent, but shows the crew chatting as they prepare for battle. My grandfather was in that same landing, and although I know that Patrick is not going to walk past the lens, I often imagine how beautiful it would be if Grandpa strolled beside the harbour in the footage. Searching for ghosts, again. The men in the video look anxious but happy. It must have been exciting. Many veterans of the Second World War have told me that at times it was a thrill to be there.

'As you know, last month we took to the water in hopes of identifying Patrick's landing craft,' Alison says.

Martin stands up and clicks a button on the screen. Two pictures of a craft appear in front of me. The dive team have uncovered photographs of 185 from the same day and same angle as the video I found. They are high-quality still images, making it much easier to study the faces of the men in detail. On the day shown in both the film and photographs, 185 had not yet been converted to an LCH. That much is obvious because the large tripod foremast is nowhere to be seen. By this point, the version of 185 that we're looking at had already been across the world from the States, through the Caribbean and into Europe. It was already a veteran. Looking at the photographs saddens me. I know how the story of LCH 185 ends, but the men in the images do not.

Martin explains that, with the analysis that he's undertaken since Normandy, a lot of new information has been uncovered.

Firstly, it's now clear to all at the table that Target 16 has without a doubt been heavily salvaged. That had been hypothesised and expected, but now we know it indisputably. Before we dived down, the multibeam sonar results didn't look good, but the side-scan sonar seemed to show the target as a boat-shaped wreck. We didn't know what to expect. When the team actually got down to the target, it was immediately clear that we had a challenge on our hands. Target 16 is in a terrible state. The conclusive evidence that the wreck has been salvaged came not in terms of existing damage, but in what parts of the wreck are missing. There are no engines relating to the propulsion of the craft on the wreck, at all. These would have been some of the sturdiest, most robust parts of the vessel and would have likely survived the initial mine explosion. The fact that these are nowhere to be seen confirms that they have most likely been lifted from the wreck.

Knowing now that what we feared is true, in order to confirm that the wreck is in fact LCH 185, we're having to scratch and claw for any definitive proof. Key features needed to be found on the dive, identifiable parts of the craft that can be compared and confirmed with the blueprints, but various moments in the history of Target 16 continue to make that difficult. The first issue is that the Germans damaged the craft in 1944, causing a huge amount of destruction. It was then destroyed a second time by French salvagers after the war. Two levels of destruction, added to the brutal degradation of seven decades on the seabed, have created a mess.

Going into the dive expedition, we hoped to identify a typical, pointy-shaped bow with a door on either side for the long walkways used for soldiers to exit quickly. This would have shown it to be a Landing Craft Infantry (Large) from which Landing Craft Headquarters were converted. Within the context of the four landing craft that sank in the area, three of which had a flat drawbridge-style door to allow tanks and other vehicles to drive straight off the craft on to the sand, finding this type of bow would have been a smoking gun. Unfortunately, the bow area was nowhere to be seen. After that realisation, identifying Target 16 became even more difficult and confusing. Nonetheless, we were able to take enough measurements, photographs and photogrammetry to study over the last two months. Despite the wreck's poor condition, drips of information we were able to extract from the data were, to our amazement, pointing in the direction of the wreck being the one for which we are searching.

Firstly, Target 16's structure is consistent with that of a flat-bottomed vessel. From the start, this confirmed that we were surveying a landing craft of some sort. It almost seems trivial to celebrate identifying the wreck as a landing craft, but if the first two survey dives in France had identified the target as a completely different type of vessel, it would have been a disaster.

Next, we were able to confirm once and for all that the wreck was upside down. Patrick vividly remembers during the sinking that he struggled to stay afloat as the bow of 185 lifted out of the water in a way not too dissimilar to how *Titanic* had lifted up before sinking; the bow was sent upwards by the weight of the sinking stern. In Patrick's view, the craft then began to 'turn turtle', meaning that it twisted until falling forward deck first. Upon diving the wreck, it was evident that Target 16 rests upside down on the seabed. Although what remains is merely a shell of what the wreck once was, we could see from the position of the machine-gun housing sticking up from the sediment that the bottom of the wreck is facing the surface of the sea. Seeing the gun housing replays in my memory often. The image of a crab stuck beneath the rim and the way the metal cone grows out from the wreck like a tentacle. Had we been allowed to excavate, there's a possibility that we would have been confronted with an Oerlikon 20-mm anti-aircraft gun buried in the sand, revealed after seven decades of slumber.

I could see ladders through the shadows during my dive. In total, five were spotted, but no hatches were seen. It could have been through one of those hatches that the radio operator had tried to rescue those trapped below. Instead, we have concluded that the lack of any hatches, which should have bookended each ladder, isn't due to damage, but because they are beneath the sand. The wreck is definitely upside down, with ladders facing the wrong way, climbing to nowhere.

The stern remains in the correct area of the wreck. The possibilities of what lies beneath are both exciting and frustrating. Any number of intact pieces of equipment, even items relating to the crew, might be buried in the sand. As the wreck is a war grave, it will instead, hopefully, be left alone. We will simply have to wonder.

With the data pointing in the right direction, things are looking positive. It's easy to get carried away as the tally of things to confirm the wreck as 185 grows, but I don't let the excitement get to me. I've seen archaeological results change rapidly too many times before, but still I allow myself to wonder, if only for a moment, whether we've actually done it. It will be such an incredible outcome if we have. Despite the wreck being the wrong way up, we were still able to locate and identify a few pieces of equipment. It isn't much, but we all did our best to gather the most information possible in the short amount of time we had during the expedition. The mass of intertwined engines, generators and motors that Martin had undertaken photogrammetry on were arguably the most important artefacts to study. They appear to be part of a single machine and are therefore the most complex piece of equipment we managed to record. It was surmised at one point during the expedition that the contraption could have been used to move the two walkways that came out from 185's bow. Now, after further analysis, it seems more likely that the gear was once used in the raising and lowering of the craft's anchor. It's still a great outcome to have learned what the objects are and how they worked, but we were hoping that, in the absence of the bow itself, linking these artefacts to the bow could have played a decisive role in identifying the wreck.

With the knowledge that the gear was not used in the bow, we need to find out where else it could have been on the craft. In the weeks since the expedition, Alison has managed to make contact with the custodian of what may be the only remaining LCI(L) in the world. After she spoke to the owner in the US, he very kindly agreed to walk around the vessel in search of the equipment. Despite him taking multiple trips up and down LCI(L) 713, which is docked in Swan Lagoon, Oregon, Alison was surprised to hear that despite a thorough search, the man couldn't spot anything resembling the auxiliary equipment in the bow of the craft. It was a shock. With measurements adding up in some parts of the wreck, but not in others, doubts had crept in towards the end of the dive expedition; it was alarming at the time, but we hoped that the archaeological puzzle could be solved on the surface after we were home with more time to properly analyse the data. This still isn't the end. It can't be. There's no way to be sure that the craft in Oregon has the exact same equipment as LCH 185. Landing Craft Headquarters were, after all, heavily modified LCI(L) in the first place. The machinery could have been removed, perhaps taken out after the war by whoever owned LCI(L) 713 in the seven decades since it was built. I hold my breath and keep hoping, but that hope soon begins to crumble.

Towards the stern of the wreck, we recorded two rudders used for steering. These were located a short distance apart from each other. One rests on the stern itself, while the other still stands upright. During the dives it was noted that these rudders both have areas of reinforcement in the form of extra ridges used for strengthening. Comparing these to the plans of an LCH shows that the rudders we should have found would have no such extra ridges. The stern itself also appears to be inconsistent in measurement to that of an LCH. Its size looks more similar to that of an LCG(L) or an LCT Mk 3. Things are suddenly looking bad.

The large structural area towards the stern of the wreck, the first part of Target 16 that I had seen upon landing on the seabed, has been identified. Rather than the water tank of an LCH, which looked to be a perfect match on the blueprints and multibeam image, the wreckage is actually part of the framework of the craft. This structure is compartmentalised into a number of large squares. What we had seen on the sonar and recorded on the wreck were four sections of the framework, but my heart breaks to realise that there were originally six squares. Whether it was through the initial explosion, the salvage dealers or simply the passage of time, the outer compartment on each side has broken away and collapsed on to the seabed. The measurements of the four sections that remain are 26 feet across, which matches exactly with the plans of an LCT Mk 4 hull, the landing craft used as the base for Landing Craft Gun. To make matters worse, the gun we saw should have had 270 degrees of armoured protection around it, but actually had 360 degrees.

With this news, my tower of speculation collapses as even more evidence cements the conclusion. When combined, framework measurements, wrong numbers of structural compartments, reinforced rudders, incorrect degrees of armoured protection on the gun, and the wrong auxiliary equipment have fought my dreams up against the ropes. When it is found that the five ladders on the wreck wouldn't have been in that area of an LCH at all, I'm down for the count.

I've thrown everything I have into the search. I have tried so hard to identify 185, vaulting every hurdle along the way. In the early days of the search, there was a high chance that, owing to the condition of wrecks in Normandy, it would be impossible to identify any target either way. Now, we are a victim of our own thoroughness. To my utter, indescribable disappointment, Target 16 is not LCH 185. I have not found Patrick's wreck. I'm speechless. So much of my life and the lives of many others have been given to Target 16. I don't know what to do. We sit at the table in silence.

'It's one more rock we've looked under. It's one more thing to knock off that isn't LCH 185,' I say to Alison.

That is true. Confirming Target 16 as not being Patrick's craft is positively proving that an unknown wreck on the seabed is not 185. That makes any attempt to find it again in the future a slightly lesser challenge. Alison explains that there is a glimmer of hope in the form of another wreck not too far from the target. It has been labelled as a trawler by DRASSM, but on the multibeam sonar it looks more like a landing craft.

'What are you going to tell Patrick?' Alison asks with tears in her eyes.

'I have no idea, I really don't,' I say. My voice is shaking as I try to hold it together.

Standing up from my chair, I say my goodbyes to the dive team. They can't make it to France for the unveiling tomorrow. I don't know if I'll ever see them again. There's a chance that we'll get the team back together and have another go at finding 185, but I know deep down that the new target isn't Patrick's craft, and I can't bear another wild goose chase.

Outside the fort, I start to panic. All that is running through my head is what Patrick will think when he hears the news. We are unveiling the memorial in two days' time. It will crush him, I'm sure of it. I run through my choices. Do I need to tell him at all? Perhaps he can see out his final years unaware of the outcome either way. What are the chances of him reading the archaeological report that we have to write up and submit to the French government? It even crosses my mind, in a brief moment of desperation, to tell him that Target 16 is 185.

Looking down at my hand as I open my car door, I realise how tightly I'm holding the papers from the meeting. It would be a lie to say that I'm not angry. At what exactly, I'm not sure, but a cloud is starting to build over me. I had an inkling on the dive trip that the target wasn't right. Measurements not being completely accurate could have meant any number of things, only one of which was that we were looking at the wrong wreck, but we all silently felt the same way as a few more strange measurements began to come up from the seabed. We kept hoping for the best. We had to, for Patrick and for the men that went down with 185, but for ourselves as well. We didn't want to let Patrick down. We wanted to be able to give him the good news that he dreamed of. Finding out that I can't do that hurts me deeply.

The drive back to the hotel drags. It is dark now and the bright lights of the seafront bounce on the sea. My stomach dances with the disappointment as my mind races between such a vast array of thoughts that I can't pin down any single one. It doesn't feel like the meeting actually took place. The outcome doesn't seem real. I don't want it to be true. So much of my energy has been put into identifying the wreck as LCH 185. I enlisted the help of others, who believed that Target 16 was the right wreck to survey. None of us, perhaps foolishly, has ever really discussed a plan in case the wreck didn't turn out to be what we were looking for.

That night, I get no sleep at all, wrestling with the moral dilemma I face. What do I do now? What happens to the search? I struggle to work out how I've ended up taking an old man, a veteran of a war fought over seventy years ago, and building up his hopes. Now, the job falls on me to let him down.

Ideas come and go, normally staying for just a few seconds. Do I leave Patrick on a high and not tell him either way? Do I tell a lie and let him think that the wreck is his? Or do I tell him the truth and risk breaking his heart? Patrick is made of stern stuff, there's no doubt about that. To have survived what he has survived, a person has to be. The news will still cause him a lot of pain. Patrick has been along for the ride the whole way. He has been on the search with me. We never told him Target 16 was the right wreck, but even back when I first started it was clear that he was gaining closure with each passing day. From seeing me return from the seabed, being taken out to the target to place a wreath and to receiving the letter from Jack, Patrick has been putting his historic hurt to bed. Confirming the target as LCH 185 would have been the final bow.

As I rub my sleepless red eyes in the bathroom mirror, pack my suitcase and head for the ferry port, I hope that his inner peace isn't about to be undone.

Chapter Fourteen

5 June 2018

I've arrived in Normandy the day before we are set to unveil the memorial. It's the week of the D-Day commemorations. It was here, during this time, that it all began for Patrick and me two years ago. He's over here with another charity, travelling around Normandy in a coach filled with veterans. They are the guests of honour wherever the wheels stop and each time I check in with him he seems to be having an amazing time. The results of the dive expedition have been eating me up, knowing that I need to break the news to the man to whom it means the most. I'm still unsure how to approach it. Patrick could be told in Lion-sur-Mer tomorrow. Maybe the celebrations will water down the bad news. I could tell him before we unveil the memorial, maybe after, but the unveiling is going to be a huge moment. One of the biggest, most important days of Patrick's long life. For over seventy years he kept the story of LCH 185 to himself. Now the memorial is a chance for all of that inner hurt to be set free and for the story of that day to be handed over to the world. To tell him the news, to potentially devastate him during that moment, would be nothing short of cruel. Instead, I'm thinking of waiting a few weeks, perhaps even a few months. When all the excitement has died down, I'll find a quiet moment to let my friend know the truth. I'm emotionally drained from everything that has happened, and so is Patrick. We both need a rest.

The atmosphere during the commemorations is something that needs to be felt to be understood. The events are equal parts happy celebration, reflective commemoration and sombre remembrance. At night behind the closed doors of old French bars, the vibe can quickly turn to that of a party. It has been an extremely stressful period since I began the search for 185, but I try as much as is possible to appreciate the few events I have time for, letting go for a couple of hours to enjoy the feeling in the air.

That evening, Dominique kindly invites Patrick and me to his house for dinner. Collecting him from his hotel after a busy day of events, I load Patrick's wheelchair on to the back seat and head along the coastline. It's a beautifully warm evening as the sun sets. This is the beginning of Patrick's big moment. We're both excited. The car journey is filled with laughter from start to finish. There's always a particular feel to seaside towns, no matter where in the world they are. I roll down my window and take it all in. The sea air is freeing. I've never not felt content when breathing it in.

We pull up at Dominique's house. It is typically French and located just metres from the beach. Driving through the gates, it feels strange to be there. At one point, it was only a dream to somehow get in touch with the mayor in order to plead my case about the memorial. Now, here I am a year later pulling into his driveway for dinner.

Patrick grabs his walking stick and hobbles forwards. I help him climb the wooden steps towards the front door. We're greeted with kisses from both Dominique and his wife Hélène. Patrick, who is prone to forget the limits of his age without a moment's notice, excitedly walks off into the house. He is thrilled to be here as a guest in the mayor's private home. Neither of us has ever been here before and have no way of knowing that there are two levels to the living room. The space between the dining table and the main living area is joined by two small steps.

It happens in slow motion. I can't believe what I'm witnessing. I watch helplessly as Patrick topples forward down the steps, hitting the hard floor with a thud. In a ball on the ground, he rocks on his side, groaning in pain. It's one of the worst things I have ever seen. From where I'm standing, it looks like he is either dead or dying.

I probably shouldn't move him, but quickly crossing the room, I use all my strength to lift him up. Unable to help himself, Patrick has become a dead weight. I struggle for a few seconds before eventually managing to drag him up and into a chair. Dominique looks horrified. I'm stunned. Patrick is gripping his shoulder and the side of his stomach. The mayor and I kneel by his side, repeatedly asking if he's OK. Patrick sits back and tries to relax. After ten minutes, he starts to come back to his usual sprightly self.

'Do you want to go to hospital?' I ask.

Patrick refuses, and refuses again each time I ask for the rest of the evening. Eventually he seems to recover and walks slowly across the room to take a seat at the dinner table. There is no doubt he is in pain, but he hides it well. It was no one's fault that the fall happened, but everyone who witnessed it feels excruciatingly bad about what occurred. Patrick is so full of life. He is a nineteen-year-old in a ninety-three-year-old's body. That's the case for almost all of the veterans I have ever met. They still want to be active and energetic, to run and dance and move with youthful enthusiasm, but their bodies stop them as our bodies will stop us all in the end. To see that inherent want to be young in such elderly men has taught me to appreciate each day that I can move freely. The fall is a reminder, not just to me but to Patrick himself, that he is frail and needs looking after. He has become such a part of the search that it's sometimes easy to forget that he is so old.

We have a commando veteran and his son joining us for dinner. It doesn't take long for us to get chatting like familiar friends. Looking at Patrick across the table, I picture having to unveil the memorial on my own with the guest of honour lying in a hospital bed somewhere, but luckily he seems to me to be his normal self. It is an enormous relief. Dominique and Hélène have pulled out all the stops for dinner. They are showing us French hospitality at its finest. We drink enough wine to float a landing craft and eat more cheese than I have ever seen in my life. It's an honour to be here.

Janette, a friend of Dominique, is at the table to translate our conversations. I'm hit with guilt watching this lady in her eighties working overtime to translate everything, but she doesn't seem to mind. Janette has lived a fascinating life. Having worked as a French teacher, she married a lecturer at Oxford and lived in England for decades. We bond over our shared recollections of my home country. After the meal, I drop Patrick off at the hotel before driving Janette back to her home. At the door, she invites me in for a drink. Inside, I ask about the war.

'Do you remember D-Day?'

'No, I wasn't here then. I lived in a small village in the middle of nowhere. It was so small that when the Allies came through, they didn't even bother to liberate it! We had all rushed to paint "welcome our liberators" across our bedsheets and hung them from the windows, but no one ever came,' she says, laughing at the memory of her childhood disappointment, although there is still a sadness in her eyes as she tells the story.

My hotel for the trip is an attic room in someone's house. It's cramped and dusty, but it's at least genuine, and it almost feels like a German soldier could stomp up the stairs and knock on the door at any second. The next morning, I get dressed for the memorial unveiling. As I put on the same suit blazer that I wore both when I graduated from university and again when I first stepped foot in the mayor's office, I have no clue whether or not the memorial physically exists. Dominique has been left with the plaque and the hand-drawn design, but that was the last I heard. Each time I asked about the situation at dinner the night before, Dominique just smiled and said in his thick accent that 'all is good', but for all I know, all may not be good.

On the drive to Arromanches to pick up Patrick, I can't stop smiling to myself. This is exactly what I've worked towards for twelve months, and the day, to my astonishment, has finally arrived. Arromanches is rammed with people. It's impossible to get my car anywhere near the pub where Patrick is having lunch. I have to argue with traffic wardens and local security, who don't believe that I'm actually picking up a veteran. Eventually I find Patrick and lead him to the car, stopping repeatedly on the way to allow a chance for him to pose for photographs and sign autographs. He's used to this by now and is always keen to please his fans.

On the drive to Lion-sur-Mer, we're halted by heavy traffic in each seaside town we pass through. The delays allow me an unwanted chance to sit and dwell on how it feels to know the truth about Target 16, but not to have told Patrick. It's troubling to keep something so huge from my friend, but as I look to his old, peaceful face, I can see how nervous he is to be heading towards an event dedicated solely to the sacrifice he and the crew of 185 once made. Now definitely isn't the time, but it still hurts not to tell him. I think about it each and every time Patrick and I meet eyes.

Arriving at Lion-sur-Mer, Patrick is clearly sore from last night's fall. He's having to use a wheelchair to move long distances, and hunches slightly over when standing. Patrick is a proud man and unhappy about being seen as frail on his big day, but such is the unfortunate reality of being an elderly war veteran. It's 6 June, but by the sea the air bites hard. The two of us head to the town hall to relax and get warm. As I cross the road, I spot a small group of people gathering around a classic sports car. I know exactly who they are, because I invited them. Patrick can't find out now, not here in the road, and while it's hard not to run over and introduce myself straightaway, I fight the urge. Once Patrick is with Dominique and happy in the company of the town hall staff, I jog back through the traffic to introduce myself.

'It's so amazing to meet you! Honestly, thank you so, so much for coming.'

The group arrived this morning from England, some in the sports car, others on motorbikes. They are all smartly dressed and ready to attend the unveiling. It's hard to believe it, but standing in front of me is the family of Jack Barringer. After we had made contact, the Barringers asked me to keep them up to date with the unveiling. I tried my best, but things were moving so slowly and then so rapidly that it was hard to keep everyone in the loop. For a long time, I had no idea when, or even if, the unveiling would occur, which meant that when I told the family that the unveiling would definitely be on 6 June, they unfortunately had no more than a week to book the trip. Despite that, here they are under the Normandy sky, excitedly waiting to meet Patrick.

I've hastily created fifty copies of an order of service that I printed off in my living room in England. While putting on my brown suit shoes, standing by the back of my car, I give the stack of papers to my mum and ask her to hand them out to whoever she can find that might be coming to the unveiling. As she disappears around the corner towards the promenade, I picture her finding so few attendees that she ends up having to give the order of services out to random passersby, roping in anyone she can find to attend the unveiling. There's still much to be done and I'm wanted in all directions, but the priority for me right now is for Patrick and the Barringer family to meet. I find the man of the hour in the main room of the town hall, regaling the staff with war stories. Walking in, I kneel by his side.

'Hi, Pat. I've had to keep this from you for a while now, but I've got some people you might like to meet. I'll bring them in.'

First through the door is Jeff Barringer and his wife Judy. Jeff is the son of Les Barringer, Jack's brother, the man who had written to Patrick asking for news of Jack's death. Les had another son named Dave, who plans to meet Patrick later alongside another of Jack's nephews, Timothy. Behind Jeff and Judy walk two men, both named John, father and son.

'This is Jack Barringer's family.' I announce.

'Is it?!' Patrick says. He is in shock.

'You remember Les Barringer? I'm his son,' Jeff says.

'Are you?!' Patrick replies.

'Yes, and I'm very pleased to meet you.'

Everyone is beaming. I'm witnessing something wonderful, moving a step back to take the moment in from afar. This isn't mine to share.

'John was Jack's brother,' Jeff says, pointing to the older man at the back.

'Jack's . . . brother?' Patrick replies.

John is wearing a similar naval blazer and tie to Patrick. He is a fourth brother of Jack Barringer, a step-brother, who I had no idea existed. John introduces himself by explaining that, like his brothers Jack and George, he too had joined the navy and, like Patrick, he had served on submarines.

'What did you serve on?' Patrick asks.

'*Tiptoe*,' John says.

'I remember *Tiptoe!*'

I watch on as two old submariners banter about their old boats. Patrick turns to Judy and asks if they have been introduced yet.

'I'm Judy, Jeff's wife.'

'Always an eye for the ladies,' Jeff says with a laugh.

'Well, this is a pleasant surprise,' Patrick says, turning to face John once again.

'Jack's . . . brother?'

Patrick's words trail off with an unmistakable weakening. It's part sadness, part joy at finally meeting Jack Barringer's family. Patrick was also unaware that there were four brothers, one of whom is still alive. Now the two sailors are face to face. The entire conversation is filled with the unspoken understanding that Jack had died on the day that Patrick had lived.

'I always went to Ranville. I always laid something on Jack's grave,' Patrick explains. Each word is said matter-of-factly and followed by a pause, making sure that the family understand that he never forgot about their relative. Patrick seems to be trying to justify his life for the past seven decades.

'So, how old were you at the time?' Judy asks.

'Nineteen,' Patrick says without hesitation.

'Wow. So young,' Judy replies.

'Green as they come. I tell you what, I grew up very quickly . . .'

Patrick's words are interrupted by a light laughter in the room. It was appropriate because Patrick had said it jovially, but he soon interrupts.

'. . . very quickly.'

Patrick's tone goes cold as his eyes fill with tears. We all nod our heads in agreement. He tells the story of the lifebelt. There is a huge weight in the air. Everyone in the room is choking up. I've heard this story countless times before but, with the Barringer family here to listen, it hits me with a fresh poignancy. It feels like Patrick has been waiting since the sinking to tell Jack's family about what really took place that day. As my friend speaks, I can see in the eyes of the Barringer family that they understand why it happened that way; why Patrick is sitting here, while Jack is buried at Ranville.

Speaking for the first time since introducing everyone, I reach into my pocket to pass Patrick a copy of the letter that Les had written to him in 1944. Patrick doesn't know, because the family attending the unveiling was a secret, that I've brought a copy for him to give to the Barringers. They have never seen it and don't know that it exists. For Jeff, the letter was written by his father in a desperate attempt to discover that his uncle would turn up alive. For John, the old submariner, it is a letter written by one brother about another.

'You wanted to give the family this, Patrick,' I say.

He had, but never thought he would get the chance. 'Ah yes,' he says.

Patrick is pleased to be given the opportunity to pass the letter to Jack's relatives. As he does, he explains how hard it had been to reply to all those years ago. As the yellowed paper is passed from Patrick to Jeff, a moment in history closes as the homecoming of a letter that had left Les's grip and followed Patrick around the world finally takes place. After sitting in a drawer for seven decades, it now finally returns to Les's children.

We say our goodbyes, for now at least, because Patrick and I have a memorial to unveil.

Together we wait a short while outside the town hall. We are joined by Dominique, a bagpipe player from the British Army and an incredible soprano named Emma Brown.

Dominique, Emma and the bagpipe player circle around Patrick to ask if he's ready. He nods silently and gives a thumbs up. The bagpiper fiercely tucks the tartan sack beneath his arm, slowly begins to squeeze out a drone and starts to march determinedly ahead. There is no turning back now. Our small procession, cobbled together in the days leading up to the event, crosses the car park towards the beach. The journey is tense. Aside from the design for the plaque, Patrick knows nothing about the memorial. From our brief conversations that morning, it's clear that he thinks that the monument is simply something small being mounted on a wall or the side of a building. After a lifetime of assuming that people aren't interested in his story, Patrick isn't expecting much.

I have no idea what to expect either, having entrusted Dominique with making sure there is an actual memorial to unveil. There is also the event itself. The many emails between the mayor and I put the construction of the memorial rightly at the forefront, but the physical structure is just one part. What if no one is here to witness the unveiling? With just Dominique, Patrick and me in attendance, it would still matter, but Patrick and the story of 185 deserve an audience. I've ended most of my chats with Dominique with the tongue-in-cheek reminder to 'Please invite people!'

Moving across the car park, I'm worried, imagining an empty event and an underwhelming memorial. As we get closer, the tension in the air is replaced with the low rumble of an unmistakable noise. I can hear a gentle but constant chatter. People are actually here. As we reach the grandiose houses on the seafront that obscure our view of the sea, the noise of attendees grows louder. We turn the corner to where the memorial should be. I come face to face with a crowd larger than I ever could have dreamed of. At the perimeter, the local police open a path through the bustling group of people to let us through. It turns out that there are so many people that my mum almost immediately ran out of copies of the order of service.

I push Patrick in his wheelchair, following the touching sounds of a bagpipe. I veer my eyes through the mass of people and spot the Barringer family looking smart in their suits and dresses. There are three other D-Day veterans in attendance with their families. Captain Philippe and the lifeboat crew are here, standing in a row like proud statues, dressed in the same orange outfits they had worn on the boat. Stephen Fisher, who helped me unravel the story of Patrick's craft, has cycled over on the ferry to be here. Among those I know, there are countless faces that I don't. Some have come from as far as the US to attend. I see a group of modern British soldiers standing to attention and members of a French veterans' association ready to raise their flags during the ceremony. Local schoolchildren, who have been allowed out of lessons to attend the unveiling, are sitting peacefully. This little patch of grass given to us by Dominique is rammed, overflowing on to the streets and sands of Lion-sur-Mer.

The bagpipe's song drifts along to announce the beginning of the event. We struggle through the crowd before reaching a small clearing. Wheeling Patrick into position, Dominique and I shuffle along towards a microphone stand. I stop to compose myself, then look forwards. There, in front of the choppy waves of the English Channel, is the memorial draped in a red cloth. The wind is picking up. Two smooth, fist-sized pebbles from the beach are keeping the fabric pinned down to prevent a premature reveal.

Dominique has managed to pull everything together in an extremely limited amount of time. He has found a local stonemason who kindly donated a beautiful block of granite about a metre high and a metre across. In the excitement of the unveiling, I don't meet the mason, who also concreted the memorial permanently into the ground, but without him and without the mayor, there would not be a monument to 185 in France. While still dressed in a suit, Dominique personally attached the plaque to the granite this morning. Not for attention, not for praise or fanfare, but because he had promised to get it done.

With a shawl in the colours of the French flag draped over his torso, Dominique begins his speech. First introducing the event, he then tells the story of the craft. Speaking with gentle authority, the mayor explains that the town is honoured to be the setting for the memorial. He speaks in French, but I understand enough to follow. I'm touched when I hear my name spoken, followed by 'archéologue'. My turn to speak seems to arrive in no time at all. It's not often that I get nervous in front of crowds, but I know I have one chance to get this right, and I'm feeling the pressure. There's a gentle tap on my shoulder before I step up to the microphone. Turning around, I see my mum. She gives a tiny wave, smiles with pride, and whispers, 'Good luck, John.'

'Monsieur le maire, my thanks to you for your moving words and for hosting this special event today,' I begin.

My French accent hasn't improved at all since meeting the mayor for the first time, but the words I've carefully chosen are the best I can give. Pausing for a moment, I pull the microphone closer to my mouth to stop my voice disappearing on the wind. I begin to tell the stories of the men whose families I've found. I speak of the lives they lived before the sinking and the lives they had planned to live if they hadn't died that day. As I speak their names, I look to the sea and wonder if they can hear.

My words are breaking up. It's so hard not to cry as I share the personal stories of those that drowned. It feels like these men are being given a brief chance to live again, a moment to call out from the past, if only in the minds of those that have turned out to remember them. As I continue to speak, I read a quote from Jack's letter home. Every few words are followed by a pause to compose myself. My eyes are filled with tears. I almost don't make it through.

'Don't you worry. I'm going grey, no sleep, I haven't taken my clothes off since we started or had a shave. What a sight. Well, Les pal, cheerio for now. Goodnight and God bless.'

'Fifteen days later,' I say, 'these men would lose their lives when LCH 185 went to the bottom of the English Channel. The list of casualties totals thirty-five, but it is likely higher. Just a handful, less than ten, survived that day and now, seventy-four years later, only one remains: my friend Patrick Thomas.'

Looking down towards Patrick, I can't speak. If I do, I'll lose my composure. Those two words get me: 'my friend'. He is my friend. It's an unlikely friendship, but it is a friendship, and I feel lucky to have it in my life. It won't be there forever, perhaps not even much longer, but right now Patrick and I are standing together as friends. I take a deep breath and carry on.

'We came together two years ago by chance, when we were both on the same trip back to Normandy. I was left off the accommodation list and he had a spare bedroom. I knocked on the door and he let me in. He told me his harrowing story and I couldn't shake the thought that it was so close to being lost to history. How could something so poignant be so forgotten? One year ago today, I told Patrick that after everything he went through back then, all the friends he lost and all the suffering those men endured, LCH 185 deserved to have a permanent memorial. Today, thanks to the belief of Mayor Dominique, the beautiful town of Lion-sur-Mer and Patrick himself, we have exactly that.'

My final words are said with vigour, but break up through tears. It is hard, but I'm determined to get out what I need to say.

'Of all the men that lost their lives that day, only four were ever given a burial. The rest were lost to the sea. Now with this memorial, the crew of LCH 185 will be remembered together . . . forever. And I am proud beyond words to stand here . . . with Patrick . . . to help unveil it.'

The instant my speech is finished, I turn my head away from the microphone, hide my face from the crowd and sob. The service isn't finished and I can't stay like this for long. I pull myself together and pass the microphone down to Patrick in his wheelchair.

'Monsieur le maire, my grateful thanks for your help in providing and locating the plinth for the memorial dedicated to those lost on LCH 185 on 25 June 1944. I was fortunate to have survived. One-eight-five was my home, and my shipmates my family. I am proud and honoured to unveil the monument commemorating the tragic loss of 185 and all who lost their lives aboard her. My grateful thanks to all who are here to witness the dedication. My shipmates will be remembered for all time by the memorial.'

Patrick unfolds the same piece of paper that he has carried with him throughout the search. By now, it is barely held together as one piece. He starts to read his favourite poem as groups of strangers huddle together to share one of the few orders of service. It is completely silent but for the waves a few feet away. The words read out by an old sailor to commemorate his lost comrades stun everyone. I hear gasps through the crowd. People are moved to tears. Those who can't speak English read along to the French version. The beauty of the translation is clear from the gentle sighs of admiration.

Emma Brown steps up to sing both the French and British national anthems. I don't have the words to the French anthem in front of me, but try my best to mouth along. The service has been put together in haste. There is no blueprint or rulebook to how a memorial unveiling should go. The order of service is just something I compiled in the days leading up to the event. As a result Dominique, Patrick and I are feeling our way through. The three of us stand in a row and then slowly step forward in unison towards the red cloth. Patrick is obviously hurting from the fall but determined to do his part with dignity and honour. His arm gripped in my left hand, we steadily walk to the memorial. Attached at the back, reaching high into the blue sky, are the French and British flags waving in the wind.

We pause for a moment. My heart races with nerves and excitement. Patrick is sombre as he moves to grab a corner of the red cloth. With what little strength he has left, Patrick pulls at it. The fabric falls away to reveal the memorial beneath. Dominique steers his eyes down to see Patrick's reaction, but there is none. He is silent, eyes glued straight ahead, squinting to read the inscription written in both French and English:

To the memory of those who perished aboard
H.M.L.C.H. 185
Struck by an acoustic mine on 25th June 1944.
Shipmates never to be forgotten.
Unveiled June 2018 by Telegraphist Patrick Thomas, a
survivor of the sinking.
There are no roses on a sailor's grave, nor wreaths upon
the storm tossed waves.
No heartbroken words carved in stone, just shipmates
lying there alone.
The only tributes are the seagulls' sweeps, and the
teardrops when a loved one weeps.

Tears once again gather in the corners of my eyes. Patrick attempts to hide his emotion. He isn't beaming with pride, but instead stands as stern-faced and firmly upright as is possible with the pain. This is not an old man that wants to be pitied. Patrick is a strong sailor doing his solemn duty by representing his fallen comrades seven decades since they left the earth. He wants to make them proud.

Emma begins to sing the hymn 'Eternal Father, Strong to Save'. The words, sang in soprano, wash over the crowd. 'O Christ/Whose voice the waters heard/and hushed their raging at thy word/Who walked on the foaming deep and calm amidst its rage didst sleep/ Oh, hear us when we cry to thee/For those in peril on the sea.' The three of us stare down at the memorial. It is beautiful; a simple and elegant tribute. I find it almost impossible to believe that the monument is right here in front of me.

We arrive back at the microphone where, with the help of his grandson Paul, Patrick once again walks back to the memorial to place a wreath. I then walk up to place my own. Earlier today, I wrote a short message to the crew of LCH 185. My mind was blank as I stared at the piece of card, until suddenly exactly what I needed to say came to me like a bolt of lightning.

I hope today has done you proud.

Behind the wreath I place photographs of each man I've managed to find. Their families aren't here to witness the event, but as with the expedition's control room, the men of 185 are watching over us. Dominique moves forward to place the town's stunning wreath of real flowers. Draped around the purple and white roses is a ribbon with 'Lion-sur-Mer' written in gold lettering over the French flag.

With that, our moment is over. It's now time for anyone in the crowd who wishes to pay their respects to do so. Emma starts to sing 'Amazing Grace' as one by one people step forward. Some are unknown to us, simply wishing to lay a poppy or a flower. I'm amazed to see strangers moved by the story. The Barringer family stand up and stroll proudly to the memorial. I watch with pride as John, Jack Barringer's brother, places a wreath. I never could have imagined that Jack's actual brother would be here. It means the world to Patrick and me. With a lump in my throat, I watch as John bends down to place his tribute. The elderly submariner rises up, straightens out his back, faces the sea, and gives a perfect salute. With that, the unveiling is over. The bagpiper fires back into action with a deep drone as we parade back out. We pass John in the crowd, who gives Patrick a thumbs up and a wink.

'Aye-aye, Captain!' Patrick calls up from his wheelchair.

Sailors never die, I think to myself, *they just get older.*

Dominique leads Patrick and the crowd towards the other memorials in the town. It's the annual tradition in Lion-sur-Mer to pay respects at each one. As we follow, I'm pulled aside by a series of reporters, camera crews and members of the public wanting to ask about Patrick's story. By the time I'm done, I've lost the congregation, and decide to stay back. It's quiet by the memorial. The flags still wave proudly as I take a seat on the bench nearby. Sitting alone, taking in everything that has just taken place and admiring what we have just unveiled, I watch as each passerby stops to read the inscription. Cyclists, runners, walkers and skateboarders all halt what they are doing respectfully to tread across the grass and read the words that Patrick and I chose so carefully. This memorial isn't just about the unveiling. It is about the lasting legacy and the remembrance by those who will pass by in their daily lives. The story of 185 will never be forgotten now. It has become a living part of the French landscape.

Patrick eventually returns. We stand together silently to read the inscription. Looking out towards the water, he asks me a question.

'It was that way, was it?' he says, pointing firmly out to sea towards where he thinks Targets 16 is.

'You're just off, slightly,' I say, grabbing Patrick's hand and manoeuvring it to the right.

'Just off that way?' he asks.

I stop his arm sharply.

'There.'

As we look to where the expedition took place, I know that I still have to tell Patrick the outcome of the survey. I can't do it now. The idea had seemed wrong before the unveiling had occurred. Now, as he basks in the glory of a moment a lifetime in the making, it seems even more of a certainty that I should wait. It will be difficult, and I have no idea what the right words will be, but I'm hoping that they will come in time. Despite the weight hanging over my shoulders, I try to enjoy the moment. This won't last forever, and neither will the time we have together.

As the sky turns to orange and the white-tipped waves of the sea draw in, for a short moment in a long life, Patrick is at peace with the events of 25 June 1944.

Chapter Fifteen

7 June 2018

After the unveiling, I catch the overnight ferry home. The ship is filled with snoring British soldiers sleeping on every chair and table on board. I manage to find a spot of floor in the corridor, where I lie for the next few hours with my eyes wide open. Back in England, I return to my day job the very next day. As quickly as the adventure had begun, it was over, and standing in the rain, knee-deep in mud, it's hard to process everything that I've experienced. The sense of deflation and the crash back to normality that came with the conclusion of the project are tough. The unveiling was an amazing moment, but it soon felt like it never happened at all. The memorial is a body of water away. It's in another country entirely. All I can do is stand in a field, close my eyes, and try to remember that, yes, that piece of granite is still being seen each day.

The results of the expedition weigh me down for months. It's impossible not to be disappointed by the outcome. I made a promise and came up short. That hurts. The search was for Patrick, of course, but it was for me as well. I was searching for LCH 185, but also searching for something else entirely. I'm still not sure what I was looking for. It's easy to daydream about the future, to hope that one significant moment in time will allow life finally to make sense, as if the future begins on a day when everything falls into place. I had no idea as I donned my drysuit in France that I was hoping to find that clarity on Target 16. I hoped that by grabbing on to that wreck all of my questions would be answered but, instead, as I sat in the back of the dinghy soaring back towards Patrick on the shore, I felt no different. I felt happy, I felt proud, but I didn't feel anything new. There was no great epiphany on the seabed. No new sense of direction. I found no hidden meaning within the rusting metal, not even the faint glimpse of a new road to head down. When Target 16 turned out not to be 185 at all, that realisation turned into something much bleaker.

In the weeks and months that follow the unveiling, I've been subconsciously set on running myself into the ground. It had all been so much to carry on my shoulders. The extreme contrasts of emotions I've been through have taken their toll. Elation felt at getting permission for the memorial, then hideous sadness at the edge of the sea as I watched Patrick burst into tears. I have reached new levels of pride having found Jack Barringer's family, followed by fresh lows of devastation at the identity of Target 16.

Britain has been enjoying a tremendous heatwave and the England football team are doing uncharacteristically well in the Euros. With the project wrapped, I take it upon myself to live the normal existence of someone my age. I enjoy time with friends, make the most of the heat in pub gardens and, in Patrick's words, drink buckets rather than pints. I'm trying to forget, trying to leave behind the year that came before. I don't want to think about death any more. I don't want to think about teenagers drowning. I don't want to see the image of Patrick in tears by the water or think about having to comfort him by the side of his best friend's grave. I can't deal with it like I could in the moment.

I want desperately to let it all go but, no matter how much I try, it never disappears.

People often ask me about the search, but I never want to talk about it. Patrick still doesn't know the outcome. How can I tell other people if I haven't told him? Instead, I always change the subject.

'Ah,' I say, looking off into the distance. 'You don't want to hear about that.'

I feel tired in every single way a person can feel tired. The burnout has got on top of me and pushed me down into the earth. After a particularly challenging time, I quit my job and stop replying to emails relating to the search. The pressure has reached a tipping point. I spend months trying to get myself back on track, taking long walks in the fields near my house for hours on end. Sometimes I try to teach myself to paint. I'm never any good, but on one occasion I paint the memorial in front of the sea. Artistically it is poor, but it feels like a small step. Every once in a while, I start to plan a new project or brainstorm ways to continue the search for 185, but each time I stop after a few hours. The pain of it all always comes back. Instead, I put away my notebooks and slam my laptop shut.

My parents take me to Southwold. It isn't far from where I live, but I've never been before. The town was where George Orwell went after he had burnt out in the Spanish Civil War. It's the quiet that I need, but staring out at the sea is just another reminder of the search. Each night, I toss and turn for hours, trying to forget about 185 while simultaneously worrying about how Patrick will react to being told the results. It will be devastating if he dies of old age while I'm trying to get myself back to a mental state strong enough to let him know about Target 16. I wouldn't be able to live with myself if that happened, but I'm just not ready.

* * *

By the time October comes around, I'm still in a bad place, but there isn't much choice. I have to tell Patrick as soon as I feel even slightly up to doing so. The day I've chosen isn't because I'm ready – I'm not at all – but because enough time has passed since the unveiling. Patrick has revelled in the excitement of the event and soaked up the admiration that came with having the story of his landing craft told to the public, but now things are quiet again. He is back to being a civilian living by the sea in Eastbourne. It feels like a now or never situation. Veterans can slip away at any second. He might live for another ten years, but he might live less than a week. No one knows. I have to tell him.

Before making the drive down, I walk to the shed in my dad's garden. The wooden walls have shrunk from the summer heat and I can peer inside through the gap. Everything is just as I left it. Pulling open the creaking doors, I see, still pinned to the wall, the map on which I circled an area where I thought the wreck could be. The paper is almost completely ruined from leaks in the shed. One by one, I remove the rusting pins from each corner to hold the map in my hand. Looking down at the circle, I feel different. So much has changed in that time. I've changed. The contrast between being full of optimism and hope at the start of the search to how I feel now is remarkable. It's upsetting to not be that person any more. I don't think I'll ever be that person again. I think anyone who had been on that journey would be forever changed by it.

I run over what I'll say in my head for the entirety of the four-hour drive to Patrick's house. The remarkable thing about our friendship has always been the way that our conversations can transcend the generation gap. We speak like mates, like he's still that nineteen-year-old that took part in D-Day. I don't think that telling Patrick the results of the expedition should seem like a presentation of archaeological data. I'm hoping we'll chat it out as friends, but there's still no guarantee he won't be distraught.

While I don't yet know what Patrick's feelings will be, I've now reached a point of personal understanding. The hideous disappointment that hit me upon discovering the wreck's identity has lessened. Target 16 isn't LCH 185, but it *is* a Second World War landing craft. I set out to discover Patrick's shipwreck; that hasn't worked out as planned, but it was always going to be a complete stab in the dark. Like finding a needle in a haystack full of needles, as I said from day one, but I have, with the help of many others, managed to locate and potentially identify a different landing craft.

Finding 185 was always going to be incredibly difficult. The Germans were sinking vessels in the English Channel with the casualness of a game of battleships. The seabed off Normandy is now a vast scrapyard of historically important, but mostly mysterious, sonar targets. Some are identifiable, but most are not. The damage inflicted on Target 16 by the enemy was crippling, and the beastly attack of corrosion on steel only added to the devastation. The post-war destruction by the French authorities of hazardous wrecks furthered the wreck's descent towards nothingness.

The vast majority of sonar targets that relate to D-Day are destroyed, if not beyond recognition, then at least to a point that requires intense and intricate study. I always knew that would be the case, but having now dived on a wreck in the English Channel, I can say first hand that the state of what is down there is nothing short of heart-breaking. There's hardly anything left. Before the expedition, I half expected, and perhaps even hoped, that we simply wouldn't be able to identify Target 16 one way or another. Maybe that would have been better for Patrick. I imagined that we'd locate a target that seemed very likely to be 185, dive on it, lay a wreath on the water above, unveil a memorial and close the trauma that had haunted Patrick his entire life. When I saw the wreck, it seemed even less likely that we could identify it as 185, because Target 16 didn't look like much at all.

Yet the results of the expedition were more conclusive than we ever hoped for. Our initial analysis of the data had been done in haste in France. The days on the seabed had been shrunk down to an absolute minimum. Since the trip, there had been much more time to thoroughly research our findings and to further explore the archives. After discovering that Target 16 was not 185, I could have left it at that. It wasn't Patrick's craft, so what else did we really need to know? Curiosity about what we had found became the new driving force of the project in the months after the dive trip, on the rare occasions I could face the subject. While the story of Patrick's craft had reached an unknown crossroads, the dive team and I now had a chance to wrap up another untold story. Target 16 is a landing craft. It is a ship. It has a story. Most importantly, it had people living and potentially dying on board. Simply to say, 'Well, it wasn't Patrick's wreck. Let's move on,' would be to not just miss an opportunity, but to miss the point. Knowing that Target 16 was most likely an LCG(L), we went on to scour more sinking reports. After a while, it looked like one LCG(L) stood out as a candidate above the rest.

Of the three LCG(L) known to have sunk in the area, 1062 was reported to have gone down closest to where Target 16 was later located. We will likely never truly know the identity of the wreck, and although I have learned that the combination of sonar targets and historical records is prone to inaccuracy, it's reasonable at least to put 1062 to the top of the list of likely craft.

Unlike Patrick and his crew, 1062 was not at Sword Beach on D-Day. The vessel had instead been used at the more westerly Juno

Beach as part of the Canadian assault. Rather than leaving from Portsmouth, the craft had left from Southampton, destined to land at a stretch of sand found on either side of the town of Courseulles-sur-Mer. It headed across the English Channel as part of the second wave of the initial attack, where the vessel's role was to provide support for the 7th Canadian Infantry Brigade with its two 4.7-inch guns, while assisting the launch of Duplex Drive tanks into the water. If the floating tanks were fired upon, 1062 would then be expected to target the gun batteries. If they launched without any enemy action, the landing craft would be tasked with firing upon the German beach defences. LCG(L) 1062 did this at the Nan Green section of Juno Beach, close to the middle of the area of attack. Like 185, the craft completed its D-Day orders without suffering any damage, successfully playing a role in a triumphant moment for the young country of Canada.

After the landings were over, 1062 was sent to join the Trout Line, where it remained for a number of weeks until, on 31 July 1944, the craft was sent to the seabed. Like LCH 185, HMS *Swift* and MV *Derrycunihy*, 1062 had hit an acoustic mine at around 06:30, which tore a huge hole in its stern. A nearby vessel attempted to tow the damaged vessel to safety, but within twenty minutes it was gone, seemingly never to be seen again. At the time of the sinking, three men were reported killed, with three missing and another two later dying of their wounds.

Upon learning this, my thoughts returned to my visit to the wreck. Floating above the sand, I had been overcome with the sense that I was visiting a cemetery, perhaps even disturbing it. Do places hold emotions within them? Can a place hold tragedy within its shadows? I certainly felt something down there. What it was, I don't know. Any shipwreck is a story of sadness and loss, whether people died or not. The entire seabed off Normandy is a site of suffering. Before the vessels started to drop, thousands of men had clambered from the shallows to the sand only to be scythed down by the German guns that awaited them. The loss of life in the area was staggering. Reports of mined vessels in the weeks that followed the invasion seem endless. So high was the number of craft being destroyed long after D-Day was over that on 16 August, when a German U-boat managed to sneak past the defensive line and cause havoc, it was unable to record whether it had sunk LCF 1, LCG(L) 831 or LCG(L) 1062.

To have likely identified a Canadian landing craft was something that had never crossed my mind at any point during the search for LCH 185. My thoughts had been set on the British story at Sword Beach. I've visited Juno before, stopping to pay respects whenever I pass by. Visiting there, or the US sector at Omaha and Utah, I ask myself a different question. Landing in Normandy was horrifying for all involved, but how did it feel to be fighting a war so far from home? I feel proud to have added something to the archaeological record of both the landing at Juno and the Trout Line at Sword. Canada, even more than Britain, is sometimes overlooked in the mainstream telling of D-Day, with its emphasis on the actions of the American forces. Juno Beach, though hallowed ground to Canadian citizens, is often overshadowed. It feels like, in the tiniest of ways, the search for 185 has changed that.

LCG(L) 1062 serves as reminder that the invasion of Normandy wasn't a British story, a French story, a Canadian story or a US story. When the chips were down, when for a few dark years the world looked to be lost to division, oppression and fear, countries across the world came together to free France and the rest of Europe from fascist rule. Not since the Second World War has the world seen so many countries shed blood together in order to rid the world of evil and to allow us to live free. In today's world, as divisive politicians gain power and the far right creep back out of the shadows with every passing day, it's more important than ever to remember just what was at stake in June 1944. Huge numbers of young men from far corners of the world fought and died on the Normandy beaches. They were fighting for a better world.

The landings were constructed of many small cogs. Each battleship, each aircraft, each landing craft, each vehicle and each person all worked in unison to undertake the task at hand. The array of landing craft in Normandy on D-Day could be considered the unsung heroes of the landings. Without them, no men or machinery could have got on to the beaches and D-Day would never have happened. While the assault on the coastline came to a close with the successful conclusion of D-Day, as troops moved inland towards victory, the ships and landing craft remained at sea. They kept the Allies running like a well-oiled machine, allowing supplies and reinforcements to pour into Europe. The craft were at huge risk from German attack. Between D-Day and the end of September 1944, 115 Allied vessels were sunk off the coast of Normandy. At least 70 of those were landing craft. Thousands of men, all with families, friends and futures, were on board. Many of them never returned home.

Each and every piece of archaeology identified off the coast of Normandy will bolster the case that they should be preserved for future generations. Our search for LCH 185 has added new information to the archaeological record. The expedition highlights one story on the seabed, just one story among many. LCG(L) 1062 is just as important as 185, because every war story matters to someone.

Since I met Patrick, we have shared many heart-wrenching moments. I know just how much 185 and the events on 25 June 1944 mean to him. I understand how much the sinking altered his life. The war for Patrick Thomas did not end on that day. His time in the Far East sits as strongly in his mind as Normandy, but the memories are different. I've never seen Patrick smile when talking about LCH 185.

He was hurt at the condition of the wreck. If it was his craft, Patrick said, then the bones of his friends had been picked up and dumped unceremoniously across the seabed. For seven decades, he pictured his shipmates lying in a deep rest, resting peacefully together within their wartime home. Each one of those men has a name, a face and a story. To Patrick, every man is a memory. He feared the destructive hand of the salvagers. When it became evident that his suspicions were right, he was overcome with emotion.

But while Target 16 not being 185 was a devastating realisation, the news came with a small chance that the place Patrick's friends once rested has been left alone. I don't know that for sure, but I also don't know where 185 is. It may be closer to the shore, resting in the shallows where sonar surveys can't reach. If that is the case, it will have more than likely been almost completely salvaged. If the wreck is further out, hidden in the deep sea, it may have been overlooked by scrap dealers and souvenir hunters. The fact that the bodies will have disintegrated soon after the sinking really doesn't matter to Patrick. I've tried delicately to explain to him a few times that there will be no human remains on any shipwreck in the English Channel, but Patrick doesn't want to hear it. In his eyes, they are still down there; if not their bodies, then their souls. He can hear them. I think I heard souls, too, when I was on the seabed. There's only one man left on earth that remembers the sounds of life aboard 185. When I or anyone involved in the search think of the wreck, we can only imagine. Patrick doesn't need to. He still sees his friends down there. If the crew can be left undisturbed, frozen in time and young forever, then that can only be a good thing.

When it comes to telling Patrick the truth about Target 16, more than anything I don't want to upset him. The two of us have already done enough crying during the search. With the unveiling of the memorial, the project had ended on a high. It was a truly touching remembrance, and it seems reasonable and kind to lean towards the most positive possibility.

I knock on the door of Patrick's home and wait the usual time for him slowly to make his way to the front of the house. He's unsure why I'm here, and his greeting is hesitant. It is as joyous as ever to see my friend, but it feels more awkward this time. There's an apprehension, perhaps a suspicion, in Patrick's eyes. I've only told him beforehand that there's some news I need pass on in person. Now, months after we unveiled the memorial, Patrick is standing in front of me. I feel sick with worry as I follow him through the hallway and into the living room. We don't have our usual cup of tea or a catch up. It's straight to the point.

Patrick leans back on the same sofa on which we had first sat together to discuss the possibility of locating 185. To our left is the dining table where we once spread out maps and photographs, when nothing was ahead of us but the unknown. Back then, the excitement of an upcoming adventure gave Patrick a new lease of life and filled me with mid-twenties energy. As we sit looking at each other eighteen months on, I'm worn out. I'm not the same any more. I think he can see that.

Sitting down on an armchair positioned slightly away from Patrick, I move forwards to speak. During our previous chats I've stuck on a dictaphone or recorded audio on my phone. This time, the thought doesn't even occur to me.

'Here we are again,' I say.

Patrick chuckles nervously.

'I've got to tell you something. I've got some news for you.'

I'm speaking matter-of-factly, partly because of his hearing, but mainly because I want to get my views across. It has taken so long for me to work out what those views are. I will only get one chance to break the news, and I want to get it right.

'Yes?' Patrick says. His voice is tired.

'When we dived on the wreck, we weren't sure what wreck it was. There was always a possibility that it might not be 185, or that we might not be able to tell.'

'Hm,' Patrick mumbles. I think he already knows what's coming. He leans towards my face to read my lips carefully.

'When the dive team did all the measurements it turned out that . . .' I pause for a moment. This is it. There's no going back from whatever happens next. Once these words leave my mouth, our journey is over. '. . . it was actually a Landing Craft Gun, rather than an LCH. It came as a big surprise.'

Patrick sits perfectly still for a moment. The room is completely silent. Sweat appears on my forehead from the heat of the house and the stress of my revelation. He pushes back into the sofa, contemplates for a while, then stares back towards me. For a few seconds, neither of us know what to say. We are lost. Maybe there is nothing else left to say.

'We still discovered a Landing Craft Gun,' I tell my friend, 'which had its own story, that had sailors lose their lives on. It was someone's wreck, it was someone's story, but it wasn't 185.'

Patrick is still silent.

'We don't know where it is,' I say.

Patrick comes forward again, eyes wide with a new look of excitement.

'Oh!' he says. Perhaps Patrick thinks I'm about to announce that I'll be donning the dive gear once more and heading back out to sea.

'. . . And that probably means that 185 hasn't been disturbed,' I say.

As it stands, that is just as likely a scenario as any other. If 185 hasn't been discovered by sonar yet, then it's probably outside the vast area that was covered during the survey, meaning that it may well be out in deeper water. Out there, it might not have been seen as a shipping hazard in the post-war years.

Patrick has been given a chance for both adventure and closure in the final years of his life. He has gone on a journey that a person of his age normally would never be able to go on. He has been there every step of the way as part of the team, a member of the very expedition that has worked as hard as it could to find his wreck.

When diving on Target 16, we hoped that it was Patrick's wreck. At that point in the expedition, the evidence pointed towards it being 185. The fact that it later turned out not to be matters little now. When Patrick headed out to sea on the lifeboat to place a wreath on the water, he was floating over Target 16, standing above the Normandy seabed. Without the water separating the veteran from the silt and sand below, beneath the boat was a battlefield scattered with wrecks. LCH 185 is down there somewhere, whether recognisable or not. The roses I tossed on to the waves paid tribute to every craft lost in the Normandy landings and to all the men whose final resting place was beneath us.

We sit together in reflection. Patrick spends some time thinking about what he's just learned. I nervously rub my hands together until they become red and sore. I watch my friend's eyes for signs of emotion. He doesn't seem to be upset, but suddenly sits up straight to speak.

'The sea . . . is never still.'

Patrick has been thinking of these words in the silence.

'Of course, everything is shifting all the time, and the sand drifts over,' he says. 'That ship, at that particular time, was my home. Of course, the crew were part of my family. But I always thought people aren't interested, it's in the past, it's ancient history to a lot of people . . . but it's still very vivid to me.'

'I feel grateful that you've given me the chance to tell this story,' I say, 'because I think it's touched a lot of people and it's really brought to light what you did and what your friends did.'

'It's through your efforts . . . it's through meeting you!' Patrick says.

'I couldn't have done it without you, Pat.'

'And I couldn't have done it without you!'

We both lean back and smile warmly.

'All because I had nowhere to stay in France,' I say, fighting back tears.

I move to the sofa and sit next to my friend where we quietly reminisce about the wild adventure that we've been on together.

As I say goodbye at Patrick's door, it feels like the same scenario as when we had parted ways after first meeting. I have no idea if I'll ever see him again. The project, for now at least, is over. It's back to reality for us both. We don't know what the future holds. No one does. Patrick has grown visibly frailer in the months since the memorial unveiling. His hearing has become even worse. It's sad to see, but such is the reality of life. I too have aged when I look in the mirror. Time is always there, wrinkling our faces and hands, ticking off the days with every setting sun. I doubt Patrick ever considered reaching his nineties as a teenager in Normandy. The man has lived longer than most people will get to live and seen corners of the world that few ever experience. He witnessed unspeakable tragedy at a young age and has ridden the highs and lows of a regular life afterwards. Patrick Thomas survived it all and lived to tell the tale. I hope we all live to tell the tale.

On the drive home I think about the words that Patrick uttered after hearing the news.

The sea is never still. Everything is shifting all the time. The sands drift over.

Epilogue

6 June 2019

From my flat in central Manchester I look down at the construction workers as they gut a building on Princess Street. It's a glorious June day, and summer is finally starting to show. I was last in this city a decade ago, but it is different now. Old buildings and derelict shells are being converted into luxury apartments. The soul of the city is still there, but it is slowly leaving the body with every elevator tower that shoots up like a flag to announce the arrival of a new development.

After I told Patrick about Target 16, there was a huge sense of relief. Not just for the information no longer being kept a secret, but because the search for LCH 185 had ended. The dive team did visit the other target they had mentioned, but it turned out to be another red herring. I always knew it would be. When people learned of the outcome with the publishing of the archaeological report, I was often asked what was next. Everyone that I spoke to wanted me to continue the search. Strangers would hear about what I'd done and contact me with tales of other expeditions that they hoped I could launch. Some were ludicrous projects to find treasure, artworks or long-lost trains filled with gold. Others were slightly more realistic, like finding plane wrecks and half-tracks buried in France.

On the day I walked out of Patrick's house in Eastbourne, the only thing I knew was that I wanted to start again. Repeating myself is not something I enjoy, and although I had many meetings about kicking off new projects, they never felt the same way that it did when I first promised to search for 185. There was a fire to that promise and a young hunger for something big. It meant so much to me, because it meant so much to Patrick. Even the most exciting ideas that were put my way didn't fill me with that same wide-eyed thrill.

I've been longing for something different. What that is, I still don't know. I've grown my hair and moved north. I've been here for six months, enjoying the time off after leaving my job. I have a Canadian work visa laid out on my desk, and as I look out of my window there's just over a week until I'll be going west to Alberta. The search and everything that came with it have been filed away to the back of my mind. Trying to find 185 took more out of me than I could ever have imagined and it has taken a long time to get my mental health back to anywhere close to where it once was. The recovery has been slow. I still don't often find myself wanting to think or talk about the search, but with each day the cloud hanging over the project slowly lifts.

I flew back to Malta at one point. It had been such an enjoyable experience to learn to dive on the island in the run-up to Normandy that I wanted to return. Although I snuck in a bit of diving, paying a return visit to the *Maori* wreck, I was there to retrace the steps of my grandfather in the build-up to the Sicily invasion. It hit me as soon as I returned from the memorial unveiling that I had put so much effort into telling the story of someone else's grandfather, but had neglected to really find out what mine had done.

Using much the same method of archival research that had successfully unravelled the story of 185, I discovered that, after serving as an airframe fitter, Grandpa had voluntarily retrained as an RAF commando. That was why he had seen his friends die. That's why he had been on landing craft. I wish I'd known that when he was still alive. I could have taken him back to the countries he liberated and shown him how much the people cared. By the time I went to Malta, the buildings he had occupied had been demolished.

On the last day, I wandered into a cemetery in a small town filled with the graves of sailors from centuries past. Those laid to rest on this volcanic island do so above ground. Hidden down a dusty track was a grave from the Second World War with two names carved into the lid of the tomb. Two men, or what little remains of them could be picked up off the floor, were inside. Bored and waiting for the invasion of Sicily, two of my grandfather's friends, comrades from his small Servicing Commando Unit, had run along the road of an airfield, kicking bits of rubbish like footballs as they went. The last thing they kicked was an undetonated mine.

As I unravelled the untold tale of my grandfather's wartime, I was reminded of the feeling of duty that had been such a deeply felt part of the search for 185. The reason I wanted to tell the story of Patrick and his shipmates in the first place was so that they wouldn't be forgotten.

While in Malta, I received a call from the BBC, who wanted Patrick and me to appear on one of its chat shows. I was flown back to London for a day. It was great fun and Patrick enjoyed every second of the limelight. Our television appearance had thrust the story back into the public eye for a brief moment, and on the afternoon after the show, as I enjoyed a cold beer in the high sun of a Maltese spring, I received an email.

It was from a couple named Gary and Noreen who had seen us on the television. Gary had been shocked to hear mention of Jack Barringer and 185 as he watched his television the night before. His father, Len Norman, had also been a telegraphist on a landing craft at Sword Beach. It was LCH 269, the sister ship of 185. When Jack Barringer had asked to swap in order to be on 185 with Patrick, Gary explained, it was Len that had taken his place. For that reason, Len was not on 185 when it sank. He survived the war and went on to have a long life, but he never forgot that the reason he had lived when many of the men with whom he had trained had not, was because Jack died in his place. The email was signed off with a photograph of Len as an old man placing flowers at the grave of Jack Barringer. I never expected to receive such correspondence from going on a chat show. Almost a year since the unveiling of the memorial, families related to the story were being brought together.

In Manchester, as midday approaches, I turn on the news. It's a year to the day since we unveiled the memorial and it is, once again, the anniversary of D-Day. Twelve months have gone by so quickly. I decided not to attend the anniversary this year. It's the first time in many years that I'm not there. With it being the seventy-fifth anniversary, the crowds will be larger than ever; it will be impossible to get anywhere without official documentation or a veteran with you. Patrick is in France with a charity, being treated like royalty, but after having such an intimate and personal experience in Lion-sur-Mer last year, I can't bear the thought of presidents and prime ministers taking the spotlight above stories such as that of Patrick and LCH 185.

Sure enough, as I watch the news coverage I'm confronted with enormous crowds and politicians being served up as the stars of the show. There's as much talk of what outrageous thing a president might say, or what tension there could be between British and European leaders, as there is mention of what the veterans actually did back in 1944. It is to be expected, but still upsetting, and I'm not sure how to feel as I watch the screen. It's sad not to be there, not to be with Patrick and the rest of my friends. Each year missed is a year closer to the end of those old boys being in attendance. I feel uneasy about not being back at the memorial too. The town, albeit with a much larger crowd, will still have a ceremony there, but it fills me with regret to think that Dominique and those that helped with the unveiling might see me as ungrateful. I erected a huge piece of granite on their beautiful seafront and then didn't come back for the next ceremony, but it's still too soon. I'm not ready to go back there. Instead, I send an email to the mayor wishing him all the best, thanking him again for everything, and promising to return as soon as I can.

Watching the anniversary play out on television, there's understandably a lot of mention of the US story. Arromanches does make a few appearances, and it brings a smile to my face to remember the good times I've spent there. To see the veterans having fun on the streets as the townspeople make a fuss of each and every one of them brings me joy. Patrick is there, somewhere, no doubt telling everyone he meets that there's now a permanent memorial with his name on in Lion-sur-Mer.

After coming to terms with the results of the survey, a bitterness crept in. To have put in all that effort and still not found the right landing craft seemed like a kick in the teeth. The project still seemed like a success, but it got to me. I know that for the rest of my life I'll have to explain exactly why I felt it was a success despite the results of the search. I'm moving to Canada in a matter of days for a new start after the long, tiring slog of the shipwreck search. Watching the commemorations feels like a reminder of a different me, the old version that felt without hesitation that he could find a shipwreck without any experience because, well, why couldn't he? I still have that sort of belief, that energy, but it's instead being funnelled into starting afresh on the other side of an ocean.

My phone buzzes on the kitchen table. I look down to see a text from a friend. While over in Normandy, he has gone out of his way to journey to Lion-sur-Mer to see the memorial for himself. My face lights up looking at the photograph of my friend kneeling by the tribute to LCH 185. In front of the granite are the remnants of that morning's remembrance service. There are wreaths, poppies, flowers and a few small wooden crosses. The British and French flags from the unveiling have been attached again and are flying high.

Opening another text, I see a second photograph. The lighting is low, but it's immediately clear what I'm looking at. I see a lamppost, one of the many that line the promenade of the town. My eyes wander up the pole until they reach a large square banner sticking prominently out on one side. At the top reads the words, 'D-Day Heroes'. In the middle is a black-and-white photograph of a youthful face, while at the bottom is the name 'Patrick Thomas'. There's also a photograph of a second lamppost a little bit further down the beach. The same writing adorns the top, with a black-and-white photograph once again in the middle. This time, at the bottom it reads 'Jack Barringer'.

The lump in my throat that appeared time and time again during the search returns once more. I can feel my eyes welling up. Dominique had asked me months ago for the photographs that I'd found of the crew. The town was planning something, he said, and they needed the images. As it turns out, the whole of Normandy has been planning to have the names and photographs of those that served and died in the area placed up on lampposts all along the coast. Photographs of the crew of 185 have been chosen to line the stretch of seafront at Lion-sur-Mer. Not just Patrick and Jack, but all of those whose faces I uncovered.

I set out to save the story of LCH 185 from the shadows of forgotten history. With every passing day that Patrick's recollections went undocumented and unrecorded, the story fell closer towards becoming just a few typewritten words in documents on dusty archive shelves to be seen by no one. By telling the tale, searching for the ship and unveiling the memorial, the story of the craft has been not only saved, but has been passed on to future generations. Patrick can't live forever. Neither can I. Neither can anyone that stops in a peaceful moment of reflection to read the words on the memorial, but the story of LCH 185, the story of Patrick Thomas, Jack Barringer and every single one of the men that lost their lives on the craft now can.

As I look at Jack and Patrick's faces proudly standing guard over the streets of Lion-sur-Mer, I realise, finally, that I've achieved what I set out to do. They are the men that make up the story. That story is just one of millions from the Second World War. It is a tiny corner of a massive endeavour on a scale almost impossible to comprehend. But that story matters as much as any other and, in this moment, on this day, in that glorious Normandy sunshine, the crew of LCH 185 have finally made it to shore, together. They are in the town and being spoken of. They are being admired and remembered. That is what matters, and that is what I will remember above everything else. Not the diving, the memorial or Target 16, but Patrick Thomas and the friends who he lost.

If I live a life as long as his, it's beautiful to know that I'll be able to tell my grandchildren, perhaps even my great-grandchildren, about that one crazy year when I went searching for a shipwreck with the last man to have survived its sinking. By then, all Second World

War veterans will be long gone and the war will be far removed from living memory. I can already imagine how unbelievable it will sound when I tell this story in years to come. Perhaps people won't believe it. It's such an unlikely tale, after all. Patrick and I have a truly once-in-a-lifetime friendship. It seems unreal, but it isn't. The story is true. It did happen and I'm lucky to have been a part of it. I took an actual veteran of the most well-known event of the Second World War on the journey of a lifetime. It might turn out to be the journey of my lifetime too. Every twist and turn along the way, and the disappointing conclusion I arrived at about Target 16 – they are not the whole story. What also matters to me is that I helped tell the tale; that I went outside and took a swing at the sky, and perhaps in doing so I found meaning on the wreck after all.

That night, for the first time in over a year, I close my eyes without the same doubts that have haunted me since the end of the search. I wonder if Patrick ever read Jack's letter, and then, at last, I sleep.

It's three days after my twenty-eighth birthday and I find myself in a cabin just outside of Canmore in the Rocky Mountains. It's the middle of November. I've been in Canada for five months. Last night, I barbecued in the deepest snow I have ever seen; now I stare out of the window as snowflakes dance down through the trees that surround me. Two deer walk with a bounce through a frozen clearing in the forest. All around are the peaks of mountains grander and more beautiful than I could ever envision. Outside, it's cold enough to kill.

After a coffee, in which I replaced the milk I'd have in England with North American cream, I open my laptop to read an email received in what for me was the dead of night. It is a message from a man named Innes Christie. Born and raised in Scotland, Innes had just returned from his father's funeral and was sorting through his belongings. In among the paper work he found a number of old maps, handwritten testimonies and a few faded photographs taken on board some sort of vessel. On one of the maps was a black cross, pencilled a few miles out to sea from Sword Beach. At some point in her life, Innes's mother had written in blue ink:

> Sword Beach is where Adam was on D-Day. He lost a lot of pals on that landing and has many sad letters from wives and mothers [of those who] were at Sword Beach along with him. Although wounded, he was one of the few who managed to get off the stricken landing craft. Seldom talks about it.

Adam Christie had been on 185 when it was struck by the acoustic mine. In the chaos, as most of his friends found themselves trapped in the bow and a small number of sailors frantically fought among themselves for lifebelts in the English Channel, Adam climbed up on to the upturned hull as the craft began to sink.

From a nearby rescue craft, sailors shouted over the screams of desperate men for him to jump away from the vessel. If he didn't, Adam would become one more digit on the number of deaths destined for the next day's report. With his arms crossed, Adam patiently sat and considered his next move. As the craft sank deeper down, he stood up and launched himself into the water, leaving the craft he had been aboard since New York for one final time. Adam's friend Frank Gammal, who had travelled with him to pick up the landing craft from the States, wasn't on 185 that day, but was killed a few days later in the same area.

I watch the deer disappear into the trees. Another survivor of the sinking had been alive the entire time that Patrick and

I were searching for the craft. He died just last week. If only Adam Christie had known, if only he had been able to come with us on the journey. Patrick and Adam could have met; two survivors reunited after all those years of wondering if there was anyone else. If Adam Christie had only known that we were out there searching for the wreck and remembering what he went through.

I move to the window and watch as fresh hoofprints fill up and fade with the snowfall. I think of returning to England, of getting the team together to head back down to the seabed. Images of the wreck still come to me at night. I can see it silently sleeping, waiting for a visit from someone else with a dream. But it seems more and more likely that 185 is gone, destroyed for good; nothing left but a ghostly outline on the seabed. It's too late. Adam Christie is gone. The wreck is gone. Patrick wasn't the last survivor of the sinking, but he is now, and he too will soon be gone. Life never goes to plan. The roads we take rarely lead to where we want to go. It's all too easy to resolve ourselves to a finale long before it has taken place, but it wasn't the wreck that needed to be found. It never was. I know that now.

Closing my laptop, I walk to the door of the cabin. I put on a thick red coat, drag a woolly hat down over my ears and cover my mouth with a scarf. Pulling my gloves up to step outside, I pause as I notice the scratches on my watch caused by grabbing at the twisted metal of Target 16 in a fight against the current. There is no decompression stop to be had, no fishing hooks to dance around, no darkness beneath my hands. All I see is the slush of snow and mud on the pavement. Stepping outside, the air freezes as it fills my lungs and the cold cracks my lips. The face of the watch disappears between my gloves and the sleeve of my coat.

Ahead, I see the frozen blue waters of a glacial lake. I've been landlocked for months. At the edge of the ice, I look up at the peak of a mountain, then carefully step out on to the frozen water. With my leather boot I scrape a gap in the snow. Staring into the darkness through the cracks beneath my feet, it reminds me of the sea, of that time I reached the bottom.

In Memoriam

*In memory of those who died in the sinking of
LCH 185 on 25 June 1944.*

Alexander Anderson
Age 19

James A. Armstrong
Age 25
Buried at Dieppe Canadian War Cemetery, Hautot-sur-Mer

Jack Barringer
Age 29
Buried at Ranville War Cemetery

Alan Raymond Barrs
Age 19

Albert Ernest Beers
Age 21

Robert Albert Bell
Age 23

William Bellenger
Age unknown

William Barclay Bremner
Age 22

John Robert Bruce Brothers
Age 19

George Albert Casselden
Age 26

Cyril Walter Clapham
Age 22

Geoffrey Dunkerley
Age 24

Arthur Greaves Dunn
Age 20

Eric Fletcher
Age 24

Verna Ford
Age unknown

Henry William Jeffrey
Age 19

Caruth Main
Age unknown

Alan Haigh Maxwell
Age 20

Matthew McIver
Age unknown

Charles John Munro
Age 19

John William Nicholson
Age 24

George Albert Paige
Age 19

Ronald Charles Patterson
Age 19

Dennis William Piper
Age 26

John James Rimmer
Age 20
Buried at Hermanville War Cemetery, Hermanville-sur-Mer

David Saunders
Age 21

James Gordon Shepherd
Age 30

Kenneth Simpson
Age 19

Norman William John Smith
Age 20

Robert Henley Tucker
Age 35

Frank Groome Waddington
Age 31

Robert Wears
Age unknown

Arthur Henry Whiston
Age unknown

Phillip John Winstanley
Age 19

Edward Yates
Age 18
Buried at Fécamp (Le Val aux Clercs) Communal Cemetery

Acknowledgements

As well as those who are mentioned throughout the book, I would also like to thank:

Daniel Oron, with whom I spent many days and nights on the road, hurtling through France towards wherever the story led us. It wasn't easy, but it was always exciting.

Jeff Shreve and Duncan Proudfoot, whose initial belief in the story allowed me the chance to write it.

Rob Crane for his research on COPP.

The families of LCH 185's crew for trusting me with their memories.

My friends and family for always being there.

Lastly, I wish to acknowledge the children of Inver Primary School, Dr Tracy Craggs, Dr James Fallon and David Sleith for their research into D-Day rehearsals at Inver, Ben Swenson for his research on Ocean View Amusement Park, John Shepherd for his work on the Empress of Japan/Scotland, and Stephen Fisher once again for his Force S expertise.

INDEX

Thompson, Fred 52
Thorne, Sir Andrew 79
Thornton, Captain 103
Thule, HMS 212
Tiptoe, HMS 270
Totem, HMS 212
Tripoli 39–40
troop carriers 34–5
Trout Line 198–9, 203–4, 207, 287
Tucker, Robert Henley 126, 312

U-boats 38, 94, 200, 206, 288
UNESCO Heritage Site status 150
United States Army 103
 2nd Infantry Division 16
Utah Beach 92, 197, 206

V-2 rockets 129
Valletta 39
Victory, HMS 59–60

Waddington, Frank 312
Walcheren 128, 129–32, 153
war cemeteries

field cemeteries 183
 Ranville War Cemetery 13, 107
Warship, HMS 129
Wears, Robert 126, 312
Western Task Force 44
Whiston, Arthur 312
Willys Jeep 182
Winstanley, Phillip 312
Woolf, Basil 127, 128, 129–30,
 131, 132, 133, 134, 153
Woolf, Ian 134
wrecks
 archaeological surveying 178, 180,
 188–90
 looting 117, 181–2
 moral issues 116–18
 salvaging operations 63, 64, 116,
 152, 181, 229, 254
 war graves 116, 118, 125, 224,
 256, 287–8, 290
 wreck diving 117, 170–2

Y Scheme 135
Yates, Edward 312